AF880081

Copyright © 2026 vga256.

All rights reserved.

First Edition.

No part of this book may be reproduced or used in any manner whatsoever without written permission of the author, except in the case of brief quotations in critical articles and reviews. The contents of this book are explicitly forbidden from usage in large language (LLM), machine learning (ML) or other AI-based training models; in other words: your AI slop-producing company will be sued into oblivion.

Any images and trademarked names used remain the property of their legal owners.

ISBN-13: 978-1-0699885-0-8

Cover and layout design by vga256.

To learn more about vga256 and tomotama, visit www.tomotama.com

Mages

&

Modems

A Childhood Well-Wasted in the Golden Age of Personal Computers, Games, and Internet Piracy

a confessional by vga256

tomotama • Edmonton

For Mom and Dad,
Who brought home our first computer in 1985 and lived to regret it.

For my Sister,
My best frenemy and co-pilot of the beloved Amstrad.

And for my beloved Wife and Best Friend,
Who knew what she was getting into all those years ago,
and *still* took a chance on me.

Table of Tales

* * *

Acknowledgements

This book would not have been possible without the loving care of my wife, who edited and patiently endured distributing review copies to my proof-readers and fact-checkers. A huge thank you to my friends and family who lived through these stories with me, and for their patience in answering my hundreds of questions about the past and correcting my many mis-remembrances. Any errors that exist in the text are purely my own and are more likely the product of corrupted memory than stylistic fabrication.

Thank you to my friend Nick, whose art and design skills came to the rescue at a critical time and much improved the cover design. And finally, thank you to my friend Brandon, whose gentle questions about emotional attachments and nostalgia on our long autumn walks encouraged me to write the book in the first place.

Preface and Fair Warning

I began writing this collection of stories as an experiment in putting together my fractured memory of the past, with the hope that it might also jog the memories of my immediate friends and family. Each of these stories are written exactly as I remember them, and include details corroborated by the people who were there. None of these stories are fabricated or embellished for dramatic effect, nor have I sanded down the rough edges of a tumultuous personal history to please other people. I sometimes use words that I have not spoken in over thirty years, and now deeply regret using them back then. There is no shortage of cringeworthy or outright offensive language in this book, but it remains intact to do factual justice to the times and places I grew up in. No one benefits from reading a sanitized narrative that distorts the past, no matter how embarrassing or hurtful. Not a single drop of AI/ML/LLM slop was used in writing this book. Any sloppy writing is by yours truly.

What am I now that I was then?
May memory restore again and again
The smallest color of the smallest day:
Time is the school in which we learn,
Time is the fire in which we burn.

Delmore Schwartz
Calmly We Walk Through This April's Day

Introduction

The Office

I stood among a couple dozen steel shelves filled with hundreds of computer games, monitors, towers, keyboards, video game consoles and cartridges, scratching my beard and trying to decide what to do with it all. It was the fifth time in as many years that I was forced to move my retro computing and gaming collection, and I was getting tired of hauling it around with me. What had started as a single narrow shelf of beloved computer games in the den of my childhood home had swollen to a hulking composite of plastic, cardboard and data crammed into every nook and cranny of the office. And it had become burdensome.

My wife sensed my hesitation and gave me a sidelong glance. "When's the last time you played any of these honey?"

Um. I scanned the rows of shelves and guesstimated that I hadn't played even half of the games for more than ten minutes, and I had brought to completion less than a dozen of them. I sensed the intimation hidden within the question: *Maybe it's time to get rid of the ones you don't play.*

My gut tightened and I closed the door, putting off the decision for another time. They could stay in the office until we were ready to move.

That day prompted me to ask myself *why* I was so attached to these silly and wonderful accoutrements of childhood that had followed me around for the past thirty years. In an age of instantaneous online gaming gratification through services like *Steam* and *GOG* there was little reason to hang on to almost a thousand games or the dozens of antiquated computer systems that could play them, when I could download most of them with a single click on my shiny new laptop.

And yet, I was so powerfully attached to each box and manual and diskette that the idea of selling or throwing out a single game felt like snipping off a fingertip with wire cutters. In the year that followed I could not bear to part with the collection, and like the character Gollum in *The Lord of the Rings,* its presence began to grow on my mind.

In the late autumn I confessed my indecision about the collection to a Buddhist friend of mine. He asked me if my attachment to the collection was with the physical objects themselves, or with the memories and emotions they represented. I was aghast. Of course! When I looked at my stained copy of *Wing Commander II* I didn't just see an intergalactic space opera flight combat game, I saw the hours I spent with my best friends in the seventh grade crouched around a computer monitor. My *King's Quest IV* box wasn't just any copy of the game, it was the one my sister and I enjoyed for over a year together in the den of our childhood home – the only evidence of which being a secret code written by my sister on the inside cover of its box. My friend suggested that maybe writing down some of these memories would help exorcise the attachments I had to the memories, and make parting with the game collection an easier task.

The Future Is Here

Today we're overwhelmed by computer technology. In all likelihood you've got the ability to play games and be on the Internet at any place, at any time, during your day. You may even be reading this book on a tiny computer the size of your hand, that is one hundred times faster than the fastest computer I had access to when I was a teenager.

For the past thirty years, computer users shaped their technology to suit their uses, as the technology reshaped those users in turn. Gone are the days where basement dwellers and Ham radio operator-types were the primary purchasers of computers who more often than not built them from parts. Today, a three-year-old can operate an iPhone well enough to buy a game from the iTunes Store, and most supermarket chains sell laptops pre-installed with Windows.

Internet access, once the stronghold of military and university élite, is now in the hands of the glorious unwashed masses. Its earliest days as a residential service delivered over noisy copper telephone lines between modems is forgotten, and in its place is always-on WiFi and wireless data; users panic when their access is temporarily interrupted by a pesky subway or elevator.

Computer and video games changed too. The 4, 16 and 256 colour palettes that characterized the vast majority of pixelated worlds I inhabited throughout my childhood have been replaced by palettes in the *billions*. Monitor resolutions inexorably grew geometrically, and games now require dedicated video hardware that can manipulate the massive data forced through them to an LCD monitor. In the process of modernizing technologies, impressionistic "pixel-art" gave way to hyper-photorealistic imagery and 3D modelling. Children today could not help but cringe at the rudimentary pixelated characters of *Space Quest* and *Maniac Mansion,* which – to many of us in the days of old – were the height of sophistication.

And yet, games and computers are not the same to me as they

were decades ago. The new games I play today feel like repetitions of old design patterns found in the classics I grew up with. There is a nostalgia in new games, as if designers and artists feel stultified in their craft and can only nod at the golden years. As I watch the latest instalment of BioWare's *Dragon Age* series hit the shelves, costing over $200 million to produce, I worry that the richest veins of imagination were prospected many years ago and today's creators are left spelunking the empty mine shafts for dust.

But perhaps it is not the games themselves that have changed. Perhaps *I* have changed, and my memories of the "good and bad ol' days" has cast a shadow on the future we're living in now. This book is an attempt at articulating the old days of computing, when simply owning a computer *mattered*. The 1980s and 1990s were exciting times to grow up in, and to me they were the peak of the computing era, even though by 1980 many of the basic decisions about how computers worked were already made. Kids who grow up today won't know the heart racing excitement of a 2400 baud modem, handshaking over quivering telephone lines to another computer hundreds of kilometres away. They won't grow up fine-tuning their MS-DOS memory configuration so they can squeeze out one more kilobyte of RAM and play their favourite space combat game.

No doubt these anachronistic voodoo rituals are at best seen as quaint, and at worst, forms of child abuse – but in the 1980s and 1990s they were the dark magicks that separated true computer mages from mere keyboardists.

I hope that my stories, told as short memoirs highlighting how computers played a role in my childhood, will bring a smile to those who grew up in such a dark and wondrous age, or at least a force a chuckle out of those who (thankfully) didn't. Each story is an experiment in "object history" – of taking a physical artifact and using it to explore the memories it evokes of the past. In my case, the objects in question are the hundreds of pieces of hardware and software I've collected over the years that now collect dust in a rarely visited office; the past I explore is my childhood. Perhaps this book, like others in its genre, will encourage others to tell the stories of how computers and video games shaped their lives, and give them an insight into the role that games may play in their future.

The book is written in three periods that roughly line up with my elementary school, junior high, and high school years. These periods in turn closely follow three periods of computer technology and their games: early home PC's like the Tandy TRS-80 and Commodore Amiga, IBM-compatibles running MS-DOS, and the age of modeming and the Internet and online gaming. Most stories are independent of each other, but all follow an arc that begins with my first family computer and ends with my last computer to run MS-DOS.

For myself, perhaps these stories will help to loosen the deathgrip I have on those old classics and let me enjoy them in a new way, freed of the emotional weight of a burdensome past.

1987: Grade Three

Tandy TRS-80 Color Computer II and Type-In Games

When I was six years old, my mother came home with what would be our first family computer. I don't actually remember the day she brought it home, but I do remember feeling perplexed by the strange white machine that occupied the corner of our living room. It was about the size of a squashed pizza box, and was made of cheap plastic – the kind you'd find in a toaster or a blender. I remembered marvelling at the design – it looked so *futuristic* compared to anything else we owned.

Just a year earlier I had seen the film *2001: A Space Odyssey* and the word "computer" was something I identified with the words "HAL 9000" and "cool". And now there was a computer sitting on a desk between our couch and the stereo system.

The Tandy TRS-80 Color Computer II was already several years old by the time it graced our living room. By now more advanced computers like the Commodore 64, Apple IIc, Atari 800, and IBM PC had flooded the American technology markets. The Commodore 64 was a runaway entry-level computer for families on a budget, and the Apple II's popularity had already peaked and was entering a gradual decline in sales. But that story is the marketing history of computers in the urban United States. Where I grew up, in the Northwest Territories of Canada, computers were only seen in movies like *TRON* and *2001*. Computers were *not* in every home, and despite Apple Computers' advertisements northern housewives were *not* balancing their chequebooks nor computing their stock portfolios on the kitchen table. In my town families were busier gutting whitefish, skinning jackrabbits and preparing cranberry jelly in the kitchen.

I lived in an old river town on the shores of Great Slave Lake. For twenty years the community had been slowly transitioning away from its reliance upon hunting, fishing and trapping. Southerners brought with them new businesses, and with those businesses came wild new kinds of technological gadgets like microwave ovens and satellite dishes.

Computers had not splashed down in the town quite yet, and there was only one place you could even *see* one: at the local Radio Shack. Yes, there was a Radio Shack that was more or less like one you'd see in the urban United States in the 1980s. I remember the acrid smell of carpet glue, fuzzy orange and brown low-pile commercial carpeting, pegboard shelves of electronic components like resistors and capacitors; and of course the smiling clerk behind the register who asked if I'd like to buy some "AA" batteries with my purchase. And like all other Radio Shacks at the time this one had a complete line of Tandy products including the TRS-80 Color Computer.

Our family bought our first home computer, a TRS-80 Color Computer II, from the minister of a local church who was upgrading his family computer. He had bought it new from Radio Shack several years earlier and spent the intervening years pirating games for it. It came with two black joysticks that had no self-centering spring, which meant that if you released the joystick it would *just sit there* until you pulled it back to its centre. A single red "fire!" button on the front of the joystick was its only other adornment, and was so stiff that it went *clack!* when depressed. There was an official Radio Shack brand Cassette Tape Recorder that was our sole data storage device.[1]

---

[1] As of this writing copying a few gigabytes of data to a USB memory stick will take a couple of minutes at most. On the CoCo II, a few dozen *bytes* of data (approximately one-millionth of a gigabyte) took five to ten minutes. The cassette tape recorder read data sequentially, unlike a modern "random access" drive. That meant if you wanted data stored at the 27 minute mark on the tape, you would have to fast-forward to the 27-minute mark before you could transfer the data to the computer.

Cassette recorders were not just slow… they were a major inconvenience. They were also cheap, and during a serious mortgage crisis due to high interest rates in the early 80s, cassettes made economic sense.

Our 'new' CoCo II sat on a student desk my dad had picked up at the local thrift store. Its monitor was a 13-inch tube television that sat on top of the machine, with a two-pronged "Computer-TV" VHF converter box hung from its backside. Behind the cassette tape recorder was a shelf of over a dozen cassette tapes all carefully copied from their original (purchased) source and hand-labeled. Neatly stacked on top of the pirated cassettes were a half-dozen game legitimate cartridges purchased from our local Radio Shack.

I did not know what to make of the computer at first, because the word had no meaning in my lexicon. It all came together when my mother inserted a game cartridge and booted the computer for the first time. My world exploded and I dragged my sister along with me for the wild ride.

We discovered games like *Pooyan, Dungeons of Daggorath, and Downland.* My mother laboriously copied down a page of obscure computer commands to a recipe card and glued the card to the computer desk. The card taught us the command "CLOAD" (which my sister and I pronounced "klode" because we did not understand it was short for "cassette-load") which allowed us to play games from cassettes like *Lurkley Manor* and *Pyramid 2000. Pooyan* gave us our initial training in lightning-quick reflexes and sense of timing that would come in handy in arcades years later. *Dungeons of Daggorath* was our first role-playing game and first-person perspective experience; the creepy *tick-tick* of the heartbeat that represented the hero's health still haunts us today.[2] *Downland* was our introduction to action-adventure games and would spark many debates with my

[2] It would be decades before modern games rediscovered the psychological impact of using a heartbeat to represent the hero's health, such as in popular action games like *Uncharted: Drake's Fortune.*

friends, years later, regarding the hero's uncanny similarity to Nintendo's "Super Mario". *Lurkley Manor* was a simple adventure game set in a spooky haunted house that taught us the basics of entering commanders into the "text parser": a skill that would come in very handy for both my sister and I years later. *Pyramid 2000* was an adventure game a bit too difficult for my sister and I so we'd stand behind my mother and watch as her fingers deftly danced across the keyboard entering commands into the text parser. For a six-year-old and a four-year-old who barely knew how to peck at individual keys, watching my mother type on the keyboard was as magical as the computer itself.

All these games would barely earn a "meh" and curt nod from gamers today, recognized as the retro obscura of a barbaric prehistory of computer gaming that no one *really* wants to go back to. But for my sister and I in 1985, these games were the only alternative to playing outside in the swampy forest across the street. The worlds depicted in these games, full of pharaoh's tombs and ancient treasures and evil old wizards and crystal caverns, were even more magical than the world outside.

After a few months of the same games, my sister and I began to succumb to boredom. It wasn't much fun getting stuck at the same level in *Pooyan* or dying in the same place in *Downland* dozens of times. Nor was dying in *Dungeons of Daggorath* much fun either; losing or extinguishing my torch in a dark corridor inevitably led to my character's heart racing to the point of a massive coronary. Buying new software was becoming difficult – the shelves at Radio Shack carried fewer and fewer TRS-80 games, and the exorbitant prices in our town meant that my family could not afford to buy new games anyway. Worse, we did not know a single family in town that owned one of these white plastic machines so copying games from a friend was not a possibility either.

Our salvation came when I discovered, buried beneath the Styrofoam panels of the TRS-80 box, two Radio Shack-branded "type-in game" books. Type-in games were listings of BASIC computer instructions – a programming language that many first generation personal computers came with. When laboriously entered into the computer one line at a time, a type-in game would in theory yield some kind of playable computer game.

Type-in books and magazines took advantage of the fact that the BASIC language was plain English and could be easily printed and sold on paper. Take the following imaginary BASIC program as an example:

```
10 PRINT "WELCOME TO MY EVIL"
20 PRINT "DUNGEON OF TERROR"
30 PRINT "    A GAME BY    "
40 PRINT "  SOME COOL KID "
50 PRINT "ENTER THY NAME"
60 PRINT "BRAVE EXPLORER"
70 INPUT$ NAME
80 PRINT "GOOD DAY TO THEE", NAME
90 PRINT "BEGIN THY QUEST? Y/N"
100 INPUT$ ANSWER
```

After typing in these BASIC commands and running the program, the player would see this:

```
WELCOME TO MY EVIL
DUNGEON OF TERROR
   A GAME BY
  SOME COOL KID
ENTER THY NAME
BRAVE EXPLORER
>SWORDMAN
GOOD DAY TO THEE SWORDMAN
BEGIN THY QUEST? Y/N
>Y_
```

Not the most exciting game, but as you can see BASIC made the first generation of mass market personal computers relatively easy to program. Every kid with a computer, some ingenuity and way too much free time could churn out a half-playable game in a few hours. Type-in magazines and books took advantage of the fact that many kids were willing to forego royalties or any kind of financial compensation just to see their homebrewed game appear in print. Many publishers, in lieu of money, gave kids copies of their games or free subscriptions to their magazines in exchange for their programs. What could be better for publishers than having some wannabe programmer mail in their hard work for a pittance? For many magazines this was a license to print money.

At the age of six I was neither programmer nor game designer. All I cared about was playing games. Compared to buying a single game off the shelf at Radio Shack which might cost between $25 and $75, a type-in magazine or book was a bargain. For $9.95 a Radio Shack BASIC type-in book came with over *twenty* games. The drawback was that the games were published as hundreds, or thousands, of lines of BASIC instructions. Someone would have to peck each line of code into the computer one key at a time. Or, in my case, *her* hands.

Somehow I bamboozled my mother into typing in an entire game from the Tandy type-in book. The game was called *Speedboat*. On the front cover was a very imaginative artist's representation of what the game *might* look like if you closed your eyes and imagined a scene from a James Bond film: a slim jet boat making a getaway on a narrow canal. The illustration practically promised that James Bond himself would crash through the wall of our living room with his jet-boat the minute we ran the program.

That's not how things played out. When I left for school in the morning I begged my mother to type in the entire computer game for me with a pleading, watery-eyed look that only six-year-olds can muster. It must have worked because when I came back home from school in the afternoon my mother ushered me over to the computer chair and sat me down in front of *Speedboat*. She had spent the entire day typing in the computer code – a couple thousand lines of BASIC commands entered on a clacky, finger-straining keyboard.

When I ran the game James Bond did *not* come crashing

through our living room wall, nor was his jet-boat anywhere to be found. In fact, I did not know exactly *what* I was looking at on the television screen. What I got instead was a screen that looked a little like this:

```
| [ ]                  |
|       [ ]            |
|   [ ]       [ ]      |
|                      |
|                      |
| [ ]                  |
|       [ ]            |
|   [ ]       [ ]      |
|                      |
|                      |
|                      |
|      {*}             |
```

If I squinted the [ ] symbols appeared to be logs or fish or bombs, and apparently I had control of the {*} at the bottom of the screen which was the speed boat. I could see at least two things wrong with the title of the game: it was neither speedy nor did I appear to be driving a boat. *Speedboat* was not even a tenth as good as the games we already had on cassette tape and cartridge!

As a six-year-old boy with a six-year-old's taste in games, I was outraged by the shoddiness of the product. Radio Shack's underpaid illustrators and programmers had betrayed me. It did not even occur to me that my mother had wasted an entire day typing in this piece of crap into the computer.

The situation became worse when my lack of knowledge concerning computers reared its ugly head. Today when you want to save a document, you just click 'Save' and your computer does the rest. But in 1985 saving a BASIC program you typed out was quite a task, especially if you did not have a disk drive; saving a BASIC program to cassette tape was an hour-long affair in itself. Owing to the fact that my mother was excited to see me play the game she had typed in, she had not yet saved it to cassette tape.

Here is where my ignorance exposed her fatal error: after a minute of disappointing gameplay I reached behind the TRS-80 and shut off the computer. In a brief flicker of the television screen I flushed ten hours of finger-breaking labour into oblivion! My mother walked from the kitchen to the living room and asked me what I thought of the game.

I replied, "It wasn't very fun so I shut off the computer."

The strained look on her face at hearing those words still haunts me to this day. Needless to say it was her first, and last, experience with computer programming. From that day onward I had to do my own damned typing.

Like most six-year-olds I was not the most patient kid. The idea of spending a dozen hours typing in some lame attempt at an arcade game sure did not appeal to me. When I tried entering a type-in game for myself for the first time I got sixty lines in before I gave up.

That autumn I made a new friend at school by the name of Joshua. Josh was an awkward blond freckled kid with coke-bottle eyeglasses and a strangely large vocabulary for someone his age. When he came over to play for the first time he spied our TRS-80 in the corner of the living room and his eyes almost popped out his thick lenses. If I thought computers were fun, Josh was absolutely in love with them. As far as I was concerned the CoCo II was just a game machine. But Josh saw much more in the machine than I did. He immediately grabbed the "Tandy Color Computer BASIC" beginner's guide sitting on the desk and began thumbing through it. A minute later he was already hammering out BASIC commands that, as far as I was concerned, were written in Klingon.

In second grade arts & crafts classes there are two kinds of kids: kids that draw things from the imagination, and kids who trace down pictures line by line. I was one of the latter both as an artist and as a type-in magazine gamer. Josh was the former: he could create things from his imagination. I watched him type out commands one at a time, and realized that he *understood* some of the meanings of BASIC commands. He understood that BASIC was a means for communicating with the computer. That became clear to me when he made a typo and the computer barked back at him:

```
?SYNTAX ERROR
```

I asked him what a "sin-tacks" error was, and told him that the computer had written that message to my sister and I all the time! Josh turned to me, pushed his glasses up on his freckled nose and said, "Oh that means I made a mistake typing. *Sine-tax* means an instruction. Like a magic word that'll make the computer do something."

I sat there baffled, unsure if what he had said was even in English. But as Josh continued to experiment with BASIC commands, I watched the computer's replies. Eventually something clicked because I realized that the computer was not like the television or the stereo system. The computer was something I could interact with, it was a little thinking machine that could understand things I typed on the keyboard. And *Josh could understand what the computer was saying back to him.*

I wish I could say that this was the moment where I decided I was going to become a computer programmer instead of a firefighter or a doctor. I wish I could say this moment sparked a love affair with computer languages. But let's face the facts: I was a six-year-old kid with a penchant for playing games. The computer was a mystical, complex machine to me and my only means for understanding how it worked was through my much smarter second-grade buddy.

Later that year Josh and his mom moved away. I lost my best friend and coding tutor. Radio Shack had stopped selling TRS-80 software and my collection of pirated (and purchased) software was becoming stale. That hole would be soon filled by new electronic competitors for my free after-school time.

IBM PC XT 8086 and Microsoft Flight Simulator

When I was in the second and third grade, my mother worked as a project coordinator at an Adult Education Centre just down the street from my elementary school. The title makes the place sound grand but the Centre was really just a shabby aluminum portable trailer with a handful of desks with typewriters on them. My mother spent our school hours assisting adults – many of them recent immigrants to the North – with reading, writing and typing. The location was perfect – after school my sister and I could walk a half-block to my mother's workplace and play until she was ready to go home.

"Play" meant different things for my sister and I, and my mother. To my mother "play" meant "play quietly, don't touch anything, and stop running around! Just find a desk to sit at and draw pictures." We were *especially* forbade from touching the very fascinating Xerox machine, which we secretly put our hands on and photocopied dozens of handprints while my mom worked.

Along the wall was a computer – it was beige and heavy-looking, like it belonged in a missile silo more than a classroom. Today I recognize this machine as a true-blue IBM XT, an early and very expensive model of IBM's Intel 8086-based computer. The government that sponsored the institution must have paid a small fortune for this metallic beast and no doubt it was the most valuable asset in the building aside from the Xerox. Along with the typewriters this computer was used to teach adults basic typing skills among other "productivity" tasks. But to my sister and I computers meant only one thing: games! One of the teachers was particularly kind to us, and when we came in after school each day he booted up the computer with their prized copy of *Microsoft Flight Simulator* – the only "game" in the Centre.

I use the word "game" somewhat pejoratively because this very early version of *Microsoft Flight Simulator* was not the most exciting entertainment product. Instead of the complex three-dimensional simulation with weather effects and radio calls we are used to today, this version of *Flight Simulator* was really just a panel of instruments and dials that would spin, blink and fluctuate as my sister and I mashed the keyboard. A few times the friendly teacher walked over and patiently showed us how to throttle the plane up and make the aircraft take off. But for us, the real reward lay in making *anything* happen on the monochromatic green phosphorus screen!

The magic of my earliest interactions with a PC were not the graphics or the rich gameplay. The magic was in the fact that I could *make something happen on a television monitor right in front of my eyes*! Today's generation of people raised in a society that takes computing for granted no longer seem to experience the glee of making a computer simply *do* something. Making the computer obey your commands felt like teaching a puppy its first trick, or the first time I mixed together baking soda and vinegar in a plastic bottle and watched it explode.

That early experience with an IBM XT gave me a foundational appreciation for computers that has stuck with me to this day: enthusiastically bashing away at the indestructible IBM keyboard makes crazy things happen. I felt fearless.

Unfortunately, while keyboard-bashing is a beloved past time of the prepubescent child, it is less so the past time of the Education Centre's director. To his eyes I'm sure that two little runts were messing up his priceless IBM with their grimy kid-hands. After a few afternoons of uninterrupted play my mother quietly shooed us off to a desk with a pile of crayons, and the computer was pointedly unplugged on our future after-school visits. Without the XT, I soon lost interest in visiting my mother's workplace and my sister and I moved on to other obsessions.

1988: Grade Four

Mattel Intellivision

I was in the fourth grade and video gaming systems were an everyday part of playground talk. During recesses and lunch hours my friends would argue over, "which had better graphics, *Sega* or *Nintendo?*" I found these conversations baffling as I did not know what the words "graphics", "Sega" or "Nintendo" meant. Rather than embarrassing myself by asking one of my friends I elected to extrapolate the meaning myself. I was familiar with the multicoloured bar chart "graphs" in my Mathematics 4 workbook, so I figured: a video game system with "good graphics" must have something to do with math and colours. In a technical sense I was right on the money: video game systems were all about displaying many colours and doing mathematical operations very quickly. But in a less technical, more fourth-grade sense, I was a complete moron.

In the mid-1980's Sega and Nintendo began a vicious battle for marketing supremacy in North America. The Nintendo had released its *Nintendo Entertainment System* (NES) in the United States (and later in Canada) as a redesign of its popular *Nintendo Famicom* game console. After a shaky start due to a video game market crash, Nintendo quickly took the lead in the North American market due to clever marketing and movie tie-ins. The NES also benefited from extremely strong "in-house" titles like *Mike Tyson's Punch-Out!!, The Legend of Zelda, Metroid,* and of course the ubiquitous *Super Mario Bros.* Nintendo also had a strong presence from "third-party" developers that produced classics like *Micro Machines, Mega Man,* and *Contra.* The gold "Nintendo Seal of Approval" sticker became the symbol for a standard of gaming excellence. Cool kids in 1987 had Nintendos in their homes and they were not afraid to brag about it.

The *Sega Master System* was a direct competitor to the *NES,* and matched it blow-for-blow in most technical aspects. However Sega's approach was to "port" or translate its large catalogue of full-sized arcade games into a smaller, home experience that could be played on a console. High quality ports like *Wonder Boy, Alex Kidd in Miracle World, Out Run* and *Rampage* were found in the bedrooms of most kids who grew up with a Sega in the house. But perhaps due to neglect of third-party developers or a lack of marketing in North America, the Sega Master System never reached the popularity of the NES and was relegated to scrappy underdog status. Kids who got a Sega for Christmas spent the rest of their grade school years defending the honour of their beloved console from the huffy Nintendo kids.

Playground talk about the video game system's "graphics" was shorthand for a game's visual art quality. A video game system with "good graphics" had flicker-free animation, high resolution with many pixels, a large range of colours or many simultaneous on-screen colours. A game system with "bad graphics" stuttered when several animated characters were on-screen at the same time, had large blocky pixels, and a very limited palette of colours to choose from.

Telling a schoolmate that their home video game system had bad graphics was tantamount to starting a playground knife fight.

I have no clear love-at-first-sight memory of the Mattel Intellivision because when it first appeared in our home I had no idea what it was. I was familiar in theory with the idea of video game systems, but the plastic brown box with faux gold trim looked nothing like our Tandy Color Computer II. Like the CoCo II, the Intellivision was a second-hand score from a family looking for a technology upgrade. *Unlike* our CoCo II which came in its original box with a lovingly curated (pirated) software collection, the Intellivision arrived in a generic Sears box with dozens of games squashed beneath a 12-inch Zenith television.

My clearest memory of the Intellivision is a plastic brown console with faux gold trim, sitting on the brown carpeted floor of my bedroom surrounded by a hoard of black cartridges. The black-and-white Zenith TV is on the floor beside it, and my sister and I are laying belly-down on the floor fiddling with the remote controllers. The controllers look like props from a *Star Trek* episode, coiling from the console with twisted cables reminiscent of rotary telephone handset cords.

A brown Mattel-branded "Voice Synthesis Module" plugged into the cartridge port and allowed several of our treasured games to speak aloud from the television. By "speak aloud" I should say "croak robotically, barely intelligible as human expression". For a generation of folks familiar with Apple's Siri, the word 'voice' in Voice Synthesis Module belongs in scarequotes dripping generously with sarcasm. Special voice-enabled games were marked by a gold cartridge label, and made the console bark incomprehensible words at the player. In *B-17 Bomber* – a very early flight combat simulator – the title screen heralded the game with an ear-ringing "BEE.... SEVEN.... TEEN... BAWMMMMERRRRR!", and during flight a narrator squawked out directives like "WATCH FUR FLACK!" In a puzzle game called *Bomb Squad*, the title screen was announced with an even worse "BOMMMM SAWWWWD!".

As my sister plugged each game cartridge one at a time into the Intellivision and experimented with the controller, I carefully read the descriptions and looked at the screen shots on the backs of each game box. Every screenshot featured impossibly bright colours – *TRON: Deadly Discs* looked particularly ravishing in its solid red and blues. *Dragon Fire* promised an incredible medieval castle full of gleaming treasures in half a dozen colours. But on the Zenith television that sat on my floor there were only monochromatic greys of different intensities. Once burned by the crafty cover art of the TRS-80 BASIC type-in book, I assumed that the screenshots on the Intellivision boxes were only imaginary artistic fabrications. It never once occurred to me that the "screen shots" were *actual photographs of each game.*

One day my sister and I conspired to steal the slightly larger television hooked up to the TRS-80. It did not cross our minds that the TRS-80 had a *colour* television. The minute we swapped televisions and turned on the Intellivision our jaws fell off their hinges. The only comparable moment I have is in the original 1939 *The Wizard of Oz* film. The first act of the movie features Dorothy and Toto in their native Kansas farm house; all filmed in a creamy monochromatic sepia. When Dorothy opens the door to Oz, the screen explodes from sepia to vibrant colour. That is precisely what happened to my sister and I. Suddenly *Lock'n'Chase* and *Night Stalker* became crisp multicoloured experiences. In *Frog Bog* the lily pads which were previously grey were now green, and dragonflies went from paler shades of grey to yellow and blue and red. *Astrosmash* – a vertical space shoot'em'up game similar to *Space Invaders* – was no longer an exercise in distinguishing charcoal-shaded enemies from the black background. After that day we received official permission from our parents to use the colour TV with the Intellivision and relegated the black-and-white Zenith to the recently unloved TRS-80.

The Intellivision never felt like a computer to us because it looked nothing like the computer in our living room – even the "Enhanced Computer System" keyboard attachment it came with did little to convince us it was a computer.[3] The Intellivision never disappointed me with its rudimentary graphics or music or sound or lack of data storage simply because it looked neither like a Nintendo nor a Tandy. And I learned a critical lesson from the colour television debacle: assume nothing about these magical video game machines and explore every nook and cranny until I have the thing figured out.

---

[3] The ECS add-on module was so famously delayed in production and release that Mattel had its proverbial pants sued off by customers who had pre-ordered and pre-paid for it; customers waited *years* to receive their modules.

Amiga 1000 and Indiana Jones and the Last Crusade

It was Halloween eve and I had been invited over to my friend David's home for a party. He and his best friend Matthew, both classmates of mine, had spent the past week designing the scariest haunted house of all time in the basement of David's house. The entire basement was transformed into the domestic equivalent of some evil carnival ride. With David's father's help they constructed a series of passages using cardboard boxes and plywood, funnelling the victim on his hands and knees through a gauntlet of boo-scares. At predetermined moments David and Matthew leapt out of hidden scare-points cut out in the boxes and enjoyed watching me shit my little corduroy pants. I honestly can say that I could not wait for the experience to be over – boo-scares are my least favourite part of Halloween.

The half hour of terror was rewarded tenfold, however, when we retired to David's father's office. For a couple of hours I was briefly acquainted with a game that to this day still eludes completion: *Indiana Jones and the Last Crusade.*

When David turned on his computer I had only a single point of reference for what a computer should be like. His Amiga 1000 bore little resemblance to the Radio Shack TRS-80 in our house. The computer case was separate from the keyboard, it used a dedicated computer monitor instead of a television, it had a strange movement device called a "mouse", and instead of a cassette recorder it had an actual disk drive! While I had no idea that a floppy disk was better than a cassette tape at the time, the ultra slim 3-½" diskettes looked as if they belonged in a futuristic science fiction film.

When David loaded up *Indiana Jones* I was immediately drawn to the rich orchestral music blasting out of the computer. It sounded *nothing* like the TRS-80! When the Lucasfilm Games logo appeared on the computer monitor I could barely take it all in – the colours were so rich, vibrant, and they were so *many* of them! John Williams' iconic *Raiders March* came out of the Amiga like there was a miniature orchestra packed inside of it. Modern gamers might sneer at the relatively conservative musical capabilities of the Amiga sound chip, but I can assure you that in 1988 it was revolutionary.[4]

Until that day the only ways I was familiar with interacting with the computer were the joystick and the keyboard. I watched Matthew's hand glide the mouse carefully around the desk – the pointer on the screen paralleled his movements! Indiana Jones walked to the exact place where Matthew's mouse pointer had pinpointed. It was a whole new way of thinking about controlling the hero – it was as if Matthew was whispering commands to Indy, and Indy was following his directions.

Indiana Jones and the Last Crusade was my first exposure to a modern adventure game. Gone were the obscure keyboard commands that I had memorized for games on the TRS-80. For example in *Dungeons of Daggorath* to ready and ignite the hero's torch to light a dark hallway I had to type in the following commands:

```
> pull right torch
You ready the pine torch in your right hand and light
it.
```

Dungeons of Daggorath used a "text parser" method of interaction. The player types in keyboard commands in a sequence and the computer interprets the keystrokes and spits a response back to the player such as moving the hero north a few feet or igniting a torch.

Text parsers in early adventure games generally used a "verb + object" approach. The verb in this case is "pull" and the object is the "torch". These older adventure games sometimes list the

---

[4] The Amiga's sound chip encouraged a generation of "MOD" or "tracker" music artists that to take advantage of its multi-track and multi-voice synthesis capabilities. Tracker artists would become vital figures in Bulletin Board System culture.

available verbs the game understands and objects might be items in the room or items in the hero's backpack or "inventory". It is the player's job to try out every verb and object combination they can think of to advance the story.

Last Crusade took a step away from the keyboard by displaying all of the available verbs and objects on-screen simultaneously along with a window where the story's action takes place.[5] I no longer had to memorize the cryptic verbs from the game manual and their corresponding keystrokes. *Last Crusade* made adventuring simple and accessible for kids like Matthew, David and I; it was the perfect gateway drug to make us adventure game addicts later in life.

I watched Matthew click furiously around the screen with different combinations of verbs and objects trying to make something happen. Even with a handful of objects in a room there might be hundreds of verb-object combinations to try. David and I crowded around him, smudging the monitor glass with our greasy kid fingers, pointing out different objects to experiment with.

Even though I was shouting out commands to Matthew I did not have a clue as to what was going on. I had not seen any of the *Indiana Jones* films and was baffled by the plucky adventurer dressed in leather and a fedora wandering around some subterranean cavern. Years later I would see *Indiana Jones and the Last Crusade* on VHS and appreciate the context: Indy was trapped underneath the palatial Venice Library exploring the catacombs of the floating city, and his goal was to find the missing inscription of the grail tablet and escape to the surface.

After hours of wandering around in circles lost in the catacombs we finally gave up: Indy inevitably ended up behind the locked gate of what looked to be a *very* important room. We had no idea how to solve the puzzle and abandoned the game in

---

[5] *Indiana Jones and the Last Crusade* is therefore known as a fully "graphical" adventure game.

favour of our cozy sleeping bags, homemade popcorn and Halloween ghost stories.

Atari 520ST and Donald Duck's Playground

My mother had set me up on a play-date with a kid who would become a necessary evil in my life for the remainder of the school year. My mother had become fast friends with another francophone mother who had a son my age named Matthieu.

Matthieu was a single child born to a relatively wealthy family and it showed. He always had the best, newest toys and had no qualms about showing them off to everyone at our school. It was no surprise then that on my first play-date at his house he was eager to show me *his* new computer.

Computer, you say?

We sat down in his family's office in front of a computer that looked very similar to David's Amiga and a bit like our TRS-80.[6] When Matthieu loaded *Donald Duck's Playground* I lost all interest in comparing the computers and sat transfixed for the rest of the evening.

The game had no on-screen instructions so we sat together trying to figure out what to do. Donald Duck waited on the main street of some one-horse town with a few different places he could visit: the toy shop, a playground, a bank, etc. Going to the toy shop began a mini-game involving processing customer orders – when a customer asked for a specific toy it was our job to direct Donald to the correct place on the wall of toys to retrieve the order. The goal of the game was to save enough money from doing odd-jobs that would allow Donald to purchase equipment for his empty playground.

I watched all of the fun happen passively as Matthieu refused

---

[6] The Atari 520ST was every bit a worthy competitor to Amiga computers. The sound chip was capable of multi-voice musical production, the monitor was gorgeous and bright, it used a mouse, and had its own graphical operating system called GEOS. Sadly, due to corporate mishandling, the machine died in the consumer world far before its time.

to give up the joystick. As I was quite the joystick hog myself this situation would not stand – I began complaining and wheedling Matthieu for my turn to no avail.

My break finally came when Matthieu was stymied by one of the mini-games that required quick reflexes. The goal of the game was to stand behind a fruit laden farm truck as the farmer lobbed fruit at Donald. Donald's job was to catch the flying fruit and deposit it into the proper basket. Each time Donald deposited fruit into the right basket he received a few cents towards his ultimate goal of furnishing the town playground with all the equipment he desired. If Donald missed catching the flying fruit, it hit the ground and exploded into gooey chunks and Donald would quack irritably. At the time I thought Donald's spastic quacking was the height of hilarity. I imagined that Donald was cursing in the cartoony $@#$*#$@*!! style I was familiar with, cursing me out for my poor reflexes.

Donald Duck's Playground is the brainchild of the legendary computer game designer Al Lowe, the (in)famous creator of Sierra On-Line's *Leisure Suit Larry* series of games. *Donald Duck's Playground* can only be described as the polar opposite of *Leisure Suit Larry.* No adolescent sexual innuendo, no PG-rated pixelated breasts. *Donald Duck's Playground* is a cleverly designed educational game that teaches kids some of the important things they'll need in life like counting change, saving money and buying toys from a toy shop. In reality: a subtle capitalist training simulator for your child's hellish future as a poor day-labouring wage slave, scrimping pennies to satisfy their materialistic desires.

Matthieu and I spent months trying to turn Donald into Scrooge McDuck before our fun on the Atari was rudely interrupted by my family purchasing a house 1200 kilometres away and moving there.

1989: Grade Five

The Move South

In the summer of 1989 my family moved south to an acreage on the prairies. My father left months ahead of us to renovate the house before our arrival; while my sister, mother and I spent the intervening time packing our belongings for the wagon drive south.

The move south warped time itself. The town I grew up in was at least fifteen years behind the rest of the known universe culturally, socially and technologically. It had no chain stores like *Toys'R'Us* and *San Francisco* (a popular joke and trinket shop); *McDonald's* was just an imaginary place seen on television ads. In my home town *Sears* was a tiny one-room office where customers ordered items from a fat catalogue and waited months for their purchases to arrive.

Our acreage was less than an hour away from a major urban centre and suddenly every materialistic desire could be catered to instantly. Instead of buying a type-in program magazine from the town Radio Shack I could visit any one of a half-dozen computer stores that sold computer games on disk. The malls had *several* different computer stores that allowed me to compare prices, or even trade-in my used computer games for new titles. I was in technoconsumerfetishistic heaven.

As happy as I was about the new opportunities I had to blow cash on computer games, the move south was full of anxiety for my family. My mother and father had left behind an army of friends and family, and a timeless Northern way of life. My sister lost a tight clique of friends. I left behind a handful of playmates and their computers; that created a vacuum in my life that demanded to be filled.

Sega Master System

Our acreage was a kilometre away from two neighbouring acreages. A family with four kids roughly similar in ages to my sister and I lived across the road, on the other side of a hilled pasture. This family became fast, life-long friends with us days after we moved in.

The second acreage was a kilometre down our dusty gravel road toward a set of green community mailboxes; it had a small white house with carefully manicured lawns and an immaculate sports car parked outside. In that white house lived a friendly, recently-divorced father and his son named Ken.

I met Ken the day his dad tried to kill himself.

My sister, mother and I were unpacking boxes in the house when we saw a young man sprinting full-tilt down the dirt road. We all walked outside to see who this guy was. He vaulted over our white horse fence and ran through our treed pasture while breathlessly yelling to us at the top of his lungs. We had no idea what he was yelling about.

He ran up to my mother and barely croaked out. "I need help. My dad's got a gun in his mouth and he wants to kill himself."

The look of panic on the boy's face was unforgettable. My mother jumped into her van and sped off down the road towards the small white house on the corner of our street. My sister and I stayed outside with the boy and he shook miserably as he introduced himself as Kenneth. He said that he lived on the acreage on the corner and that he would be on the same school bus ride as we were when the school year started in a month. Not knowing what else to do or say, we stood around chatting about the upcoming school year.

After an hour my mother came back and told us everything was going to be okay. She explained to us that the man was sad about his divorce and had promised not to hurt himself or anyone else. She drove Kenneth home, and the rest of the night was spent in an eery silence as we all processed what had just happened.

A week later, Kenneth came back and re-introduced himself to our family as if the incident had not happened at all. It was an early lesson for my family in acreage culture: learning how to pretend nothing was wrong despite everything being wrong.

A couple of weeks later, just before the school year began, Ken invited me over to his house. He introduced me to my neighbour Steven, who lived at the acreage across the pasture. Both boys were older than me – Ken was in the eighth grade and Steven was just about to begin the seventh grade. Both were lanky and tall for their age. Ken wore wireframe glasses reminiscent of the glasses the character "Wheels" wore on the Canadian television series *Degrassi Junior High,* and thanks to a stonewashed jean jacket managed to pull off a badass teenager look even with the Coke bottle lenses. Steven had an athletic build, green eyes and was becoming a teenage heart throb for the girls in his grade. Both boys were walking hormone dispensers.

I followed the boys down into the basement which had been converted into a dark cave of teenage angst. Posters of bikini babes and metal rock bands were clumsily pasted on the 1970s-era wood panelled walls, and a small television and VHS recorder were huddled together in front of Ken's waterbed. It was the quintessential man-cave for a thirteen-year-old who was into chicks, beer and heavy metal. I was far outside of my comfort zone.

Ken and Steve sat down on the waterbed which gurgled and sloshed under them.

Ken reached across to a futuristic black and red unit in front of the TV which read "SEGA MASTER SYSTEM" and pressed a button. "Let's play some Sega, man."

Sega. Was this the same mysterious "Sega" that the rich kids on the playground had argued about in my home town?

A blue SEGA logo flashed across the screen before loading a car racing game called *Out Run.* I watched as Ken and Steve took turns flooring a red convertible sports car down an endless highway. The smooth animation and sheer speed of the game was incredible – it was nothing like the games I had played on the computer. Ken hooked up his television to a stereo receiver and it blasted *Out Run's* catchy driving music and sound effects to the point of hurting my delicate ears. A year ago I thought nothing could top the quality of music and graphics I had seen on a full sized Amiga computer.

When *Out Run* wore thin Ken plugged in a cartridge called *Gangster Town* and both boys took turns shooting at the screen with a "Light Phaser" – a plastic gun that allowed you to shoot enemies on the television! Every time they pointed at a prohibition era-themed gangster waving a pistol and pressed the trigger, a bullet exploded on the screen and the character was blasted into oblivion. Years of fighting with cheap joysticks and awkward Intellivision controllers made the Light Phaser unimaginably cool and completely novel!

After a couple of hours a classmate of Ken's showed up, dressed in stylish white *Reebok* 'The Pump' hi-tops and zebra-patterned *Zulu Airwear* sweatpants. He had a six-pack of beer with him in tow, and the three sat on the waterbed drinking and belching. After a few minutes the new guest leaned back and turned to Ken, "Hey let's watch some porno. Still got your dad's tape?"

Ken dug under his bed and fished out an unlabelled VHS cassette. A moment of brotherly concern crossed his face and he turned to me, "Sorry man. This is for older kids. You can't watch."

Despite not having a clue what "porno" was, I tried to play it nonchalant. "Hey I'm cool. Can I have a beer?"

The three of them gave me a sympathetic chuckle. Steven shook his head, "Sorry man. Your dad would kill me."

They repositioned the chair I was sitting on so that I was no longer facing the television. After hearing the groans and moans coming from the speakers it did not take long for me to figure out what the word "porno" meant. The three boys nursed their beers and made comments about the naked people carousing on the screen. When I realized there was no way I could sneak a peek at the naked ladies they were ogling I beat a hasty retreat in fear of publicly sporting a boner in my sweat pants. When I walked up the stairs from the basement and said goodbye, all three boys were completely transfixed by the television and said nothing as I left.

That day I decided that the Sega Master System was the best video game console on Earth. The Sega was not just cool because it had bright and colourful games. It was cool because *teenagers who were into cool adult stuff played it.* Despite never seeing a Nintendo Entertainment System, there was *no* way it could be as cool as the Sega. If I wanted to join the cool kids club I needed a Sega and I needed one right away.

Apple //e

The summer full of packing and unpacking and family drama on the acreage came to an end too quickly. The school year was upon us and my sister and I began attending a school located in a village a forty-five minute drive from our acreage. The village had about 200 residents and half of those attended our tiny school. At the tender age of ten I had become extremely shy and self-conscious. Attending a new school meant making new friends, meeting new teachers and dealing with a whole new way of "down south" life I was unfamiliar with.

On my first day I was thrown into the deep end of the pool. The one-and-a-half hour ride to the school in a big yellow bus was a social ecology of rumour-mongering, teen romances and fights among three dozen farm kids. My sister and I occupied a seat together and tried to look impassive as we overheard the other kids talking. Most of them had been riding the same bus to school their whole lives and us "new kids" were the talk of the town. Although they were farm kids like us this new environment was metropolitan in a way I could not have imagined. These kids had *Nike* "Air" and *Reebok* "The Pump" shoes. They talked about "bands" they liked and which songs on the radio were "rad" and which ones "blew". The high school students at the back of the bus appeared to have broken out of a federal penitentiary; they scrawled dirty words in ink on their jeans and shot orange peels at one another with deconstructed Bic ballpoint pens. My sister and I, dressed in our non-brand name duds and black rubber boots were about as cool as day-old oatmeal.

When I got to my new fifth grade home room class I was scared shitless. The teacher, Mrs. L, introduced me to the entire class.

I was a goofy, short, dark-skinned kid with a bad curly black mullet and missing baby teeth. All 30 pale faces and blonde heads turned towards me and I turned a beet red.

A few of the girls began whispering and giggling as they goggled at the new kid. I sank into my chair, stammered a quick hi, and gratefully sighed when the teacher told me to find a desk and continued on with the roll-call. A group of four boys my age waved me over to an empty desk near them.

Those boys became the closest friends I had for the next ten years of my life. Their names were Robert, Trevor, Chris and Donny. Seeing my embarrassment somehow singled me out as a potential new gang recruit and playmate. To this day I suspect that the only thing we all had in common was that we all were wearing matching polyester sweater and sweatpants combinations that must have driven the ladies wild. It is a wonder that any of us married later in life.

Thinking back to that day and the years that followed, their names are synonymous with the happiest childhood memories I have. If this crew had not taken pity on me that day, I would have never fallen in love with computer games quite the way I did. These boys became the central figures in my exploration of computers in the 1990s.

At the end the first week of the fifth grade, Mrs. L announced that she would be holding a special draw for the use of the classroom computer. *Computer?*

I was so busy playing soccer and Connect Four with my new friends that week that I had somehow overlooked the computer tucked away in a corner of the classroom. I turned around in my chair and stared: propped up on an old student desk with a fat beige keyboard sticking out of it was a computer I had never seen before. I squinted and made out the playful logo of a colourful apple with a bite taken out of it.

Mrs. L continued, "I want everyone to put their name on a piece of paper. Every day we'll draw one name out of a hat and the winner gets to use the computer at lunch recess. We'll start the draw again when we run out of names."

I do not think she had finished saying 'computer' before I had my name written out on a slip of paper and charged to the front of the class and jammed it into her hat. Most of the class reluctantly added their names to the hat, not quite sure why anyone would *want* to use the computer in the first place. Thinking back to that day I suspect most kids simply wanted to *win* something, regardless of what it was. My friends – Trevor, Robert, Chris and Donny – all added their entries to the hat, and for the next few minutes we speculated on the games we could play on it.

A nasal, sneering voice rang out before us, "I'm gonna win you know. You guys don't even know how to play games. I already know how to get the trident in *King's Quest*."

We turned around to face the voice that had thrown down the glove. It was an evil, mature sixth grader who had nothing but contempt for us prepubescent fifth graders. It was Donny's older brother, Carl: renowned egotist, braggart extraordinaire, and (apparently) computer game whiz. I did not know what *King's Quest* was but I knew that Carl talked a bigger game than he could possibly muster. He was one of those kids that knew how to push every one of my red buttons and excelled at doing it to everyone else too… especially his brother Donny.

My friends and I devised a plan to prevent Carl from winning the draw. Each of us boys convinced some of the other students in the class to give *us* their turns on the computer if they won; in exchange our benefactors received a payoff in the form of *Old Dutch* brand ketchup-flavoured potato chips. The plan was ostensibly perfect: each of us would have at *least* two turns on the computer for a total of ten turns. This would force Carl to watch *us* play his precious *King's Quest* for most of the month! With a class of 32 students, almost 1/3 the population of the entire school, there was a very good chance that one of us would get to play on the computer on the first draw.

The next morning Mrs. L dug into the hat and retrieved the first name. "Okay guys – everyone do a drum roll! – the winner is… Carl!" I turned around in my plastic chair and glowered at Carl. He had the most spectacular shit-eating grin that only black hearted children can muster.

Carl played *King's Quest* with a group of his sixth grade

friends that day. My group of friends and I went outside to play soccer, thus refusing to give him the satisfaction of making us watch him play.

It took us a week to realize that we had massively underestimated Carl's Machiavellian brilliance. A week later he won *again*. Mrs. L frowned quizzically. There were many shouts of "No fair!" and "He already won!" from the outraged class. She dug into the hat once more and began laughing. "Oh Carl..", she chided in her unconditionally compassionate voice. Carl gave his best sheepish grin, the calling card of the career criminal pleading 'boys will be boys' to our lenient judge, and earned a finger-wag sentence.

Apparently Carl had won the draw by his superior sixth-grade understanding of probability: he simply added twenty multiple entries of his own name to the hat. He did not care if he was caught for winning twice – he just wanted to get on the computer *before we did*.

None of our scheming against our master criminal arch-enemy mattered the second I saw the Apple //e computer boot up for the first time. It had a colour monitor and *two* 5-¼" disk drives![7] Whomever won the draw that day sat down in the plastic orange chair, picked out a diskette from a box of hand-labelled copies, slipped the disk into the drive and locked its plastic tab, and hit the power button.

The computer emitted a high-pitched *BEEP!* and we watched the disk drive chatter away with a loud *Chkhhkh-khkhkhkkh-khghkghgh-kgkgk-ggggg!* as it chomped at the disk in some strange

---

[7] The Apple // is an engineering masterpiece. Its designer, Steve Wozniak, created an "open architecture" design that allowed prospective engineers to add their own expansion devices to the computer. Even without a floppy disk drive the Apple // could store data on cassette tape via a cassette interface, just like the Commodore 64 or Tandy TRS-80. For its time the built-in color graphics and speedy disk drive interface were exceptional, making it an ideal platform for computer games.

waking routine. When the drive detected the disk it began grinding with a gentle *mrrrr-RRRRrr-RRMmRm-RRm-MRmRR* as it loaded the game. A crowd of classmates gathered behind the chair and waited eagerly to see which game the winner had picked.[8]

Our favoured choice was *King's Quest II: Romancing the Throne,* a Sierra On-Line graphical adventure game. The player assumed the role of a hero by the name of King Graham who ambled around the medieval land of Daventry, controlling his movement with a set of up, down, left and right arrow keys. There was also a text parser interface that required the player to type in keyboard commands like "pick up trident" or "talk to troll". Since there was only enough room for one person at the keyboard at a time, kids crowded around the player and barked out back-seat-driver commands while the poor player hammered them into the kludgy text parser. Chaos ensued whenever one of the kids who did not know how to type on a keyboard took the driver's seat, and King Graham died over and over as the kid repeatedly drowned him in the castle's moat. Kids behind them cried out, "No! Go right! No not there! You'll die if you go left!" or "You're not even trying! Give someone else a try!"

After a few months the lure of the Apple // wore off. New personal computers were breaking into the market and kids were beginning to talk about them on the playground. The brands "Packard Bell" and "Tandy" were spoken of reverently and the Apple // was becoming a name of yesteryear. By the

---

[8] The Apple // computer was introduced by Apple Computers in 1977. Keep in mind that it was now 1989 and the computer we were fighting over was already twelve years old! The computer most likely got into our classroom thanks to a brilliant Apple marketing plan: the company sold (and donated) computers at an "educational discount" to educational districts in North America. The plan was devious – children self-indoctrinated themselves with Apple software and later begged their parents to buy an Apple // for the family home.

end of the first semester, the Nintendo Entertainment System and Sega Master System were everywhere and every family had some kind of gaming console in their living room. I did not even mention to my friends that my sister and I owned a Mattel Intellivision – this was scoffed at as a passé product of the early 1980s. The 1990s were just around the corner and the new generation of video game consoles like the Sega Genesis were almost upon us.

My family was effectively two video game console generations behind, and as far as I was concerned, we needed to catch up *now*.

Nintendo Entertainment System

Robert, Trevor and I became fast friends a few weeks into the first semester of the fifth grade. It turned out they had a younger sister who was in the same grade as my own sister, and they had become friends too. For our parents this made visiting one another's houses very simple – they just loaded all of us kids up into the family car and drove us a few miles away to visit.

I will never forget my first sleep-over at Robert and Trevor's house. My mother drove me over to their farm on a cold November day – the wind was vicious and had drifted snow over the dirt roads. When I arrived the front door to the house was locked. Robert and Trevor's mother exited from a side door and apologetically greeted us outside.

"The boys are in the garage. That's their temporary bedroom while the house is being renovated."

I dragged my backpack and sleeping bag through the door to their two-car garage. Inside it was dark, lit only by a couple of table lamps and a television. Robert and Trevor ran up and jumped up and down, pleading to their mother loudly, "Mom can we have pizzas please?"

My mother laughed at the sight of them, and when she was convinced I would be safe amongst my new friends, she embarrassed me by giving me a hug in front of them. I barely managed to squirm away.

The garage-gone-bedroom was every pre-teen boy's dream. Robert and Trevor shared it with an older brother by the name of Larry who occupied a large bed in one of the car bays. The other bay was a shared space for all three boys, with a small brown faux-woodgrain Sears television propped up in front of a large comfy brown couch. The floor was a patchwork of carpets and rugs clumsily arranged to protect our tiny feet from the freezing concrete underneath.

Trevor jumped onto the couch and bounced up and down. Robert pointed at the television and yelled to his older brother

Larry, who sat on his bed reading comic books trying to ignore us.

"Hey Larry, can we play your Nintendo?"

He yelled back nonchalantly, "Alright. As long as you little shits don't wreck it. Or I'll whup ya."

Nintendo?

On a shelf underneath the television was a large grey box the size of a toaster laying on its side. The lid was partly open and I could see a video game cartridge protruding out of it. It was too dark inside of the garage to make out the label on the game.

Trevor had a controller in his hands and he was deftly moving a character on the screen around what appeared to be a mine – a series of ladders and rails. The character could even climb into a mining cart and zoom off down the rails. It took a minute to recognize the iconic whip and fedora on the character – it was Indiana Jones on another one of his grave-robbing adventures, this time in the cavernous depths of a mine in India! The game was an adaptation of *Indiana Jones and the Temple of Doom,* a film I had recently seen. I had been enamoured with the film's gross-out scenes including a hand extracting a beating heart from a man's chest and people eating chilled monkey brains – the kinds of outrageous movie scenes kids gossiped over on the school bus.

Trevor, Rob and I took turns playing a handful of Nintendo games like *Super Mario Bros., Xevious, The Adventures of Bayou Billy, and Wrestlemania. Wrestlemania* was particularly entertaining because it allowed for two players to compete in a wrestling ring, complete with the characters from the WWF and their copyrighted theatrics. After an hour our WWF wrestling bouts descended into each of us imitating WWF characters like Hulk Hogan, The Million Dollar Man, and The Ultimate Warrior. Fake wrestling matches broke out on the couch until their mom arrived with McCain-brand frozen personal pizzas fresh from the oven.

When the sleep-over ended a day later I was sad to leave my friends. It was the most fun I had since my sister and I had moved to our acreage. When I got home that night I replayed the weekend in my imagination and thought about all of the games I had played on their Nintendo. I was impressed by the Nintendo Entertainment System. While it did not have the adolescent appeal of the Sega that so sorely mattered to me at the time, the games themselves were colourful, musical, exciting and just plain fun! I begrudgingly admitted to myself: it was a hell of a lot better than our Intellivision, and I could not wait for my next chance to spend time with my new friends *and* their Nintendo.

The bus ride home was the nexus from which almost all of my computer adventures began. The one-and-a-half hour ride back to my home from school turned the yellow school bus into a miniature space colony where friendships were forged and shattered in a single ride. The youngest kids sat in the front where (purportedly) the ride was less bumpy and therefore less apt to cause one of them to barf all over their seat-neighbour. The oldest kids sat at the very rear of the bus pretending to enjoy the wild bouncy ride over the deep ruts in the muddy roads, and definitely enjoyed being out of the bus driver's view so they could commit any crime their cruel hearts desired. As a fifth grader I earned a seat in the middle with other kids my age – this area was effectively a purgatory.

Behind me sat two boys I recognized from my class. They were sixth-graders, infinitely wiser and more mature than I, and I naturally was afraid of them like any child who valued his own life. The boys were named Chad and Fraser.

Fraser was a wan-faced boy who always looked like he was on the verge of vomiting on the bus. He was quiet and studious around adults, but in the company of likeminded kids he was a fountain of energy and enjoyed getting attention from his peers in any way possible. He first got *my* attention when he held a daily ritual sacrifice of his mom's home-made submarine sandwiches in the classroom.[9]

Each morning, Fraser's mother laboriously prepared one of the finest deli sandwiches to grace the classroom of our tiny

---

[9] Submarine: A foot-long, torpedo-shaped hunk of bread filled with assorted meats, lettuce, cheeses, tomatoes and mayonnaise. In Western Canada the quintessential 'sub' has ham or turkey, cheddar cheese, mayo, mustard, chopped iceberg lettuce, tomatoes, pepper and salt. The name varies from region to region, but the fundamental magic remains the same.

school. And hours later Fraser gave his sub away to one of his classmates in a classroom ritual, which went like this: Fraser waited until lunch hour when the teacher disappeared to the staff room, and yelled out "OKAY, SUB-TOSS!" Us filthy street urchins gathered behind him in a crowd, reaching up to the skies with our grubby little paws yelling 'Me!', 'No! Over here!' Fraser donned the dramatic pose of a bride tossing her bouquet to a clutch of desperate old maids, faced the chalkboard, closed his eyes, and tossed the submarine over his shoulder into the air behind him. Reaching hands fought over the flying German bomb as it careened towards us. There was always a fumble, much scrambling to the Asbestos-infused tiled floor, and one of us grimy ragamuffins emerged victorious and munched on the glorious tubular treasure.

Fraser's desperate antics for attention and friendship quickly warmed him to me, perhaps because I was new to the class and desperate for friends myself.

The boy sitting beside Fraser on the bus seat was everything Fraser was not. Chad was a calm, blue-eyed and blond-haired boy who drew the attention of any girl in the room. Chad's good looks, easygoing demeanour and interest in horse-riding made him dreamcandy for almost every girl in our class and he knew it. The only thing Chad and Fraser had in common was that they lived on acreages a five-minute bicycle ride apart, and in those days that was enough of a foundation for a lifelong friendship. And I lived just a short bike ride away from both of them, too.

Unlike most of the other older kids on the bus, Chad and Fraser were far more approachable. I poked my head over the backrest of my bus seat and introduced myself. It did not take long for us to get on the subject of hockey, and when they found out that I liked ice hockey and knew how to skate, Fraser suggested a get-together at his house later that evening. Fraser introduced me to what became a nightly ritual that cemented our friendship over the next three years: the evening shinny hockey game.

Most weeknights, and every weekend, Fraser invited Chad

and I over to play hockey on his outdoor rink. In the spring, summer and autumn the rink was a diamond of dirt and weeds that we played on with a fluorescent orange ball and sticks. In winter, Fraser's father flooded the area with water from a garden hose and turned the small dirt patch into a gorgeous ice hockey rink, supporting skates and a sponge puck.

Regardless of the season or the weather, we gathered after supper at his house and played a three-man game of hockey. Each night began the same way: as we laced up our skates an argument ensued over who would have to be the goalie, and who would get to fire pucks at him. Inevitably, Fraser cowed down to our manipulative cajoling and donned the flimsy foam goalie pads and plastic mask that his father had purchased at Canadian Tire.[10] Chad and I would spend the rest of the night hurling orange sponge pucks at Fraser, occasionally goading him into an on-ice fight by winging a puck at the family jewels. It was good, clean, puerile, fun.

After an hour our feet would freeze in our skates and we would retire to the comforts of Fraser's walk-in basement. His father graciously built a fire where we could warm our frozen skates, and we huddled in front of their 27-inch wood-panelled television set. We alternated between *Blades of Steel* and *Super Mario Bros. 2* on Fraser's Nintendo Entertainment System, the loser handing off the controller to the next player.

This ritual went on for months until the day that I heard a sickly, electronic "BOOOOOOOP!" come from a nearby room. I inquired about the source of the sound and Fraser absently replied as he played *Mario 2*, "Oh that's just my mom on the computer."

A computer, you say? Why was I not informed of this important addition to your household?

I watched as Fraser's mom left one of the rooms down the hall

---

[10] Canadian Tire was an automotive tire chain that expanded to carry bicycles, auto parts, sports equipment, and even video games/systems.

next to the bathroom and walked upstairs. Fraser made it clear that he had absolutely no interest in the computer as he was feverishly tapping buttons trying to get past a particularly intense level of *Mario 2*. Here was my chance to sneak a peek at a computer!

I announced ostentatiously that I was going to the bathroom and padded down the basement hallway. I walked past the bathroom door to the room his mother had walked out of, and peeking inside of the dark room I found the gem: an unattended Apple Macintosh 512K with a glowing monochromatic screen. The screen currently pictured the silhouette of a city skyline at night as it filled in pixel by pixel.[11] Unable to contain my curiosity, I moved the mouse and the skyline disappeared, revealing a beautiful desktop environment.[12] I had heard of Macintosh computers before but I had never seen one in the flesh. Fraser's "Mac" was undeniably better looking than any computer I had seen before. The 3½ inch disk drive and monitor were smoothly integrated into a bevelled plastic housing, and the keyboard and mouse were angular and clean looking. Everything about this computer screamed professional, friendly, and *expensive*.

Not satisfied with just seeing the computer I began rooting around in a nearby box of diskettes. Who would notice if I did a

---

[11] This is likely the ubiquitous screensaver by Berkeley Systems called "Starry Night". A screensaver is a program that constantly changes what is displayed on the screen to prevent "burn-in" on glass tube monitors, the kind used prior to our LCD screens.

[12] The early Macintosh user interface was based on the Xerox Palo Alto Research Center's (PARC) "Alto" model of computer. Although Microsoft borrowed a very similar interface for their own Windows desktop environment, the Macintosh had a cleaner, gentler, interface from the very beginning. Fonts were rendered with anti-aliasing, dialog boxes and buttons were rounded and bevelled instead of completely square, and the system played cute audio cues to accompany system events. The Mac 512K that Fraser's family owned had a high resolution 7-inch black-and-white monitor built into the stylish form-fitted casing.

bit of snooping? After inspecting a dozen disk labels in front of the harsh light of the monitor I found a disk label that piqued my interest: *Dark Castle.* I quietly slipped the diskette into the drive with a *snick!* and lo' and behold, a little *Dark Castle* diskette icon appeared on the desktop. This truly was far ahead of the computers I had seen so far, which were all operated with complex keyboard commands.

I had no idea what to do next. It took a minute to figure out how to use the mouse to move the cursor around the screen. I hit the <enter> key on the keyboard when I managed to highlight the *Dark Castle* icon. I watched in amazement as the disk drive began to mumble and whirr and the game loaded in front of me.

Dark Castle's title screen artwork blew me away. It was so crisp and sharp. The game promised a medieval horror story set in a haunted castle. It was the kind of artwork that belonged on the cover of a VHS movie. I became so entranced by the visuals that I had hardly noticed the noisy explosion of thunder from the Mac's single speaker as lightning lit up the castle on the screen. I froze.

One room away, Fraser paused *Mario 2* in the living room and the basement became deathly silent. I panicked. How do I turn off the sound?! Hell, how do I turn off the computer?

Fraser yelled out, "Hey what are you doing?"

Uh-oh. I searched everywhere for a power button, but could not see anything behind the monitor's glare in the dark room. The floppy drive made grinding noises and the computer began playing a demo of one of the levels. A little monster skittered across the screen of some medieval dungeon yelling "NEENER NEENER NEENER!"

The door flew open and the light flicked on. Caught red-handed.

"Oh geez. Mom's gonna *kill* you if she sees this!"

Fraser reached behind the computer to turn it off when we all heard footsteps booming down the staircase to the basement. *Shit.*

Fraser's wan face turned a dull green. His mom stomped into

the office where all three of us boys stood like deer caught in the headlights.

"What did I tell you about the computer Fraser?" Her eyes bore into him like steel drill bits.

"I uh… wasn't… I didn't DO anythingggg!" Fraser cried.

"And what did we talk about earlier? About lying? You're grounded right now, mister. You boys have to go home. Fraser is in a lot of trouble."

Did you ever notice that parents always seem to react differently to their kids when friends are around? Fraser's parents wanted to prove to the neighbourhood that they were finer-bred than most. That meant showing everyone that their only son was strictly disciplined for any small error, with quick and decisive punishment. They surmised, correctly, that Chad and I would go immediately home and tell our parents about what had happened… and this would become neighbourhood gossip amongst the parents over coffee the next morning. You see how acreage-family politics worked back then?

Fraser's eyes welled up with anger at the injustice of it all, and Chad and I fled the house with our skates slung over our shoulders into the chilly night. On the walk home, Chad kept repeating that Fraser had not touched the computer himself, and that this was all my fault. Why did I have to go messing around with someone else's computer anyway?

I had no good answer to that.

The next day, Fraser sat alone and inconsolable in his bus seat. He refused to speak with either of us, but it did not take long to find out he was grounded for a week and instructed to come home and do homework after school, with a Draconian 9 o'clock bedtime. There would be no hockey nights and Nintendo games for the rest of the month.

The grounding did not last. The storm blew over a week later and we were eventually invited back to Fraser's house. The nightly hockey games resumed and the NES once again became our virtual battleground. Only once, a year later, did I surreptitiously inquire about the Macintosh in the office. Fraser looked at me blandly without replying, searching my eyes for guilt and repentance. I saw the look on his face and knew the thought behind it: he had covered for me and I still owed him big.

Sadly, it was a debt I would never repay. A couple of years later, citing concerns over the quality of his education in our hillbilly secondary school, Fraser's parents forced him to attend a City school fifty kilometres away. The family moved away from the acreage, marking the end of our hockey nights and my last chance to mess around with his mom's Mac Plus.

Zenith 8086 XT Personal Computer

A few months after the Macintosh incident, I noticed that there was one boy in our neighbourhood of acreages who notably did *not* ride the bus with us and instead attended a school in another county. At the end of the road close to the highway lived a boy named Barrett, who was Chad's age. Barrett's family eschewed relationships with lesser farmers, perhaps because his family was undeniably affluent compared to the blue-collar families in the area like ours. His mother was a university professor, she drove a Mercedes-Benz sedan, and Barrett was often seen riding around on a Honda trike that his father bought for him as a birthday present.

One day Barrett invited Chad and I over to his house. I met Chad at his house, and we climbed on to his little Honda motorcycle, riding double. When we arrived I noticed an enormous white satellite dish that dwarfed the front lawn of Barrett's house. Inside the large house we found a huge *Sears* rear-projection television hooked up to a satellite receiver. In an area where "cable TV" still does not exist today, and where most homes still sprout a wind-vane style TV antenna from the roof capturing what one friend called "PeasantVision" over-the-air television signals, a satellite dish in 1989 was the ultimate symbol of wealth. Our farmhouse was lucky to receive four public broadcast channels when the weather conditions were *just* right; Barrett's television received over a HUNDRED! The television even had a remote control, which was years ahead of our wood-panelled television with a knob. *You could change the channel from the couch!* Barrett's home looked more like a Hollywood film director's house than a farmhouse in the boonies.

It did not take us long to discover that there was a "scrambled" Playboy channel on the satellite dish. If I turned my head, crossed my eyes, and squinted, I could occasionally make out a nipple or a few short'n'curlies. At least that's how my pre-teen imagination saw it. While Barrett and Chad tried to guess their way past the satellite scrambler's passcode to unlock its pornographic treasures, I wandered downstairs to the basement.

In the lavishly dark basement I found a leather-panelled bar, a pool table, and in the corner – bingo! – a small grey Zenith-brand computer. I immediately fingered my way through a pile of pirated diskettes on the desk: it was all games! Remembering the Mac incident with Fraser, I called upstairs, asking if I could turn on the computer.

Barrett yelled back, in the midst of boyish giggles, "Sure I don't care!"

His voice was muffled by the sounds of ecstatic moaning. I guessed correctly that they had successfully unscrambled Playboy.

The computer booted and I was greeted by an obscure A:\> prompt. I looked at the labels of the diskettes and picked out one that read "SOPWITH.COM" on the label. I typed SOPWITH.COM on the keyboard and hit enter. The disk drive whirred.[13]

A minute later I was greeted by a cloyingly cute arcade game featuring a puttering Sopwith Camel bi-plane that flew all over the screen, shooting at enemy buildings on a landscape. Hearing the grainy *pew-pew! thukthukthuk!* of the tinny computer speaker, Barrett and Chad came downstairs to investigate. For the next few hours all three of us took turns playing *Sopwith,* and then turned our attention to a CGA conversion of the arcade classic

---

[13] *Sopwith* was originally a "booter"-type game. Booters were MS-DOS computer games that needed to be inserted into the computer *before* boot, and loaded prior to the operating system. There was no executable file on a booter disk, which was an anti-piracy feature. You just inserted the diskette, turned on the computer, and the game would load. The fact that the executable file SOPWITH.COM existed is evidence that this was a pirated copy of the game. Crackers created .COM executable files that bypassed the booter copy-protection routines.

Moon Patrol.[14]

In between gaming marathons I experimented with the other diskettes in the pile. One disk prompted a mystery that took me 30 years to solve. The disk was labelled "JOLT!"... when I ran JOLT.COM, the computer screen went black, and a lifelike photo of a Jolt-branded cola can appeared on the screen. The aluminum can rotated in a perfect circle, showing each side of the can in bright photorealistic graphics. Compared to *Sopwith* and *Moon Patrol* on the same computer, it was like stepping into a Georges Seurat painting. The next day I bragged to my friends at school that Barrett's computer had "graphics so good it looked like TV", and I was met with skepticism at best, and more often downright incredulousness at an obvious lie. They all demanded evidence of the Jolt cola can – a soda pop brand they recognized from American comic books – but I did not have a copy of the program myself. I begged Barrett to borrow the disk to prove my case, but after half a dozen attempts it was clear he had no interest in helping me out.[15]

* * *

[14] Color Graphics Adapter (CGA): A video graphics standard introduced by IBM in 1981. CGA is capable of two standard resolutions: 640x200 with two colours, or 320x400 with four colours. There are several colour palettes available in CGA mode, but the most common (and the one in use with this piece of software) palette had cyan, magenta, yellow, and black.

[15] JOLT.EXE is a "demo" – a program created by hackers meant to show off programming and artistic talents. Thanks to the wonders of Internet archival, I found JOLT.ZIP three decades later. It is compiled with the GRASP animation system and can be downloaded from TEXTFILES.COM.

A screenshot of the Jolt demo program running in DOSBOX.

In our captivated state we collectively failed to notice a car rolling down the driveway. I distinctly heard a door opening and a female voice call out, "Hi! Who's home?", and thought nothing of it. I absently thought that this must be Barrett's mom, home from her college professor job. Barrett and Chad took one look at each other and bolted out of their chairs upstairs. Someone had left the 50-inch television on the Playboy channel with the volume cranked.

Before they made it halfway up the stairs I heard the TV click off. I prudently hid downstairs, dug my heels into the carpet, and focused all my attention on *Sopwith*. There was a lot of yelling coming from upstairs – I made out "Go to your room!" and "I can't believe you guys! Jesus Christ!" A minute later I heard Chad's motorcycle fire up and speed away. He had left me behind!

I can't tell you how afraid I was to go upstairs. I heard a lot of clanging pots and pans coming from the kitchen, and in my home that meant mom was REALLY angry! I quietly stepped along the stair stringers, trying not to make a squeak as I made my escape. I spied Barrett's mom pacing around in the kitchen on the far end of the house, slamming cupboards and muttering under her breath. I crept quietly through the living room to a side door that opened onto their back deck. I slipped over a little deck gate and sprinted down the driveway. When I got to Chad's house a few minutes later I did not stop to visit, and climbed on to my bicycle and pedalled hard for home. I sweated out the next couple of hours waiting for a phone call from Barrett's mom: 'your boy was caught watching pornography!' She never did call, but it was a long time before Barrett invited Chad and I over again. All for a brief, but intense, fling with an IBM clone.

Amstrad PC2086/30

Every person has a brief period in their life that they see as their halcyon days. For some it's the languid summers of the 1950's, redolent of Coca-Cola and banana seat bicycles with baseball cards in the spokes. For others it's the golden years of retirement and slow hours spent fishing with their grandchildren. For me, those perfectly indolent yellow years were bookended by a single computer: the Amstrad XT Personal Computer. And those days began the day… The Day… my mom came home with one.

If I could remember that day in picture-perfect clarity I would encase it in a sapphire jewel and preserve it forever and never let my happiness leave me. But the truth is that all I have are a few foggy images of the day the computer showed up at our farmhouse.

The urban centre that all us farm kids visited occasionally was known by everyone as 'The City', located fifty kilometres away, was a forty-five minute drive to the downtown core from our acreages. One day my mother announced that she was making a trip to the City to buy us something special. When I asked her where she was going she replied, 'The Brick', and I immediately lost interest in anything she had to say afterward.

The Brick was a Canadian furniture store chain that advertised itself on television as a bargain furniture warehouse that was *CRAZY! CRAZY! CRAZY!* with *MIDNIGHT FURNITURE SALES FOR ONE NIGHT ONLY, ONE NIGHT ONLY, ONE NIGHT ONLYYYY!* You get the idea. Even if hitching a ride to the City was a treat in itself, the idea of walking around a furniture store for hours while my mom checked out prices on coffee tables rang absolutely dull to me. I skipped out on the trip, and my sister went with her instead.

When they returned several hours later I was called outside to help bring in the groceries. When I got to the family minivan there were several bags of groceries and a couple of curiously large boxes with the words *Amstrad* emblazoned on the sides.[16] I had no idea what was inside of the boxes but given their sheer weight I suspect they were electronic in nature. Heavy is good. That was enough to make my knees a little wobbly and my head spin trying to guess at the contents.

When we got inside my father told us to carry the boxes to the den. The den of the house was a second living room or office, separated from the rest of the house by a brick wall from the main living room. It was a long, narrow, carpeted room with an old upright piano at one end and my father's oak teacher's desk at the other end. My mother's bookshelves lined the wall behind the desk and were stuffed with hundreds of books we had dragged with us from our hometown the previous year. Prior to that moment the den had been a place primarily for book-keeping my father's carpentry business.

But today the den had its entire function in our home transformed. My father helped us clear-off his antique desk and made space for the two large boxes we were carrying. He hovered over us as we unpacked the boxes, chiding us for our careless kid-fingers. 'Hey, be careful with that! It's expensive!' Eventually I pulled out a few layers of Styrofoam and gazed at the new family member: it was *gorgeous*. The second I saw the

---

[16] Twenty years later I learned a little more about the mysterious Amstrad logo. Amstrad was a British computer company that had made a splash in Europe with its cheaply priced computers that competed with the BBC Micro and Sinclair Computers. Amstrad desired to make a dent in the North American PC market by remanufacturing their PC's with 120 Volt power supplies, and developed a relationship with The Brick to sell them. So why the hell was a furniture store selling computers in 1990? The simplest answer is: because they could. In the 1990s computers was finally catching on in Canada. To their credit the owners of The Brick hoped to latch on as an early adopter of the computer craze before it exploded into a billion dollar consumer industry. Unfortunately for my family, the chain only sold Amstrad computers for a year before divesting themselves of their products and closing the computing department of the store.

plastic vents on the sides I knew that it was a computer: a *new computer*.

We unpacked the monitor and put everything on the huge desk. The incredibly shiny plastic still smelled factory-fresh and all of the cords were still wrapped in plastic and foam, with elastic bands holding them together. My dad told us that we were only allowed to use the computer if we read the instruction manual from front to back. Today I realize how incredibly hesitant he was about the whole affair. The expression on his face at the time was the kind seen on adults who are looking at something they don't understand: they believe that if something is electronic and heavy, it is likely very expensive and definitely fragile. The fact that my father, in his lifetime, used a computer less than a dozen times is evidence that he was likely scared shitless that we'd break something and he wouldn't know how to fix it.

When it was all set up the monitor fired up with a magnetic *bongggggggg!* and the computer *whirrrrred* up to speed. To this day I can remember the exact sound of the boot-up sequence. I'll spare you any attempt at characterizing the sounds textually, but it was mostly composed of the hard drive head seeking back-and-forth in rapid succession punctuated by a few happy chirps. Yes, you could *hear* a hard drive head moving in those days! Every time the read/write head moved – like a turntable needle – a tiny red LED on the front of the PC blinked as the computer made soft chirping sounds. To readers today it is unimaginable that your hard drive would have a blinking LED light to indicate whether it was busy reading or writing. But in 1990 the LED was the perfect diagnostic tool. You could tell, for instance, if the computer had completely "locked up", by watching (or listening) for hard drive activity. Like a car, the different sounds and sights the computer made indicated its overall health.

In those days computers were intensely personal creatures – they were called "personal computers" or "family computers" for a reason. Having a computer in the 1970s, 1980s and early 1990s meant that someone in the home was a technogeek. The early IBM PC clones like the Amstrad did not come with fancy pre-installed software, emergency system recovery partitions or 1-800 tech support stickers pasted on the case. PCs were strictly for people who were unafraid of hacking their way through a jungle of complex command jargon and temperamental hardware. Computer owners had to look after their prized creature like it was a rare endangered species of bird that was sexually attracted to fire. Fixing damaged hardware meant waiting days or weeks for a replacement part. (In our case, we would learn that Amstrad computers were manufactured across the ocean in England, which meant months for parts to arrive!)

In retrospect, I finally can appreciate my father's hesitation as I booted up this very expensive piece of equipment. He was waiting for something to fizzle and catch fire, and send his $3000 investment in smoke. (Neither of us could predict that I would do *exactly* that in a few years - but we'll get to that story later.)

As the blurry monitor focused and warmed up my entire family crowded around watching it for signs of life. The computer went through a boot-up sequence, checking all 640 mighty kilobytes of internal RAM and…

… as you probably guessed, after that first boot, *nothing much happened*. The computer sat like a puppy dumbly looking at a stick I held in my hand, showing a single white-lettered prompt on a black background.

```
C:\>_
```

We all waited for a minute watching the cursor blink, hoping the computer was in the midst of some housekeeping before it blew us away. When nothing happened it was clear more research was in order. Relieved that nothing had exploded, my dad wandered off to the living room to catch the rest of the Toronto-Montreal NHL hockey game. My mom went back to studying for a university exam and told us to tell her when we got the machine working.

King's Quest IV: The Perils of Rosella

My sister couldn't handle the waiting any longer and told me she had a surprise: my mother had let *her* pick out a computer game at the store! My heart sank. What on Earth did my *sister* know about computer games? It wasn't fair! *I* was the one that played games on an Amiga and IBM and Atari. I began grumbling and she replied with a smug look that younger sisters delight in, "Well you should have come with us to the City then!"

It got worse when she pulled the computer game box out of the Radio Shack bag. The front cover was absolutely awful: a princess riding a white unicorn while two flying gargoyles tried to wrench her off the shiny saddle, against a distant background of a castle shrouded in clouds and moonlight. It was exactly the kind of thing my sister – who was a *My Little Pony* and *She-Ra: Princess of Power* and *Jem and the Holograms* devotee – would blow money on. At the time it was, without exaggeration, the worst thing that had happened to my life up to that point. Little did I know that this awful-looking game would become one of my favourite adventure games and consume my life for the rest of the year. The game was the incredibly popular *King's Quest IV: The Perils of Rosella*, the fourth instalment of the popular *King's Quest* series by Sierra On-Line.

While she opened the box I held back tears of rage and wrestled with the thin Amstrad PC Installation Manual that came with the computer. It gave some basic instructions on cleaning and caring for the computer but not much else. I found a sealed package of six diskettes with the official Amstrad logo. Ah ha! The first disk, labeled "Setup and Installation Disk" had instructions on how to get the computer up and running. The label had a few brief instructions printed on it too: "Insert Disk and type A:SETUP". Perfect!

The installation procedure involved listening to the computer churn through the diskette bit by bit and waiting for an "Insert

Disk #2" prompt, "Insert Disk #3" prompt, and so on until all of the diskettes were arranged in a neat pile beside the PC. Forty minutes later I was greeted by the *Windows 2.0* interface. Neither my sister nor I knew what the point of Windows was, but it sure was fun trying to figure it out! We ran every program we could find and experimented with them. My mom wandered in every hour to check on us and smiled at how much fun we were having. I would excitedly point out icons and files and say, "Hey mom! Watch this!" and then run a program for her. If you remember Windows 3.1 (a pre-cursor to the ubiquitous Windows 95) you might remember a graphical user interface that didn't do a whole helluva lot. Now imagine a graphical user interface that could do 1/100th of what Windows 3.1 could do and voila – *Windows 2.0*! No *Paint* program. No games like *Minesweeper* or *Solitaire* or *Freecell*. Nothing but a lame *Clock* and *Notepad* program, neither of which were very functional.

Exploring Windows programs soon wore thin and my sister and I were told to go to bed. My sister told my mom we hadn't even installed the game she had got for us, and that excuse bought us an extension of a "few minutes" to our bedtime. We managed to stretch the extension to an hour by turning off the light in the den so my parents would think we were already in bed.

I got to work. My sister couldn't sit still in her chair while we guessed our way through the Sierra On-Line Installation program. The program asked a half-dozen questions about our computer that we had *no* idea how to answer correctly. Do you have VGA, EGA, Tandy, CGA or Hercules graphics? Do you have a Disney Sound Source, IBM PC speaker or Roland MT-32 sound device? Do you want to install this to the hard drive? If so, what letter is the hard drive assigned to? The *only* question we had a fairly solid answer to was, "Do you want to use your Microsoft-compatible mouse?" I looked at the plastic teardrop-shaped gadget on the desk – I had no idea if it was Microsoft-compatible, but it sure was called a mouse!

The interrogation lasted much longer than it should have. I was terrified of "breaking the computer", as if there was some magical combination of configuration choices that would send this $3000 pile of circuits to the scrapheap. When the installer program finished we both held our breath and typed "SIERRA" and waited for the magic to happen.

Magic *did* happen. A Sierra On-Line logo appeared on the screen and then the PC speaker blasted out an ear-piercing bleepy-bloopy fanfare throughout the house. The title sequence had a richly animated royal red banner complete with sparkling golden letters.

In my rush to judge the game by its cover I had not paid much attention to the company that developed and published it, and had forgotten all the joy I had from *King's Quest II* on the classroom Apple //e. This was a *Sierra* game which meant it was going to be of the highest quality I could imagine and just plain fun! Sure it had princesses and castles and unicorns and flying gargoyles, but it probably had a bunch of other stuff that didn't suck too!

The fanfare music lasted a couple seconds before my dad yelled out from the living room to shut the damned thing off and go to bed. Busted by the PC speaker. We turned off the computer. (Days later we figured out that there was a volume control knob for the PC speaker, proving necessary for our future gaming expeditions past 10 o'clock at night.)

The next morning I woke up before anyone else and wandered to the den wrapped in my blanket. I huddled myself in the huge 1970s faux-leather office chair, blanket wrapped around me like a shawl with my feet tucked inside of it, and got back to work. I figured that I had at least a half hour before everyone else was up and I was sent out to ride the bus to school.

I booted up the computer and…

```
Keylock Detected. System Halted.
```

Halted? I thought I had done something to break the computer the previous night, but after a quick inspection I noticed that the metal key stuck into the side of the computer was missing. I flipped open the Amstrad PC2086 User Manual and looked for a diagram of a key, the type you'd see used in an old deep-freeze freezer. There it was – if the key was removed from the desktop case, the system would no longer accept keyboard commands! It didn't take long to realize that my dad had sabotaged my plan to sneak onto the computer. He might not have known anything about computers but he sure knew what a metal key was for.

I snuck up to my parents' bedroom and snooped around while my dad snored loudly. Sure enough he had left the little silver key on a nightstand beside him. Light-fingered pilfering made short work of his clever ruse and I crept my way down the staircase to the den.

I quietly pulled the *King's Quest IV* diskettes from the disk box and inserted one into the computer. I braced each disk with my fingertips so I could muffle the metallic *snick!* as the diskette locked into place in the 3-½″ floppy drive. Ten minutes later I was ready to assume the role of Princess Rosella.

I heard my father yawn upstairs and I froze. Out of time! Damn! I shut off the computer as the introduction sequence was loading, and re-locked the computer with the key. When I walked into the living room my mother was already up and gave me a sly smile. I made an excuse about waking up early to do some homework, and when I heard my father go into the bathroom I snuck the key back on to his nightstand. It was the kind of cheesy drama that could have played out in one of the adventure games I would come to love on the Amstrad. All that work for a few seconds of joy… but it was worth it.

The bus ride to school, and the return ride home, were excruciating. With no access to the Amstrad for the next ten hours (a lifetime!) my imagination was filled with the beepy-boopy sing-song introduction music to *King's Quest IV*. Every minute at school felt like an eternity and when I got within a few kilometres of my house my heart began racing. The cool autumn morning had become a breezy autumn afternoon when my sister and I began racing down the half-kilometre acreage driveway.

"First one to the house gets to play *King's Quest*!", I yelled as I gasped for breath.

It didn't matter that my sister beat me to the house because we immediately began installing *King's Quest IV* together and watched the introduction sequence from beginning to end. We took turns learning to use the arrow-keys to walk the heroine of the adventure, Princess Rosella, around a beach in the magical land of Tamir. Blue waves washed in along the beach.. birds circled around a fisherman's wharf in the distance, whose chimney plumed with grey smoke.. a few screens away a character reminiscent of the mythical cloven-hoofed Pan danced around playing his flute.. a crew of dwarves worked tirelessly in a mine searching for gems. It seemed like every single area was populated with a living creature that we could speak to. Tamir was not just a convenient fairy tale setting – to us kids it was a *whole world* that was living inside of our new computer.

Each day after school began the same. I re-installed the game from diskette and we sat side-by-side, one in the big chair at the keyboard and one in a little chair to the left, became the co-operative style that we played games together for years afterward. The person in the little chair gave out commands and commentary to the person in the big chair; the person in the big chair did all the keyboarding. After an hour the roles were reversed usually because someone's fingers needed a rest.

Like most kids we delighted in typing all kinds of naughty and hilarious phrases into the command parser. We lived for the moments that the game would recognize our silly command and reply with some polite rejoinder like, "That is not very Princess-like of you, Rosella!"

King's Quest IV kept us constantly occupied for the rest of the year trying to solve its puzzles, until we found out that we could purchase an official "Sierra On-Line Hintbook". Sierra hintbooks provided step-by-step solutions for every puzzle in a game, often doling out the information in tiny morsels rather than systematic "walk-throughs" that spoiled the whole experience.

In the pre-Internet era hintbooks were as valuable as gold, because the only other source of hints and strategies for games came from other kids at school. We didn't know a single person who had a computer, never mind one who also had a copy of *King's Quest IV*. One trip to the City and ten bucks later we cheated our way past a handful of vicious little puzzles that had us stuck for months. We could not help but keep reading the hintbook after that, and cheated our way straight to the end of the game.

The schmaltzy ending to the game fulfilled our expectations and brought closure to the story – it was the first time we had ever "beat" a game together. When the endgame sequence was over the game presented us with a "secret code", and my sister wrote down the code on the inside cover of the tan Sierra game box. We had *no* idea what the secret code represented and spent days afterward trying to use the code in the game… we typed it as a command into the text parser hundreds of times in different locations hoping that it would trigger some special event. It became a mystery that neither of us solved for twenty five years.

One day, a couple of years ago, I found a copy of *King's Quest IV* in a thrift store. I could not resist buying it, thinking back to all the fond memories I had playing it with my sister. This copy appeared to be brand new, and still had a promotional sticker affixed to the front cover:

"Win a trip to a Medieval Castle in England!"

The sticker turned out to be an advertisement for a promotional contest Sierra On-Line was running: when you finished the game you called a 1-800 number and gave the receiver the secret code from the end of the game. This put the player into a grand prize draw for a trip to England.

By the time our family had bought the game, the draw was long over and the promotional sticker on the box had been removed by the manufacturer. Apparently none of the programmers at Sierra On-Line had thought to remove the secret code message before it was reprinted in the budget re-release my mother had bought for us.

What the heck is a Hard Drive?

If you're a bit of a geek you might be wondering – why did I re-install *King's Quest IV* every single day? Was there a problem with the original installation that necessitated re-installing the game every time my sister and I wanted to play it?

At the time I had no idea that the Amstrad PC had a fancy thang called a h-a-r-d d-r-i-v-e. In my kid-mind I thought that 'installing' was synonymous with 'loading', so taking five or ten minutes to load the game was completely normal – this seemed especially true after playing games on the TRS-80 and Apple // for years. The only thing capable of loading a game instantaneously was an Intellivision or Sega, and those machines were just *different* than computers.

That misunderstanding about my computer meant that every time I wanted to mess around with *Windows 2.0* I went through the five-diskette installation procedure over a forty minute period. *King's Quest IV* took mercifully less time to install and was ready in about ten minutes. There was no techno-literate person to say, "Hey kid, computers don't work like that anymore!"

It took two months for me to realize that the computer had an internal memory storage device that could permanently store programs after the computer was turned off. Whenever a program asked if I had a hard disk drive, I thought it was referring to our 3 ½" floppy disk drive. Weren't "floppy disks" those wobbly huge diskettes that the Apple // computer used? It took a few re-reads of the Amstrad User's Guide to understand the differences between these different mediums for data storage, and even then they seemed muddled to me.

You see, at that time how else was a computer user to know? If something wasn't printed in the Amstrad User's Guide in a 32-point boldfaced font, or if you didn't have a friend that was a computer hacker, there was no way of knowing what these contraptions were capable of. None of our friends had computers, and *none of their friends even knew anyone who had one either*. At the time, to my knowledge, our family was the only one with a computer in their home in a twenty kilometer radius.

The day I realized that "Drive C" was the hard disk drive, and "Drive A" was our floppy disk drive, was a revolution in my understanding of computers. All of a sudden I learned that I could copy files between each, and more importantly that the hard drive was *much* faster at loading programs than the disk drive was. I called my sister over to the computer to demonstrate.

"Hey, watch how fast I can make *King's Quest* load..."

I typed in the command SIERRA and the hard drive whirred as usual, displaying the familiar Sierra logo.

"Um. So?" She was nonplussed.

"But... I didn't use the disks. See? *No disks!*" I pointed at the pile of floppies beside the case.

She shrugged.

After a couple of hours we figured out how to use the command "cd\sierra\kq4" to get us to the right location on the hard drive, and then run our beloved game. After that my sister no longer needed me to "load" *King's Quest* for her on the computer so she could play it – I had hacked my way out of a job.

That fundamental misunderstanding of the storage properties of the computer's hard drive came to haunt me only a few months later when I began to experiment with MS-DOS 3.3 commands.

Dangerous Experiments in MS-DOS 3.3

The Amstrad PC came with an unbelievably well-written *Microsoft* MS-DOS 3.3 User's Guide that I read daily, like a devout Christian reads passages from the Bible. Each day after school I rushed down the driveway to read through *Microsoft's* holy scriptures and ponder their many uses in my life. The MS-DOS command guide was organized alphabetically, beginning with strange commands like APPEND and ending with even stranger sounding ones like XCOPY.

I pored over the book for months and learned the ins and outs of every command by simple experimentation: I ran the command and watched what happened next. I learned how to modify the AUTOEXEC.BAT and CONFIG.SYS files to yield a little more usable RAM for my games, similar to how a racing team does a "weight reduction" on their race car to lighten the load.[17] I figured out how to change the MS-DOS command screen resolution with the MODE command to my delight, making it squished-up and tall, or short and squat. I learned the value of the command @ECHO OFF, and how to create a RAMDISK out of the meagre scraps of memory available to me.

A few months into my MS-DOS seminary training my mother showed up with a box of ten fresh 3-½" diskettes. The salesman at Radio Shack suggested that she "back up" all of her original

---

[17] Anyone who grew up with MS-DOS games will remember modifying their AUTOEXEC.BAT and CONFIG.SYS files to squeeze just a little more memory out of their computer. MS-DOS games of the early 1990s required between 500Kb and 600Kb of conventional memory. On a computer with only 640Kb of memory, that was a big hunk of space. Some games, like *Ultima VII: The Black Gate* wanted every single scrap of memory available. Freeing up memory meant paring away unneeded device drivers and TSR (Terminate and Stay Resident) programs that chewed up valuable memory real estate. MS-DOS 6.22 introduced the MEMMAKER program which attempted to automatically free up extra conventional memory – often with mixed results.

purchased disks, because floppies were not the most reliable storage medium. Putting a floppy disk near any magnetic field – say, a television set, might randomize its bits completely… and in a house with two pre-teens this was bound to happen. The fresh diskettes were clearly marked "UNFORMATTED" on the box, and that meant a bit of detective work before I figured out how to use them. Five minutes of digging through the MS-DOS guide later I found the FORMAT command and formatted each diskette in turn.[18]

I learned how to use the DISKCOPY command to make duplicates of each of our computer programs, and spent hours laboriously copying productivity software like *Easy Working Eight-in-One* and *The New Print Shop*. I eventually ran out of blank disks and patience for the tedious process and my mind wandered back to MS-DOS commands. What would the computer do if I told it to FORMAT *itself*? Would MS-DOS even allow that? Would the Amstrad adopt a HAL 9000 voice and berate me, "I can't allow you to do that, Dave"? Would the whole hard drive implode and shrink into a black hole?

Surely the all-knowing and all-seeing Mr. Bill Gates and his team of deities at Microsoft would never allow the operating system to harm *itself!* Still, why not try it? The worst thing that could happen is that I would have to re-install a few games and my mom's word processing programs. And she stored all of her personal files on floppy disks anyway, so what's the harm?

```
C:\>FORMAT C:
This will destroy ALL data on Drive C. Are you sure?
[Y/N] Y_
```

---

[18] Formatting a diskette means preparing its magnetic surface for use with a specific type of computer architecture and/or operating system. Formatting allows people to use standard 3-½" or 5-¼" floppy diskettes on a range of different computers. For instance, when a 3-½" disk is formatted to work with an IBM PC it will *only* work on IBM PC's; when a diskette is formatted to work on a Macintosh, it will *only* work on Macintosh computers.

* * *

My thumb hovered over the enter key for a minute. Ever have that tickle in the back of your mind RIGHT before you do something very, very stupid? Or feel the horror of watching the car door slam shut as you realize that your keys are still inside of the ignition? I had that very same feeling and happily ignored it. I hit enter and waited for the implosion!

The hard drive chattered away for a couple of seconds and was returned to the C:\> prompt as if nothing had happened. I scratched my head, disappointed. I ran the DIR command to view the directory list and was pleasantly surprised to see zero files listed! None at all. I ran a command called CHKDSK, which showed the current free space on the computer, and was shocked to see a *ton* of free space – the entire hard drive was erased! It was like walking into your apartment after you've packed all of your boxes for a move and realizing just how darned big the whole place is. Why hadn't I thought of this brilliant move weeks earlier when I was deleting games just to make enough space to install other ones?

A minute of self-congratulations was all I needed before I began re-installing all of our games and programs. I did not want my sister to walk in asking to play *Hoyle's Book of Games*, only to find out that I had deleted it. It took a few hours but by the time I was done everything looked pretty much the same. I had even freed up one extra megabyte of free space in the process. Score!

My mother walked in and asked to use the computer. I hung around nervously to see if she would notice any differences, and was relieved when her *Eight-in-One* word processing program loaded without an issue. I walked over to the kitchen to fix myself a celebratory overflowing bowl of *Froot Loops*. By the time the bowl was spilling over its edges with sugary goodness, my mom was calling me back to the den for help with the computer.

"I can't find my paper. I saved it here but it's not showing up."

I sighed impatiently. My mother always stored her files on

floppy disks, and sometimes forgot to insert her diskette into the drive before trying to load her document.

"Mom, you have to put the disk in the computer first."

She sighed irritably. "No, no! Your mother is not that stupid! You told me to stop putting my files on these disks because they go bad. You told me to save my files to the computer."

Oh God. I *did* tell her to start saving her word processing documents to the hard drive, didn't I? My face flushed with a cold sweat and my heart began pounding uncontrollably. I tried to mask my panic attack by shooing her away and telling her that I would fix the problem if she just gave me a few minutes to figure out what was wrong.

"Well, hurry. My paper is due in the morning and I already asked for two extensions from my professor." She disappeared into the kitchen.

Okay, think fast. If there is a FORMAT command surely there is an UN-FORMAT command right?[19] I flipped through the MS-DOS manual with sweaty fingers. There must be some command that could reverse the electromagnetic holocaust I had unleashed upon the hard drive hours earlier, and if not – I better learn how to build a time machine fast.

She came back, expecting me to have worked my magic. I looked up at her with a look of sheer dread in my eyes and said,

---

[19] Many years later, versions of MS-DOS came with UNFORMAT and UNDELETE commands that proved invaluable to families with troublemaking children. The FORMAT and DELETE commands do not *physically* destroy data, but instead delete the filenames/titles of each file. In other words: the sequence of ones and zeroes that comprise the file are still on the hard drive, but the name of the file no longer shows up on the directory listing. This would be like removing every street sign in a city – the city still exists, but there is no way of finding an exact street address. Data recovery programs take advantage of this fact and allow a user to recover their data by sifting through tons of raw data and recovering it piece by piece. But data recovery was in its infancy in 1990, and good consumer-grade software would not be released for a couple of years.

"Mom I think I deleted your files by accident."

True enough. Deleting *her* files was an accident – formatting the hard drive was not however. I thought this quick apology might buy me some sympathy.

Her eyes turned into steel ball bearings, her jaw set in a hard line, and she stomped off to the kitchen. I was a dead man. My mother would go to college tomorrow, paperless, and some dull professor in a tweed jacket would point her out in her classroom seat and scream, *"That one!"* She would be drawn and quartered publicly by a team of harnessed graduate students, in front of a cackling dean cracking a whip. The tattered remnants of our family would fall into poverty, living under some City bridge like common trolls. All because of a deleted term paper.

She came back a minute later with a stack of hand-written notes in her elegant script, and thrust them in front of me on the desk. My mother belonged to a different generation than me. Whereas I typed my entire course assignments out on the computer and printed them off, she believed in handwriting essays first before committed them to typewritten text on a machine. It was an old habit ingrained during the age of typewriters and correction fluid. The stack of papers in front of me was her hand-written version of the paper.

"You're going to type up that entire paper before you go to bed tonight."

I choked back tears and nodded. It was nine o'clock at night and she normally left for school at seven in the morning. I'd have to work fast to get it done in time. She picked up the phone and left a message on the professor's voice answering machine, pleading her case that she might be late due to some computer problems at home. I felt even worse.

For the next few hours I hammered away at the keyboard as fast as my little fingers could manage. I do not remember finishing the paper, but it was well after midnight by the time I made it to bed. The next morning I woke up to the familiar *screeeee! screee! scree! screeeeeeeee!* of our faithful dot-matrix printer.[20] I stumbled up to the den after only a few hours of sleep and found my mother hovering over the printer, coaxing it to print faster with anxious waves of her hands and curses. A few minutes later she tore the last page out of the printer, gave me a quick peck on the head, rushed out the door into her car and sped off up the driveway towards the City.

My shoulders sagged with relief and I turned off the computer. That day marked the end of my mad scientist MS-DOS experimentation – Mr. Gates had granted too much power to this eleven year old.

---

[20] This particular printer was a monochrome Star NX-1000 dot-matrix. A dot-matrix printer works by impacting individual wires mounted on a print head, through an ink ribbon, onto a sheet of paper. The print-head's wire tips approximate tiny dots, that, when crammed together in a fine mesh, look something like a printed letter font. Like most dot-matrix printers of the time, the NX-1000 used "line-feed" paper that was a perennial favourite of kids: this paper had perforated edges that wound around a spiky spool that carried the sheet through the printer. After printing the paper required you to tear off the perforated edges, making one heck of a mess and ton of fun for the average kid. Dot-matrix printers were unbelievably loud compared to modern inkjet and laser printers. Many businesses and schools placed dot-matrix printers inside of sound-proofed Plexiglas housings just to muffle their racket.

Police Quest II: The Vengeance

The fifth grade was well into the final semester when my sister and I began to search for new games after completing *King's Quest IV*. One of the sixth-graders in our class, Carl – the scallywag that had beat us to playing games on the Apple // - was beginning to grate on my nerves. Each day he would come up to my gang of friends just to brag about his computer gaming skills on his Tandy 1000 – a computer he thought was superior to any computer anyone else had at home. As far as my gang was concerned, anything Carl said about himself likely contained a truth to bullshit ratio of 1 to 9. But in all of his bragging three games consistently came up: *Silpheed* (which we pronounced "sliffeed"), *Thexder* and *Police Quest*. According to Carl and his brother Donny, these games outstripped any Sega or Nintendo game out there.

One day I had to know for myself if any of these games could possibly live up to Carl's hype. I proposed a trade: One of his games for my copy of *King's Quest IV*. I even brought the box with me in my backpack as proof that I had the goods. He agreed to bring *Police Quest II* with him the next morning, as *Thexder and Silpheed* were probably "too hard" for a sucker like me.[21] I ignored the jab and signed off on the deal – I was just happy to have secured my first legit computer game trade.

Carl and I agreed to convene behind the school near a brown play-hut to conceal our exchange like we were making a drug deal. We were not worried that anyone would care we were trading computer games. We were each concerned that someone

---

[21] Years later I learned that both *Thexder and Silpheed* were Sierra On-Line arcade game titles. In the late 1980s, Sierra began publishing arcade-style action games to capitalize on the popularity of this overlooked genre in their company's catalog. While Sierra never became a household brand for arcade games, both *Silpheed* and *Thexder* were well-liked by audiences.

would see us as friends – I didn't want my gang to find out Carl and I were on good terms, and he didn't want his sixth grade friends to find out he was associating with a puny fifth grader.

I handed Carl the *King's Quest IV* box and in return I got a handful of disks. I balked and demanded, "Where's the rest of it?"

He whispered, "I had to leave the box at home. My parents'll skin me alive if they find out I brought *Police Quest* to school. It's *that* good you know. You only need the disks anyway."

I stuffed the disks into a compartment of my vinyl backpack and walked off like nothing had happened. I was irritated with Carl's cheap ploy to keep the box and manual for himself. I had planned to dig through the box on the bus ride home. But he was right – the disks were what mattered.

On the bus ride home I daydreamed about *Police Quest II: The Vengeance*. Over the past few months, Carl had ticked off all its highlights: finding a dead body, conducting a murder investigation, chasing down speeders on the highway, and SCUBA diving in a river. "It's like you're a real cop. *I saw a dead guy!*"

I ran down the driveway, pulling the diskettes out of my backpack as I went. When I rushed into the den, the whole minute I waited for the computer to boot seemed like an hour, and the familiar Sierra On-Line install program grinding away on the diskettes felt like an eternity. My first computer game trade – I had just gotten a game for *free!*

When the game finally loaded my spine and legs buzzed with electricity. This was great! Seconds after seeing the Sierra On-Line logo I was greeted with a question, not unlike the type I had seen in *King's Quest IV.* It presented me with a criminal's mug shot, and asked me to enter the criminal ID number. This was clearly a "copy protection verification" question that required me to look up the proper code in the computer game manual that came in the box. Verification questions ensured that the player had actually purchased the game and had not pirated the disks from a friend. Or, in my case, traded with a frenemy.

I was crushed. Carl had screwed me by not giving me the box and its manual, and there was no way to guess the answer to the verification question. My heart exploded with rage and I imagined all the terrible things I would say to him the next day at school. I was so angry that I grabbed the phone book and looked up his parents' phone number.

In those days even though Carl's family lived only a few kilometres away from my acreage, their phone exchange was considered long-distance from us. Many years earlier the planners at the telephone company made an inconvenient decision to simplify the division of local calling areas in the acreages we inhabited: if you lived north of the Trans-Canada highway you were in the (363) telephone exchange, and if you lived south of the highway you were in the (662) exchange. The Trans-Canada highway bisected many communities so this meant neighbours separated only by a few hundred feet were forced to call long distance to contact one another. It was often cheaper to drive or walk over to their house just to ask a simple question.

For that reason my parents strictly forbade my sister and I from making long distance calls to our friends without asking for their explicit permission first. Neither of my parents were home at the time and as far as I was concerned, this truly was an emergency. I found Carl's number in the phone book and dialled. He picked up the phone and was genuinely surprised to hear my voice.

"Hey. What's up?"

I grumbled, trying to contain my rage, "I need the *Police Quest* manual. You didn't tell me there was an ID number check at the start!"

"Oh that's easy. Just tell me what the guy in the mug shot looks like and I'll give you the ID number. We can do it over the phone right now."

I described the man in the mug shot: black hair, a pointy black moustache and dark eyes. He looked like a pretty mean dude.

Carl searched the manual and exclaimed, "That's Jessie Bains!

Here type in this number…"

Evidently there were a number of different mug shots of criminals, some with blond hair and black hair, some with blue eyes and brown – each corresponding to an entry in the manual, and each entry with an ID number below the suspect's name.

I typed in the number and it worked. I thanked Carl, despite feeling irritated over having to call him in the first place. A typical Carl move.

"Just call me whenever you need the ID number. I can't give you the manual or I'll be in hell with my parents y'know."

I hung up. He was right. This was something easily solved by a simple phone call. Besides, my parents would never care about a one-minute phone call a couple of times a week. My father made long-distance calls all the time practically anyway! He'd hardly notice a few extra calls to a nearby farm.

Police Quest II was every bit as good as Carl had promised. It *was* like being a real cop, carrying out all the minutiae of police work that I had not imagined went on behind the scenes. It quickly became an obsession for me, and my other games paled in comparison.

Over the next few weeks I called Carl almost every day after school to get the ID number and sometimes ask for a quick hint to a puzzle or two. I liked to think these were one-minute calls, but in reality they were more like five to ten minutes long.

At the end of the month I was called into the kitchen by my father in a stern tone. He jammed his stubby index finger into a stack of paper in front of him, like it was a fat cigar burning a hole through it.

"Explain to me this fucking phone bill. Your sister said it wasn't her. Who's this you're calling? 363…" His eyes were like coals and burned a violent red light through me. "Look at this! Every goddamned day! One dollar here. TWO dollars! Three-fifty for this one!"

I felt my knees weakening. There was no way out of this jam. I admitted to calling Carl for help with the computer and did not beg for leniency with the irate judge. I was going to get the book thrown at me regardless of how I pleaded.

My father tabulated the calls along the margin of the phone bill and they added up to over fifty dollars. This was more money than I'd receive for my birthday and Christmas put together. There was no way I could pay him back and he knew it.

"You're going to work every goddamned cent of this off with chores. And you're off that fucking computer for a month!"

A month? I knew I had done something wrong, but a month away from the computer might as well have been a year. It was *so* unfair, especially because I was *so* close to beating *Police Quest II*.

For the next week I diligently helped out with extra chores around the acreage, earning a dollar or two every day when I could.

By the end of the week my father's fury cooled. On the weekend I asked him if I could use the computer and he said that I could, as long as I had completed all my chores. The month-long computing ban sentence was commuted to a week, although it took me several more weeks to repay him for the phone bill.

In the end it would have cost me less to buy a brand new copy of *Police Quest II* from Radio Shack than trading it with Carl. It would be almost ten years before I bought my own copy of the game (*with* the manual so I could pass the copy protection questions) from a flea market and got to see the ending to the story. Lesson learned: never, ever, trade games with guys like Carl.

The family den, circa 1990. I had just completed GhostBusters II and asked my sister to take a photo as the credits rolled and slimer danced around, to prove to my friends that I had finished the game. Top: Amstrad PC2086 and Star NX-1000 printer. Bottom left: GhostBusters II box, on top of a box of tractor feed paper. Bottom right: Yours truly, feeling smug.

1990: Grade Six

Tandy 1000

The fifth grade was finally over and I was free to burn away my summer playing video games and eating *Froot Loops* in front of Saturday morning cartoons until my roof of my mouth was bleeding. At least that was the plan, until my father announced that he had secured a construction contract in our old home town thirteen hours away.

Our family finances had been in the red ever since we had moved a year earlier and this was an opportunity for my father to get us back in the black. My mom had elected to take summer university classes so this presented a childcare problem: my sister and I could either stay with the neighbours for the summer, or we could go up North with my father. We ended up with a split decision in the end: my sister would move in with her best friend and neighbour, and I would go up North with my father and help him out however I could.

I was pretty excited to drive back to my old home town – I hadn't been there in a year and longed to regale my northern friends with exaggerated stories about my (comparatively) metropolitan life down south.

Leisure Suit Larry in The Land of the Lounge Lizards

My father and I arrived in our old home town in the early summer. He began work on a construction contract he had won from a married couple who were teachers at my former school. One of the two teachers, Mrs. O, had been my fourth grade homeroom teacher two years earlier and her personality had all the charm of a rusty battle axe. My father enlisted me as his gopher/day-labourer whose job was to run around the job site tracking down wayward measuring tapes and hammers, because honestly, a gangly eleven-year-old was not good for much else. Keeping me with him on the job site was cheaper than paying for a babysitter, and Mr. and Mrs. O gave me permission to watch television inside of their house when I wasn't working. The only stipulation was that I was *not* to go up the flight of stairs to the second storey where the bedrooms were. Out-of-bounds. *Verboten.*

To an eleven-year-old that word translates to: *just be extra sneaky.* One day while my father was talking with the couple outside of their house, I began my reconnaissance of the second floor. Bedrooms held nothing of interest. Bathroom: nothing. There was a trap-door to the attic but that was out of reach. In a recessed bay window, I hit pay-dirt and unearthed the crown jewel of their house: a Tandy 1000 personal computer!

The Tandy 1000 looked a little like our TRS-80 and Amstrad, but a little slicker and better built with metal instead of plastic.

I peeked out of the bay window that overlooked their front yard. My father was regaling the couple with one of his half-true/half-fabricated stories trying to squeeze a laugh out of their sour old faces. They'd be there for a while so there was time for me to peek around their computer. I looked around the old desk the computer sat on and found what I was looking for: a plastic box full of 5-¼" diskettes! I thumbed through them and was disappointed with the predictable pile of copied disks with titles like "Typing Tutor" and "Finances 1987". The teachers had a history of being old curmudgeons at the school and they no doubt used the computer to balance their chequebooks and force-feed their children educational software. I doubted I would find anything worth playing in the box.

I was about to give up when I saw a creamy tan-coloured label of what could *only* be a diskette manufactured by one company: Sierra On-Line. Stamped on the label were words blurred by greasy thumbprints: *Leisure Suit Larry in the Land of the Lounge Lizards*. My heart raced. Yes! If this was even a tenth as fun as *King's Quest* I was in for a great time. And the phrase "lounge lizard" promised something a little ribald and filthy. My pre-teen mind could only guess at the secrets that lie within.

I booted the computer, and not much happened. Unlike the Amstrad PC at home, this computer did not have a C:\> drive, and operated purely from its single floppy disk drive. I inserted the *Leisure Suit Larry* disk in the drive and set the MS-DOS boot disk aside. It ran MS-DOS just like my Amstrad at home, but this appeared to work a little differently than my own and I had no MS-DOS User Guide to refer to. I tried to guess my way through.

```
A:\>START GAME
Bad command or filename.
A:\>HELP
Bad command or filename.
```

The guessing game went on for a few minutes until I thought back to my own computer at home. What was the magical command my sister and I had to type to play *King's Quest*? Oh yeah!

```
A:\>SIERRA.COM_
```

The disk began to whir in the drive. I felt like a million bucks. I was David Lightman cracking a military supercomputer in *WarGames*. I was Gandalf the Grey opening the gates to the mines of Moria with an elvish word in *The Fellowship of the Ring*.

I was Indiana friggin' Jones swapping out the golden idol for a bag of sand in *Raiders of the Lost Ark*. These are the moments of supreme larceny that separate the mere pickpocket from the master of locks!

I took another peek out the window while the game loaded. My father was waving the couple towards the house, pointing at some flaw on the exterior of the home. I had a couple of minutes at best.

The screen finally went black and after the familiar Sierra On-Line logo, I got what I could have never imagined: a single box asking me to enter my age. Suspecting some kind of trickery I lied and entered "99" in the box.

The game began asking me trivia questions about American history. What year was Abraham Lincoln born in? Who invented the Cotton Gin? This was *nothing* like the kind of game my imagination had conjured up.

I spent the next minute trying to guess the correct answers to the game. There was no way *Leisure Suit Larry* was some lame trivia game – this was obviously some kind of Sierra On-Line "verification" test that probably needed me to look up answers in the game manual. I feverishly searched around the desk for a manual of some kind. I heard the door crack open downstairs and my father's voice boomed into the house. I turned off the computer and monitor and beat a hasty retreat down the creaky staircase to the living room. I'm sure that the owners were suspicious of my flushed sweaty face when they entered, but my dad still held their attention with another one of his rambling cock-and-bull stories.

We left an hour later and I spent the night ruminating about the secrets locked away in that diskette. How could I possibly answer questions about American history without the manual? I thought back to the computer and the desk, imagining how cool it would be to guess the right answer and crack the Tandy. And then it hit me: I had forgotten to eject the *Leisure Suit Larry* disk from the computer! I could only guess at what happened that night. The owner likely went to use their computer and found the disk in the computer. They would call the cops, who would lift my fingerprints from the disk, tracing it in some global criminal database for bad little kids who snooped around in other people's computers, and then come arrest me in some televised media circus where my dad would cover my head with a coat while the cops escorted me to an idling cruiser. No more summer. No more games. The government probably had a special little prison for kids who played games they weren't supposed to.

The next day my dad asked me to come with him back to the house and I demurred. I told him that I was sick and wanted to stay at my aunt's for the day. I sweated things out for the entire day and when he came back and mentioned nothing about Mr. and Mrs. O's computer I only became *more* worried. The police were probably collecting all kinds of evidence so they could really nail me to the cross when I was taken to court.

After a week my father stopped asking me to accompany with him to Mr. and Mrs. O's home, and I breathed a sigh of relief. Maybe messing around on other people's computers without their permission wasn't such a good idea. I couldn't handle a guilty conscience.

Space Quest III: The Pirates of Pestulon

When the home renovation project for the two teachers came to an end, my father won a large contract with a local business owner. The project involved renovating some run-down low income duplex residences for an infamous and unscrupulous businessman named Norm, who also owned a small grocery store. Owing to my limited carpentry skills and skeletal biceps at the tender age of eleven, I barely lasted a week helping my father demolishing the interiors of the shabby rooms that reeked of smoke and pet urine. To keep me occupied for the rest of the summer my father persuaded Norm to hire me as a junior grocery clerk in his store.

I made a handshake deal with Norm: I would work an eight-hour shift beginning when the store opened and would leave when my dad was done his work for the day for three dollars an hour. In retrospect, paying me three dollars an hour was illegal at a time when the minimum wage was set at $5.75... but this concern was moot considering that hiring an eleven year old kid was even more illegal.

Child labour laws notwithstanding I was one happy kiddo. My lifelong dream of running around the store with a pricing gun in my little hand was finally fulfilled, and I was given an *official* store butcher's smock which was three sizes too big for an adult man and fifteen sizes too big for a scraggly kid. The only other employee in the store was a woman in her late teens who found the idea of a prepubescent boy-grocer adorable.

The owner, Norm, tasked me with making bags of ice, using an ice-making machine in the basement of the store. He told me to bag the ice and let him know when it was done, and we'd carry the bags up to the store cooler upstairs. I treated ice bagging like a mini-game: it was a competition to make as many bags of ice in an hour as I could. As it turns out, a kid with nothing else to do with his time can make a *helluva* lot of ice in an hour. Norm eventually came down to the basement to figure out what I was up to, and found that I had made over sixty bags of ice. They were piled around me like a dragon's hoard.

"Who'n the hell's gonna buy all *that?*" He shook his head. "Next time just make five bags. We barely'll sell that'n a week!"

After the ice fiasco I was demoted to janitorial duty, a fitting foreshadowing of how my summer would end. I was handed a toilet brush and mop and told to clean the employee washroom. I imagine what Norm really meant to say was, 'clean the employee washroom for the first time since the building was erected'. If you've ever seen the film *Trainspotting* this washroom was the Canadian sister to "the worst toilet in Scotland". By the time I finished cleaning, my smock was covered in every kind of human filth imaginable. I hung up the fouled butcher's smock in the manager's office that doubled as an employee lounge late that afternoon and mopped the floors until my shift was over.

When I waved good-bye to Norm he was standing behind the meat counter, weighing slabs of meat on a scale for a customer. He wiped his gloveless hand on the rubber surface of his chest, smearing it with blood – *he was wearing the very same unwashed smock I had cleaned the washroom with hours earlier*. I quickly exited the store before I barfed.

By the end of my first day I was already feeling imaginary cash burning a hole in my pocket. At roughly $12 per day working at the grocery store was going to add up to one helluva haul by the end of the summer. Wisely, my father told Norm to pay me in full at the *end* of the summer instead of giving me weekly cheques, so I couldn't squander my pay piecemeal. By the end of the summer I had earned almost two hundred dollars which Norm grudgingly thumbed out to me one twenty-dollar bill at a time. Cash-in-hand I ran straight to the local Radio Shack and eyeballed the only shelf of IBM PC-compatible games in a 1200 kilometre radius.

When I think back to the games on the shelf that day I can only remember the one I bought. It practically leaped off the shelf into my arms the second I spotted it. It had a man munching on a cheeseburger, sitting in the captain's chair of a spaceship, which was being chased by insectoid spacecraft, all in view of an intergalactic diner whose lemon yellow marquee looked suspiciously like the golden arches. The box cover art practically promised that I'd be rolling around in my chair laughing my little butt off. A year earlier I had seen the Mel Brooks classic spoof film *Spaceballs (1987)* and was enamoured by its satirical take on *Star Wars* and *Star Trek*. The cover art made me think 'this game *must* have been made by people who loved *Spaceballs* too!' If you haven't guessed it already, I was gawking at the adventure gaming classic title *Space Quest III: The Pirates of Pestulon*. The princely price tag of $64.99 almost made me balk until I saw that it was made by Sierra On-Line. I couldn't tear open my Velcro-locked wallet fast enough.

I was in pizza face paradise. I didn't even *care* that I wouldn't have access to my family computer until my father and I made the return drive south several days later. On the ride home I gingerly slid the box out of its shrink-wrap and goggled at the contents of the familiar tan-coloured Sierra box. There were fake postcards from imaginary intergalactic locations like a black hole and the planet Arrakis; and there were a pair of cardboard sunglasses with tinted plastic lenses and a fake alien nose, not unlike a Groucho Marx gag facial prosthetic. I put them on and looked at myself in the mirror – I looked just like one of the Two Guys from Andromeda pictured on the back of the box. Hilarious! The game so far spoke to every ounce of humour in me and all I thought was: *the Two Guys who made this game must be the funniest people I've never met.*

That evening I examined every square inch of the box and re-read the manual several times. I wasn't the most patient kid and within hours the desire to actually *play* the game was giving me itchy fingers. I tried to load the game on my aunt's IBM XT-class computer – a glorified word processor. Not only did it have an amber monochrome monitor but it did not even have enough RAM to load the game. Damn.

The next day, by complete happenstance, I got a call from my friend Norman, a boy who had been in my Boy Scout troop years earlier. He had heard I had returned to town for the summer and invited me to his house for a sleep-over. After a long day of playing outside we retired to his bedroom where my prayers were answered: there was a beautiful, shiny, Tandy 1000 computer sitting on a desk beside his bed! I immediately called my father and asked him to drive across town with my copy of *Space Quest III*. Like the FedEx service all parents effectively are, my dad showed up with the game and a few cans of pop and bags of chips for our sleep-over. I double-checked the system requirements on the box cover: Yes! Just like *King's Quest IV* it was made to be played on "IBM PC *and* Tandy-compatibles"!

For anyone that is not familiar with this ubiquitous computer, the Tandy 1000 was one of many "IBM clones" that emerged in the late 1980's. The term "clone" means a computer that is designed to ape the functionality and software compatibility of the IBM PC. IBM clones of the time – like Tandy and Compaq computers – generally had similar graphics, memory and sound capabilities as their true-blue IBM masters. The Tandy 1000 had a few aces up its sleeve compared to other generic clones. The Tandy 1000 had its own advanced graphics hardware and "three-voice" sound hardware that gave the machine improved graphics and sound even over its IBM predecessor. It had a joystick port and a volume knob too, which made it similar to my Amstrad PC at home. All of these technical details are especially relevant to what transpired in Norman's bedroom that night.

Norman and I delicately inserted the first *Space Quest III* disk and a few minutes later watched as the introduction sequence rolled. The three-voice sound system fanfared a bombastic musical theme for the game and the Tandy's crisp sixteen colour EGA graphics made our eyes pop out. But that wasn't what blew our minds.

A minute into the introduction of the game, the camera cuts to a close-up of Roger Wilco, intrepid hero of the story. Roger awakens from a long hypersleep in an *Alien*-like sleeping pod. His eyes open groggily and he says to the audience in a thought balloon, "Where am I?"

The speaker from the Tandy exploded in a scratchily enunciated digitized voice: ***WHERE AM I?***

Our eleven-year-old jaws hung open and we stared at each other and yelled "no way!" in chorus. The Tandy *spoke!* We had never in our lives imagined that, like HAL 9000 of *2001: A Space Odyssey,* one day a computer might speak to us. We couldn't believe our ears. In fact we *didn't* believe our ears. We both agreed that our minds were probably playing tricks on us from all the cans of pop we had guzzled and empty bags of chips strewn across the floor.

After watching the introduction sequence we walked Roger around the screen for a few minutes in the way familiar to all Sierra On-Line "3D Animated Adventure Games". Norman fought with the keyboard controls and became exasperated with trying to control the character's movements. He said finally, "Hey let's play with the joystick instead."

We changed the game's settings to use the Tandy's joystick instead of the keyboard and re-ran the game. The introduction sequence played, but this time when Roger Wilco's thought balloon appeared with 'Where Am I?', the computer did not make a sound. We both looked at each other. Hadn't we heard his voice the first time we played the game?

We reloaded the game, this time cranking up the volume knob on the Tandy so we wouldn't miss a sound. This time the speaker bleated out the *Space Quest III* musical theme and we heard from the hallway, "Norman! You guys go to bed! It's past midnight!"

Busted. Norman shut off the computer and we both whispered for an hour arguing about if we had *actually* heard Roger speak the first time. Norman was convinced we had imagined it, and I was convinced it was some kind of installation setting I had messed up when we re-started the game. Sadly, we had spent so much time trying to make Roger speak again that we had only played the game for a couple of minutes.

When I left Norman's house the next morning I had to wait

another week to play *Space Quest III* on my own computer. When we arrived at our acreage I immediately installed the game on our Amstrad and tried it out. To my great disappointment Roger did not speak a single word on our computer either. Norman must have been right: it had been a hallucination. Worse, the PC speaker music of my Amstrad was clearly inferior to the Tandy's rich three-voice synthesizer. Perhaps Carl had been right months ago: Tandy computers really were superior to other IBM clones.

But that disappointment did not tarnish the gleam of the adventure game that became my personal touchstone for humour and entertainment. *Space Quest III* was the game that demanded all of my attention throughout the sixth grade. It became the game I played for comfort when I was sick, the game I showed off to friends when they came to visit me, the game I thought about when I went to bed at night, and the game I played alone when no one else took an interest in it.

But it was the least favourite among my friends and with my sister. No one appreciated its grisly yet hilarious Roger Wilco death animations or its thinly-veiled parody of *The Terminator*, mockery of McDonald's Restaurants, and lampooning of *Ms. Pac-man*. My sister either didn't get it or didn't care, and most of my friends found the science fiction setting boring. Even my friend Robert, whom I saw as having the most similar taste in humour to me, gave the cheesy jokes his lowest rating ever: a mere chuckle.

Thinking back, I owe a large part of my sense of humour to the Two Guys from Andromeda. Their love for cheesy puns and dark sarcasm did as much to formulate my sense of humour as *The Simpsons* did with its over-the-top ironic view of the world. Every few years I discovered some cleverly not-so-hidden pop culture/science fiction reference stuffed into the game. Roger Wilco's ship - the "Aluminum Mallard" – was a pun on the historical aircraft the "Spruce Goose" (and *Star Wars'* Millennium Falcon) - and curiously similar in design to the Winnebago-styled space ship at the heart of the film *Spaceballs*. An evil robotic villain in the game named "Arnoid the

Annihilator" was an obvious reference to Arnold Schwarznegger's role as *The Terminator*. Or Monolith Burger's play on McDonald's. And so on.

Space Quest III became an unspoken piece of me that I kept for myself, and yet the game remained subtly implicated in every joke I made for the next thirty years. Until I had the pleasure of meeting true *Space Quest* fans online in my thirties, I never spoke a word of the game to anyone.

I suspect that everyone has a game (or film or book or piece of music) in their life that no one else seems to love as much as they do. It becomes a quiet part of them, waiting to be shared with special others some day.

There was an outstanding mystery to *Space Quest III* that haunted me for decades however: the damned ghost voice of Roger Wilco that Norman and I had stumbled upon. In my early thirties I discovered, thanks to a brief page of technical errata buried in the technical manual for the Tandy 1000 computer, the solution to the problem. As it turned out, the special Tandy 1000 three-voice sound system shared resources with the joystick port. *Either* the joystick *or* the sound system could be activated, but not both at the same time. When one was activated the other was automatically disabled. When Norman and I had turned on the joystick port to make the game easier to play, the computer automatically turned off the sound system!

When I finally got my hands on a Tandy 1000 of my own twenty years after my sleep-over at Norman's, I grabbed my pile of bit-rotted *Space Quest III* disks and tried it again... *this time with the joystick off*. For the first time in two decades Roger Wilco croaked out those three fateful words: **Where Am I?** Norman and I finally had our answer, thus solving the riddle of the Tandy ghost voice. Norman, if you're out there somewhere: we weren't hallucinating! It was real!

Amstrad PC1512 and Computer Porn

It was the sixth grade and I had graduated to membership among the elementary school's elite. In our five-six split class, sixth graders were undeniably older, wiser and smarter than their juvenile fifth grade underlings. I even had a few solid connections with seventh graders like Chad and Fraser thanks to our hockey nights, which gave me some street cred amongst my peers.

My parents were both busy with their respective careers and my sister and I became latchkey kids. On weekdays my sister and I were expected to either let ourselves into the house, or spend after-school time at one of the neighbouring acreages with friends.

My go-to friend for after school play time was always my friend Chad. Chad was a year older than me and he was into all the cool stuff that boys thought girls liked boys for: motorcycles, music, girls and horses. He was an actual *teenager* and he even had a few blond whiskers growing on his acne-splotched upper lip. I on the other hand was into the stuff that nerdy kids were into: computer games, science experiments and the Sega Master System. Chad introduced me to the un-nerdy stuff boys were supposed to like, and I introduced him to the dorky stuff that no one was supposed to like. I hate to admit it but at the time I was the Milhouse van Houten to his Bart Simpson.

On days that I was home alone, I hopped on my Honda 50R child-sized motorcycle and sped over to Chad's house, which was a 1960s double-wide trailer. Hanging out together was an exercise in boredom management – with so few things to do around his acreage we spent most of our time getting into all kinds of trouble (usually without getting caught). An abridged list of unsupervised play-time activities: home-made "bombs" consisting of an ice cream bucket filled with every industrial solvent found in his garage and a match, taking turns driving my motorcycle while the rear passenger shot a .22 calibre rifle at passing hay bales, trespassing neighbouring farms and exploring abandoned farm sheds, searching his brother's bedroom for a mythical *Hustler* magazine stashed away like treasure... it was all harmless fun for a teen and pre-teen. But make no mistake: we would have been in a heap of trouble from our folks if we had been caught doing any of this.

A few weeks into the sixth grade Chad's father came home with a special surprise for his family. Like all farmers, Chad's dad tried to keep up with the Jones' and bought his family all the niceties that other acreage owners were buying for their kids. Apparently, Chad's father had learned that his son had been playing computer games over at my house, and this meant that his family needed a computer too.

Like my own father, Chad's father knew diddly-squat about computers. It was the early 1990's and Canada was going through a national recession. Money was tight and Chad's father had no intention of blowing thousands of dollars on a hunk of plastic and silicon. Over coffee at his oilfield day-job, Chad's father overheard a co-worker looking to sell his Amstrad computer for a few hundred bucks. He called my father immediately and asked if five hundred dollars for an Amstrad computer was a good deal. My father, who figured a computer was a computer, told him it was one hell of a deal after spending $2500 on our Amstrad just a year earlier.

Today, before making any kind of technological purchase, most people would think to enquire about the age, condition, and technical specifications of a used computer before pulling the trigger. But two troglodyte-dads on a budget figured that the Amstrad logo and the word "computer" was warrant enough to make a sale.

Chad's father came home with the computer and set it up inside of a tiny hallway closet in their trailer. The computer had no mouse, and it had a smaller monitor than our computer.

There appeared to be no hard drive, only two 5-¼" disk drives.[22] It appeared to be inferior to our own Amstrad computer in every way, but it *did* have the same grey-and-red Amstrad logo at least. Chad and I sped over to my house, doubling on my motorcycle, and grabbed a handful of the 5-¼" diskettes I had in my Sierra On-Line game boxes. We tried them one at a time, and none of them appeared to work!

The computer did not come with manuals nor operating system disks, and my own 3-½" MS-DOS disks didn't fit in the drive. There appeared to be no way of booting the thing. The computer sat there for days. No one knew what to do with it and I was hesitant to experiment with it in fear of breaking it.

A week later Chad and I had one of our sleep-over nights which included playing *Atari 7800* games and watching *WWF Wrestling*. An enduring favourite was playing *One-on-One: Dr. J vs. Larry Bird* – a basketball game – on the Atari. Slam-dunking on the net caused the glass to shatter and fall down, sending a janitor on to the screen who spasmodically barked at us as he swept up the mess. When the potato chips and *Coca-Cola* ran low, we snuck out of his bedroom to raid the kitchen for more snacks around midnight. In the hallway we heard an oscillating hum inside of the tiny closet in the hallway. The computer was on! We slid open the noisy accordion door to the closet and heard and saw what male preteen eyes pray for, but are rarely ever granted: nude female breasts.

Well, I *think* they were breasts. They appeared as two very bright magenta dots in the centre of two round yellow circles. Below and above that were, if you squinted and turned your head sideways: the head, groin and legs of a very nubile redheaded woman with a sultry pout on her… face? The eyes of that lusty, busty, cartoony, pixelated redhead dared us to "hit any

---

[22] The Amstrad PC1512 came with an Intel 8086 8MHz CPU, dual 360KB floppy drives, non-standard CGA graphic card, and 512 kilobytes of RAM. It was the kind of entry-level machine that was out of date the minute it left the assembly line in 1985.

key on the keyboard" and unlock the naughty secrets inside!

I'm sure some of you are concerned about two preteen boys exposing themselves to hardcore pornography well before their time. But I can only stress the surrealism of the experience: it was a low-res four-colour CGA graphics cartoon woman on a computer screen. It was barely discernible *as a human being* never mind as a nude woman. To this day I suspect my eleven-going-on-twelve imagination fabricated more sensual details in that image than any talented pixel artist could have pushed to that crappy monitor.

But nude CGA ladies were still nude ladies and we didn't need to be told twice. Just imagine the hoard of nudity waiting for us on that diskette! Chad hit a key as instructed, and bam!, we were prompted to enter a four-digit passcode. We checked over our shoulders nervously, worried that one of his parents would see us hiding in the closet at midnight, giggling quietly at the computer screen. We closed the accordion door behind us and crammed ourselves together in the closet. That night, and every night for the next week, we tried dozens upon dozens of passcodes to get past the lock screen. It got to the point that Chad asked his father what year he and his mother were born in, hoping that the passcode was one of their birthday years.

Eventually the disk disappeared from the floppy drive. Chad's father must have caught on to our late-night spelunking and likely returned the smutty disk to the care of the oilfield co-worker who gave it to him.

We rationalized our disappointment. Why on Earth would anyone want dirty pictures on the computer anyway? It made as much sense as washing your kitchen dishes in the toilet tank: sure you *can*, but why would you want to? Dirty pictures were for *Playboy*, *Hustler* and scrambled satellite television channels! Computers were for computer games not sexy adult stuff! It would be a few years before we found out how wrong we were: we could have never imagined the massive torrent of pornography that would one day flood a thing called The Internet.

AdLib Music Synthesizer: The Christmas Meltdown

Over the year I became the nerdy equivalent of a bar-fly at the nearest Radio Shack. Every weekend on trips to the City I returned to Radio Shack's shelves, and gazed at the new releases. One day, as I browsed through the glut of Sierra On-Line and Activision titles, I spied a new rack of larger boxes that didn't look much like games. Radio Shack was slowly expanding into computer upgrades and peripherals.

Just within reach of my puny sixth-grade stature was something I had only seen in magazines: a sound card. I was familiar with the concept of a sound card from the Sierra On-Line product catalogue packed in every game box: sound cards allowed the computer to express more realistic music and sound than the beepy-boopy PC speaker was capable of.

This particular sound hardware, the AdLib Music Synthesizer, promised everything and then some. The technical specifications on the back of the box made me drool: polyphonic digital music that sounded *just* like real musical instruments! And it came with a music composition program that allowed me to make my own music. I saw the price tag and winced. It was $200 – more dough than I had earned the entire summer. That left only one financial avenue: the bank of mom and dad.

Making withdrawals from this particular bank required serious tactical knowledge. A personal loan was out of the question. It was already a week past my twelfth birthday so an extravagant birthday present was a dead end too. The only option left was Christmas which was a couple of months away. I needed a strong pre-Christmas marketing campaign to secure any hope of getting that AdLib.

My mother walked into the store and I casually guided her over to the shelves and feigned surprise.

"Oh wow! Look! I've *always* wanted one of these and they finally got one in."

I grabbed the AdLib box off of the shelf and poured on a sales spiel that would have embarrassed a used furniture salesman. By the time I was done my pitch I had practically promised her that the AdLib would balance her chequebook and do the dishes.

Moms, especially my mom who had grown accustomed to these 'One time only! Act now!' sales offers, are correctly suspicious of their pre-teen sons by nature. She smiled sympathetically and said, "We'll see." As I put the box back on the shelf, satisfied with myself, she asked me how much it cost.

I carefully pursed my lips and mumbled, "Um. One ninety-nine ninety-five."

"What?!" she exclaimed and shook her head. As she marched out of the store I stayed on her heels trying to chase down my only chance of achieving musical nirvana. I was about to lose my sale, I had to do something.

Over the next five weeks I became Ralphy from *A Christmas Story*, trying to get his Red Ryder B.B. gun for Christmas from his parents. I cajoled, persuaded and called in every favour from the White House I could muster. The AdLib was the only thing I wanted for Christmas. Mom and dad could combine my Christmas presents for the next three years. They could ask the entire family – aunts, uncles, grandparents – to pitch in. C'mon, help me out!

Nothing worked and a week before Christmas I visited Radio Shack with my mom for one last-ditch attempt. This time I took the emotional road and put on my best Dickensian quivering-bottom-lip-poor-little-orphan routine. If my mom and dad didn't buy me the AdLib there would be no Christmas on 34th street this year. No Christmas for Tiny Tim. No three wise men. No baby Jesus.

"Oh, my son. It's too much. We can't afford it right now." She smiled sadly and hugged me. My routine had failed and nothing was going to get me that music card.

I was inconsolable the entire ride home and stared out the passenger window. I went on a five-day vow of silence in protest of the Worst Christmas Ever. My mother and father dutifully ignored my mute tantrum and went on as if nothing was wrong. The world was so unfair! I only wanted this *one* thing and my parents wouldn't buy it for me!

Little did I appreciate that a recession had hit Canadian families in the 1990s, and ours had been pummelled particularly badly. Despite working seven days a week my father's construction business was failing to bring in enough to support a family of four. My mother was taking an extra-heavy load of coursework at the university to expedite her degree so she could get a job as soon as possible. She began working odd-jobs on weekends for pocket cash. We were in a serious financial crisis and my parents were going into heavy personal debt. But no one spoke a word about it and suffered in silence, as many parents do, while their kids begged for the latest and greatest toys. Knowing this now, I feel even more regret for what I did next.

It was Christmas Eve. My mother's family tradition was to open their gifts on Christmas Eve followed by a late dinner. My father's tradition strictly observed opening presents on Christmas Day. Most years they'd split the difference and allow us to open one present on Christmas Eve and the rest on Christmas morning.

I inspected the boxes of gifts under the tree. There was a part of me that truly believed my month-long political demonstration had been effective and they had secretly bought me the AdLib. A minute's inspection was heartbreaking: none of the boxes were even close to the right shape, size, or heft. In fact, I only had one gift under the tree with my name on it. It was large and extremely heavy, like it held a collection of Encyclopaedias. My sister had *four* presents. This was totally unfair, borderline criminal, and practically a declaration of war.

My mom, dad and sister gathered around the Christmas tree a few minutes before midnight. I was nowhere to be found. After a few minutes my mom went into the basement to find me curled up on my bed, hugging my blankets like a toddler and his teddy bear. She asked me what was wrong and I broke down in tears. As far as I was concerned it was the worst Christmas of any child's life anywhere in the world. My father and sister, hearing the commotion in my bedroom, called us upstairs.

When I arrived, tears running down my face, my father gave me a dirty look and said, "If you don't stop your crying we aren't opening any presents tonight!"

This opened the flood gates. "I DON'T CARE! I DON'T WANT ANY OF THIS STUPID STUFF ANYWAY!" I shrieked and threw a massive tantrum.

The minor storm that was brewing became a hurricane. My sister was yelling at me, which made my father yell at her, which drew my mom in between us all trying to mediate. Round and round it went, like the sketch from *The Simpsons* where Homer, Bart, Lisa and Marge are all choking one another.

Finally my sister forced the large, heavy gift box onto my lap. "Oh, quit crying already! They got you your stupid game or whatever!"

I looked at my parents, truly confused. They stood there half-enraged and trying to suppress laughter. I opened the huge box gingerly amidst angry tears and inside found a large cement brick and several hardcover books. Beside them, wrapped in an old tee-shirt, was the AdLib Music Synthesizer.

My jaw hung open and my tears vanished instantly. I hugged the box and began apologizing profusely to everyone around me. I mumbled excitedly that it was the best Christmas ever and I'm sorry I was being stupid and crying but you told me I wouldn't get one and that was a rotten trick to pull and yeah I'm really surprised and, and…

My dad clapped his hands together and barked out a huge laugh. "Hahaha! It worked!" He was always trying to baffle me with clever gift-wrapping ruses at Christmas, and usually I saw past his cheap subterfuge. This time he had masterfully put one past me. Putting the cement brick in the box was an evil and brilliant ploy.

I immediately ran over to the Amstrad and slipped open the rear plastic cover to expose its single ISA slot. After a few terrifying moments trying to figure out which side of the card faced outward, it slid into the slot with a satisfying pop. Although I did not have a pair of powered speakers for its headphone jack, I did have a pair of GameBoy earbuds that I wore around the place like old jeans. I turned on the computer and immediately re-ran the Sierra On-Line installation program for *King's Quest IV*. I HAD to know what the music sounded like!

The opening fanfare did not disappoint. The thin, metallic trumpets the AdLib produced were even better than the real thing as far as I was concerned. I handed my sister the left earbud and we both listened along and smiled at each other as the game played its musical themes. It was like finding a fifty dollar bill under your pillow from the Tooth Fairy. It was the discovery of the New World. It was the first time someone dunked an Oreo cookie in milk. It was everything the box had promised and more.

My parents shooed us to bed an hour later and I clearly remember hearing the introduction music to *King's Quest IV* ringing in my ears as I fell asleep.

The next morning I awoke early and went straight to the Amstrad. Every single game I owned supported the AdLib, which meant that the rest of the Christmas holidays were spent re-configuring my games to take advantage of my new hardware. *Space Quest III* was an instant hit with me, as the music now surpassed even the Tandy three-voice versions of the music I had heard at Norman's house a year earlier.

For the next two years the AdLib was my music card of choice. Sure, the Sound Blaster was technically more impressive with its digitized samples, but I didn't have one of those.[23] The

[23] The AdLib Music Synthesizer was not a "sound card" per se. The AdLib used a cheap, off the shelf Yamaha OPL-2 music synthesizer chip to reproduce musical instruments. Unfortunately the AdLib could not reproduce "digital samples" – that is, it could not play back pre-recorded sound like people's voices or a car horn honking. The Sound Blaster in contrast had a newer Yamaha OPL-3 music chip, and supported digital sample playback. Today, some retro gaming

AdLib was my Christmas miracle and became my workhorse for many of my MS-DOS days.. that is, until the day the Amstrad met its early demise at my hands.

enthusiasts argue over the preferred musicality of both cards. For me, the AdLib has an unforgettably buzzy musicality that define the games I grew up with.

1991-1992: Grades Seven & Eight

Not-so-Boring Beige Intel 486 DX-33

It was the seventh grade and finally computers were spreading throughout Western Canada, even to the little rural communities that surrounded our acreage. As far as I knew, Carl, myself and a handful of other kids were the only people in the school with computers at home. This was about to change in a big way.

My two best friends, Robert and Trevor, continued to visit for the occasional sleep-over, but our tradition of playing outdoor sports was quickly transforming into indoor gaming.

When they visited my house we sometimes played a game of *Tank Wars* or *Wacky Wheels* – two shareware titles that had deceptively simple but fun multiplayer support. Otherwise the Sega Genesis was now our go-to for sports titles like EA Sports' *NHL Hockey* and *Lakers vs. Celtics in the NBA Playoffs*. My collection of single-player PC titles like *Out of this World, Space Quest III* and *Ghostbusters II* got no love when my friends visited, as sitting there watching one person play a game wasn't much fun. Even when I offered to let them play these games on their own as I sat to the side, they didn't show much enthusiasm for them. That is, until they day *they* got their *own* computer.

One day, Robert and Trevor came to school saying that their parents had bought a new computer to do their farm business accounting on. When I asked them about the technical aspects of the new computer they had no idea what kind of computer it was, but assured me it looked pretty cool. It stood upright on the desk instead of flat, and it even had a set of its own powered speakers!

I *had* to know what this shiny new beast was like, so I did the one thing I always did when I wanted to hang out with my best friends on the weekend: I invited myself and my sister over to their house for a sleep-over. I asked my mom to ask their mom if we could have a sleep-over on the weekend, and let the moms do their negotiations for driving responsibilities. A day later we had a date: my sister and I were to stay over Friday night after school and return Sunday morning before their family went to church. Two whole days with my best friends *and* their new computer!

That Friday the bus ride home from school felt excruciatingly long – I couldn't wait to get over to their house and get a peek at the new machine. I spent an hour packing and re-packing my backpack with everything we could possibly need for the next two days: Game Boy. Nuby Magnifier with Light attachment. Sega Game Gear. *Out of this World*. *Stunts*. *Space Quest III*. *Taz-Mania* for the Sega Genesis. A Frisbee. By the time I was done there was barely room for a single change of clothing in my backpack.

My mom drove my sister and I the five kilometres to their home and dropped us off. With renovations to their farmhouse complete, my friends were no longer living in their garage. Entry to the house was now through a side-door which had a shiny newly-tiled mudroom.

Our usual sleep-over routine went like this: I kicked off my shoes into a pile of teenage Nike and Reebok footwear along the wall. Trevor and Robert poked their heads around the corners of the hallway ten feet away and everyone broke into excited grins. We converged in Robert's bedroom for a quick warm-up game of *NHL Hockey* on his Genesis, while McCain's personal pizzas baked in the oven in the kitchen at the opposite end of the house.

Except, today was different. Trevor and Robert were curiously absent when my sister and I pulled off our shoes in the mudroom. I only heard what sounded like video game music coming from the second storey of the house. I rushed up a spiral staircase where I found my best friends completely engrossed in front of a brand-spanking-new computer.

If the Amstrad was my idea of a PC fit for lords, their new computer made me look like I was a 14th century serf clawing around in the muck while they rode by on their massive stallion. It had a much larger monitor, and the computer proper was a *tower* that had buttons and LED readouts on the front. I watched as the screen showed an incredibly realistic cartoon animation of a tiger-man barking out a line of dialogue.

"Prince Thrakath!"

The Sound Blaster brand powered speakers erupted with the growling voice of the tiger-man. *It spoke!* The silhouetted tiger-man in the scene gestured with its right hand, claws extended to another figure standing nearby. The animation was so *smooth*. A close-up revealed the tiger-man's facial features, covered in decorative piercings. I secretly hoped that their new computer wasn't as good as mine, but this completely obliterated our Amstrad.

Trevor, Robert and I sat transfixed as we watched the rest of the cinematic story play out in front of us. The sound, music, animation and graphics were beyond anything I had seen shown on a screen outside of a movie theatre, and destroyed the comparatively adolescent capabilities of game consoles like the Super Nintendo and Sega Genesis. When the introduction sequence finished it revealed the title of this amazing mystery game: *Wing Commander II: Vengeance of the Kilrathi*.

Trevor sat at the keyboard and Robert read from a large card showing all of the keyboard commands required to play the game. It took us a few minutes to figure out how to launch into a space battle, and when we did our jaws dropped at the 3D graphics. They were so smooth and life-like compared to the handful of 3D games we had experience with up to that moment. We were decisively routed after a minute of dogfighting in our spacecraft and Robert, seeing that our ship was ready to explode, hit the "eject" button on the keyboard. Instead of seeing a Game

Over screen, to my delight the game continued with a cinematic sequence that carried the story onward.

Although Robert and Trevor were hardly enthusiastic about space combat simulators, especially one with such complex keyboard controls, we all knew that *Wing Commander II* redefined our understanding of how cool video games could be. Eventually we figured out how to fly the spacecraft using the mouse, which proved even more ungainly than the keyboard, and Trevor and Robert soon began digging for different games to play in a large box of software.

"Hey this one looks cool." Trevor pulled out a brightly coloured animated game called *Dragon's Lair II: Time Warp*.

I showed my friends how to install games from the floppy disk to the hard drive, and we impatiently waited as the floppy drive grinded byte-by-byte through each disk.

Dragon's Lair II was even more impressive, cinematically, than the last game. Not only were there digitized audio clips for each scene of the game, the animation was incredibly life-like, reminding me of Walt Disney cartoons like *Fantasia*.[24] Sure the gameplay was a little repetitive, seeing the hero Dirk the Daring die on every screen, but we absolutely loved watching the hilarious death sequences which were half of the fun.

This computer clearly had better hardware than mine in every respect. I flipped open the owner's manual and goggled at the specifications: a Super VGA video card, a Sound Blaster sound card, a 486 DX-33 CPU, a single-speed CD-ROM drive, and *four* megabytes of RAM. I *had* to find some game that brought it down from Mount Olympus to live among mere mortals like my Amstrad. I installed *Out of this World* hoping that its cinematic

[24] In fact, the game was animated by none other than Don Bluth Studios, the ex-Disney animators behind *The Secret of NIMH* and *Anastasia*. Unbeknownst to us, *Dragon's Lair* was an incredibly popular arcade game that ran on a laser disc player, and had been out for years. The hand-animation and simple control formula proved lucrative, spawning sequels to *Dragon's Lair* and the *Space Ace* series of games.

sequences would cripple it.

Instead of crippling the machine, the game played even smoother and with better quality sound than I had ever seen! The Sound Blaster card inside of their computer was evidently better than my beloved AdLib, and the faster CPU allowed the game to play at a much higher frame rate than I was used to at home. It turned out that my Amstrad was so slow that the game played in slow-motion at home compared to the perfectly smooth animation I was seeing now.

We spent the remainder of the night installing every single game we could find. One disk, borrowed from a friend was labelled *Barbarian* and proved to be a hilarious two-player combat game featuring half-nude warriors with the physiques of characters from *Conan the Barbarian* comics. When the game title screen appeared, the PC speaker scratchily croaked out a digitized PC voice saying, "BARRRRRBARIANNN!" To three immature boys like us it was the height of hilarity.

Halfway through the evening of antics I noticed a curious button labelled "Turbo" on the front of the PC's tower. Robert and Trevor warned me not to touch anything on their computer as their parents were (prudently) concerned I'd break something on their new investment. While the boys ran downstairs to get us more root beer I couldn't resist the urge to push the Turbo button.[25] Not a whole lot happened, except that a red LED turned off below the button. I loaded *Wing Commander II* and immediately noticed a difference: the game was playing so

[25] The infamous Turbo button on 1980s and 1990s PCs did not "speed up" the computer. The Turbo button was a clever device to "clock down" the CPU so it ran at a slower speed for specific programs that only ran properly slowly. This function proved useful for many old computer games that had CPU-sensitive timing algorithms, such as Sierra On-Line adventure games of the 1980s and 1990s. In Turbo mode a 486 DX-33 ran at 33 MHz, but in "normal" non-Turbo mode the computer ran like an IBM XT 8086. Think of depressing the Turbo button as pulling the emergency brake on your car: it only slows you down.

sluggishly that it was in slow motion! Robert and Trevor came upstairs and saw that the game was now almost unplayable.

"What'd you do?" Robert looked at me accusingly.

"Watch this."

I pressed the Turbo button again and the game speed returned to normal. It did not take long for us to make a game out of the Turbo button – in the midst of a critical moment in *The Simpsons Arcade Game* or *Wacky Wheels* someone would press the turbo button and throw the player's sense of timing off completely. It was about as cruel as stepping on your car's accelerator as someone is trying to open the passenger door, driving a few feet, and then stopping again.

When this tedious prepubescent prank wore thin, we clambered down the spiral staircase before 10 o'clock and quietly played *NHL Hockey* on the Sega Genesis until bed time. I barely slept that night with the sounds and sights of *Wing Commander*'s Kilrathi ships exploding in my head.

Saturday morning meant a few hours of glorious cartoons thanks to the Disney Afternoon program on our local television station. I drifted off into daydreams of *Wing Commander II* as we watched episodes of *Raw Toonage, Tailspin* and *Darkwing Duck*. Their computer even used MS-DOS 5.0 which was two whole versions newer than the MS-DOS 3.3 used on our Amstrad. In every way their computer was better than mine. Coming home to my own computer the next day, for the first time ever, was full of disappointment.

Dr. Sbaitso and the Sound Blaster

Beyond the computer's incredible speed it was the Sound Blaster sound card and speakers that became a preoccupation of ours. Only a few months earlier I had spent entire days daydreaming of how great the AdLib music synthesizer card would sound on my Amstrad. And here was a sound card that outstripped the AdLib in every way – it produced digitized audio samples and voices like I was watching a movie, and its music was just as good if not better.

After a few hours of much needed outdoor time burning off preteen energy I eventually hornswoggled my way back to the computer waiting upstairs. This time I was intent on understanding the musical capabilities of the Sound Blaster. We grabbed the pile of diskettes with the Sound Blaster logo and installed all of them. Robert dug a plastic microphone out of the box which plugged directly into the sound card. Could this thing really play our voices back over the speakers like a Karaoke machine?

The truth turned out to be even better. Not only could the Sound Blaster record our voices, but it could also produce voices of its own. I dug around in the C:\>SB\ directory and found an executable file by the name of SBAITSO.EXE. We ran it and were greeted by a bright blue screen full of text, and more importantly, a computerized voice rang out loudly over the speakers:

```
HELLO I AM DOCTOR SBAITSO FROM CREATIVE LABS.
PLEASE ENTER YOUR NAME.
>_
```

The cursor blinked patiently and waited for us to enter a command just like a DOS prompt. I experimented:

```
>vga
```

* * *

The mechanical voice squawked out in reply to our utter astonishment and delight:

```
HELLO VGA. I AM HERE TO HELP.
TELL ME ABOUT YOUR PROBLEMS.
```

We all looked at each other and broke out laughing. It could talk and even pronounce our names! We took turns entering our names and listening to the hilarious mispronunciations of them all. DR. SBAITSO was incredible! We had never imagined that a computer could be capable not only of producing a fairly lifelike human voice like HAL 9000, but also responding to us interactively as we typed.

Experimenting with the program revealed that it was a simulated parody of a stereotypical psychologist.[26] Anything we typed in reply to the dear doctor would earn a response in equal measure:

```
>i am happy
Why do you think you are happy?
>i love you
Let's not make this about me. Tell me more about
yourself.
>i love butts
I understand that you love butts. Tell me more about
this please.
```

The conversation continued on in this circular fashion, and tormenting the program's text parser with curses, insults and indelicate requests became a delightful game in itself. After an

---

[26] The SBAITSO program was based on a much earlier manifestation of a computer psychiatrist program called ELIZA. Although decades older, ELIZA had a similar design: it responded in a querying format reminiscent of Rogerian psychologists of the 1960s, encouraging the user to volunteer more and more information about themselves. Dr. Sbaitso took the same formula and added a computerized voice with a healthy dose of sarcasm.

hour our interest was waning, until Trevor discovered the dear doctor's most important function:

```
>say cathy loves mike
Cathy loves mike.
```

Our jaws dropped. The doctor could be commanded to speak! He was like a genie that could grant our infinite wishes!

```
>say my name is robert and im gay for mr dressup_
```

Robert caught on to the juvenile homophobia I was pecking into the keyboard before I could complete the sentence, wrestling the keyboard out of my hands. All three of us fought over the keyboard, trying to hit the "y" and "enter" keys to complete the puerile declaration. Robert eventually won the tug-of-war, deleted the phrase, and began typing out his own comebacks. The circus went on for a few minutes until we were all doubled over with laughter and wiping tears from our eyes.

"Does anyone want to make a... prank call?" Robert asked as he waggled his eyebrows at Trevor and I.

Of course! It would be perfect! Like those spy movies where a device modified a voice over the phone so the person at the other end didn't know who it was. Robert ran downstairs to get a phone book while Trevor and I schemed over who we'd prank call first. We both thought of the same person at the same time: Mike.

Mike was a boy who lived on an acreage equidistant to our homes, and had been a classmate of ours since the first grade. At school he was known informally as "Mike the Spaz" owing to his explosive temper that could erupt at the drop of a hat. Students delighted in tormenting poor Mike, trying to trigger a spaz with mean-spirited jabs and vicious name-calling. Although we were not strictly friends, Mike was a fellow farm kid so we were all on a long-lasting ceasefire agreement with one another: we did not tease him and he was pretty nice to us. But this was a particularly sweet plum, and the lowest hanging fruit is always the easiest to pluck.

The plan was simple. Robert would dial Mike's number and hold the phone receiver in front of the computer speaker. I'd hit the "enter" key and we'd all lean in to listen to the inevitable profanities that would erupt from the phone. We had nothing to lose. It was 1992 and caller ID was nonexistent in our area. Mike would have no idea where the computerized voice came from.

I typed a nasty phrase into *Dr. Sbaitso* and watched Robert dial Mike's phone number. I cranked up the volume on the computer speakers, and when we heard a voice answer I hit the enter key. The doctor's voice blasted out of the speaker into the handset:

```
MIKE YOU ARE A SPAZ.
```

We heard someone swearing on the other end and Robert immediately hung up. The plan had went off without a hitch and we rolled around on the floor laughing uncontrollably. For the rest of the night we schemed a list of prank calls to enemies in our local calling area, including teachers and students we thought were particularly deserving of a tongue lashing from the doctor.

The next morning my sister and I climbed back into our family van and went home. The Amstrad was still there, waiting faithfully like an old dog for its owner to come home and give it attention. I loaded up *Out of this World* and sighed irritably as the game played in slow motion. The Amstrad didn't even meet the minimum system requirements to play *Wing Commander II*. The golden halo that surrounded the machine had faded and now I knew the bitter taste of technoenvy. Like Martin Luther of the Protestant Reformation, I would have to nail my proclamation to the front door of our home and let all ye people know: this family has lived in the dark ages of computing for too long! We need a 486!

Photo circa 1991. Left: Rob, Right: Yours truly, with a Sega Game Gear on his lap. Out of frame: Trevor.

Apple //e Revisited

By now I was firmly entrenched in my PC fanaticism and my gaming shelf had swollen. Each month I expanded my library to include the latest game I could afford. *Out of this World, Railroad Tycoon, Ghostbusters II,* and *The Simpsons Arcade Game* never left the Amstrad's hard drive until the machine's untimely demise.[27] Sure, my gang of buddies and I were playing plenty of Sega Genesis and Game Gear games by now, but home for me was still on a PC.

In the eighth grade our school began offering a beginner's computing course for the first time in the history of the school district. Computers were finally making inroads in Western Canada, and educators believed that the next generation of student needed to know how to operate these strange gadgets. Twice a week my buddies and I packed into Mr. M's computer lab of thirty Apple //e computers for "Computers 8".

In 1978 when the Apple // became North America's hottest home computer, Mr. M's "Apple Lab" would have been breathtaking. But it was 1992 – fourteen years after its launch – and the green-phosphor monochrome monitors were on their last legs. Kids were buying Sega Genesis and Super Nintendo consoles with their summer job money, and these systems had games with bright, colourful palettes, sprite rendering effects and advanced multi-track music synthesizers. To my comrades in Computers 8 the Apple //e's must have looked and felt like

---

[27] *Out of this World* was originally released in Europe as *Another World,* the creation of auteur developer Éric Chahi. The game is a work of art deserving of its own book. Chahi's custom development environment on the Amiga 500 is one of the best examples of a game engine perfectly matched to the production of the final game. I highly recommend reading Éric Chahi's official "Another World" website where he discusses the development process of it in much detail: http://anotherworld.fr

Ford Model T's compared to their Formula One race cars idling at home. But to me, a computer was a computer! It meant another three wonderful hours in front of a glowing monitor every week.

The first half of the hour-long class was computing theory. Mr. M put handwritten notes up on an overhead projector, expounding upon the virtues of Arithmetic Logic Units (ALU), Random Access Memory (RAM) and Boolean Logic Gates. I glanced around at my classmates every few minutes and saw the utter disdain on their faces. But I was in heaven. This was the kind of hardcore stuff I could never learn about on my own – the real, mathy stuff that happened inside of those silicon chips! I was sold. This was instantly my favourite class, and Mr. M was the coolest teacher in the school.

The remaining half-hour was devoted to hands-on computing. Students learned basic typing skills for the first few weeks, and progressed to word processing and other boring make-work projects. Each student had a "data disk" which stored all their student assignments. At the end of the class, students handed in their data disks to Mr. M who loaded them up and graded the assignments.

One day Mr. M introduced a new program called *Color LOGO*. *Logo* was a drawing program that introduced the basics of computer programming, allowing kids to draw pretty pictures on the screen using rudimentary fragments of code.[28] Imagine

---

[28] LOGO was created by the cognitive psychologist Seymour Papert, who believed that children could improve their intellectual skills by interacting with computers. In its original form LogoScript was a simple programming language that children could use to direct a "turtle" around on the floor. The turtle was in fact a small robot on wheels with a plush turtle glued on to it. When children instructed it with the "pen down" command, the turtle would extend a small ink pen using a servo-motor to the floor. By moving the turtle around with its pen down, children could draw geometric figures on a paper-covered floor. *Color Logo* on the Apple // took this idea and get rid of the

controlling an electronic paintbrush one instruction at a time by entering a sequence of commands:

```
PEN DOWN, FORWARD 5, TURN RIGHT, FORWARD 5, TURN
RIGHT, FORWARD 5, TURN RIGHT, FORWARD 5, PEN UP.
```

This simple program draws a square, beginning from one corner and proceeding to the next with a series of right turns. "Pen up" and "Pen down" control when the imaginary pen is contacting the imaginary paper. More complex programs could draw intricate geometric figures in multiple colours, *if* the computer had a colour monitor. Ours did not.

The version of *Color Logo* we used had a simple menu system to navigate through the program:

```
[L]oad a program
[S]ave current program
[E]xit
```

After ten minutes of tinkering around with drawing I had finished my assignment and *Color Logo* was boring me to tears. It felt like something for kindergarteners. I had already written more complex Microsoft GW-BASIC programs on my computer at home, and LogoScript was a lot less powerful than even BASIC. Mr. M was busy helping a couple of stragglers trying to run their programs so this meant I had plenty of time for some real fun.

I exited *Logo* and ran the CAT command on the diskette, which showed all the files available to me. I noticed beside the LOGO program that it was not a "binary" program, but a program written in BASIC.[29] This meant that I could take a peek

---

electromechanical turtle and simply put everything on the Apple // screen, adding colour support.

[29] Binary: Computers only process information in terms of zeroes and ones – or "on" and "off", just like a light switch. Binary is a computer's lowest level of language, meaning that it can process this information

at the programming code that *Logo* ran on. It also meant I could make modifications to the program. I have no doubt that the original purpose of writing the program in BASIC was to ensure that teachers and parents could modify the program themselves, making customized versions for their schools and homes. But I had much more devious plans in mind.

I used the LIST instruction to view the program's source code and was pleased to see thousands of lines of instructions spill down the screen. Whew – this was going to take a while to go through line by line! I leaned forward and began parsing through dozens of pages of code, skimming each line for something interesting. The vast majority of code was full of BASIC commands I didn't recognize, probably related to specialized graphical routines on the Apple //e. I have to admit, I felt like a real badass.

Finally, pay-dirt: I found the series of instructions that made the title screen. I quickly noted down the line numbers of the BASIC instructions I planned to modify and walked over to Mr. M.

A couple of months into the semester Mr. M and I were getting along famously, jibing at one another for our devotion to PC's and Apple computers. To him I was a "DOS guy" and to me, he was "Mr. Mac". We had developed the kind of ease found between a mentor and apprentice, and this gave me a few privileges other students didn't have... like staying in the computer lab over lunch.

"Do you mind if I work on my assignment over lunch?" I

---

very quickly. In contrast, a program written in a higher-level language like BASIC must go through a series of translation steps before it can be rendered as binary information to the computer. Programs written in BASIC run much slower than binary programs. On the other hand, BASIC programs are much, much easier to write and understand for human beings since they are written in the English language, and not zeroes and ones. *Color Logo* for the Apple // was written in BASIC so that everyday people could modify and extend the program without specialized tools or training in machine language.

asked, in my most syrupy tone.

He smiled in the knowing way that grandparents do when they let their grandkids get away with murder. He winked, "Hah. Let me know what your top score is in *Lode Runner* later today."

At the end of class he locked me inside of the lab for the entire lunch hour. I was so dead set on hacking *Logo* that I had forgotten about playing *Lode Runner* on the old beast. (Next time). Today I had more Machiavellian plans to unveil.

I spent the next forty-five minutes feverishly modifying BASIC code and testing out the results one instruction at a time. My plan was working perfectly. Someday soon I was going to be celebrated as the boy genius who hacked the Apple //e and saved the class from the doldrums of *Color Logo!*

My little scheme required a bit of burglary. I went through the box of student data disks and pulled out the diskette of a boy named Kurt. Kurt was a tall, quiet, lanky, pale, carrot-top whose parents were members of the Jehovah's Witnesses church. Kurt had a good sense of humour and endured no shortage of teasing about his ginger complexion and could take a nasty joke. I copied my modified LOGO program to his diskette and placed his modified disk back in the box. The program was modified with the kind of humour an immature eighth grade boy like me found hi-larious. Today I feel unbelievably ashamed, but here's what happened in uncensored form:

Two days later the class filtered into the room and grabbed their data disks. I picked a computer two seats away from Kurt and asked my friends Robert and Donny to sit on both sides of me. I wanted my buddies to bear witness to my skilful hijinks so no one could deny how brilliant I was. Mr. M instructed everyone to load up *Logo* and get to work on their new assignment.

At the time I had no idea what a "Jehovah's Witness" was. I knew that Kurt never stood during or sang during the mandatory "Oh Canada" national anthem each week, and that it had something to do with his religious beliefs. But what I didn't know at the time was that cursing was considered a sin of equal viciousness.

Kurt loaded his program and his jaw dropped open. He turned beet red and immediately switched off his monitor. Twenty-nine students had *Logo* running with stuff on the screen, and Kurt's was the only computer that was dark.

Mr. M barked out, "Hey! Kurt! Load up your assignment and get to work!"

Kurt's voice was barely a croak. "I can't. My disk's broken." He sounded like a wounded animal.

Kurt turned his monitor back on and swivelled it toward Robert and I, away from Mr. M. He stared directly at me, eyes wet with tears, knowing I could only be the culprit. The title screen of his copy of *Logo* now read:

```
[F]uck off!
[S]uck my balls!
[K]urt is a fag!
```

I waited for Robert and Donny to laugh but they were both silent. An outspoken girl named Katie walked by and said as she read Kurt's screen, "That's mean. You guys are idiots."

No one found it funny. Not Kurt, not my buddies, and especially not the girls in the class. If my friends and I were already considered socially awkward in junior high, we were now outed as homophobic social outcasts with no sensitivity to other human beings whatsoever. Worse, Kurt had lied to Mr. M to save my butt, fully knowing that I had done the evil deed. I owed him big time.

After that coding fiasco I did not touch another line of BASIC code until I was a grown adult, and it mercifully put an end to my homophobic teasing.

Return to The Land of the Lounge Lizards

It was one of those rare weekends where I got to spend two nights over at Robert and Trevor's house and already had the weekend planned out in my mind: I would sit down at their computer and play *Wing Commander II* every second I could. But when I got there both of my friends made it clear that they found the game mind-numbingly boring and wanted to play a new game that their older brother, Larry, had bought: the new 256-colour remake of *Leisure Suit Larry*. There was a problem: the game had a security check screen that they were having trouble getting past. I flexed my fingers and smirked. This was the kind of job I was made for baby!

When they loaded up the game I found that the security questions were, in fact, multiple choice questions about pop trivia and history. The game began by asking the player's age. Had I not seen something like this before? Yes! This was exactly like the *Leisure Suit Larry* age verification questions I had encountered years earlier, and made a comment to that effect. Trevor grabbed a bright pink box from behind the computer.

"Yeah, it's called 'Leisure Suit Larry in the Land of the Lounge Lizards'. Here, check it out." He handed me the box and I broke out in an excited smile. This appeared to be the game that I had tried to play in my old home town on a Tandy 1000 two summers ago.

The age verification process was intended to ensure that the player was above the age of eighteen. The logic was that if you were above eighteen years old, you'd be able to correctly answer three multiple choice questions about pop movies and music stars. The questions for 18 to 25 year olds baffled us – many of them were about 1970s and 1980s bands or films we had never heard of.

Just for fun I selected "66 to 99" when prompted for my age. The game chirped at my venerable age with, "Warning! This game may be hazardous to your health!" prompt, and began peppering us with trivia about *really* old American history from the late 19th and early 20th century. There was no way we'd be able to answer these questions without asking our grandparents. We spent twenty minutes guessing at the answers until suddenly it clicked: *Where in Time is Carmen Sandiego* came with a thick, condensed encyclopedia that might have at least a few answers to the questions. One of us sat at the keyboard reading out questions as the other two scoured the encyclopedia's pages for answers.

I am fairly sure that the developers of the children's educational title *Carmen Sandiego* never intended for their prized encyclopedia to be used by a few teenagers to play a smutty adventure game about sexually transmitted diseases, hookers and booze. Our ploy worked and over time and through a process of elimination, we created an exam key for most of the age verification questions.

The game itself turned out to only tease the player with the *prospect* of cartoony nudity, but for three teens the mere suggestion of nude female breasts was titillating enough. Part of the allure of *Leisure Suit Larry* was the persistent fear of being caught by my friends' devoutly Christian parents, who would have skinned us alive if they had seen us playing the game. Every time we heard feet creeping up the spiral staircase to the loft where the computer was located, we'd quit the game and innocently poke in commands at the MS-DOS prompt.

Leisure Suit Larry would seem tame compared to the average adult animated cartoon shown after 9PM on network television today, but in the 1990s its ribald sense of humour and lovingly pathetic protagonist made it an instant hit for a few lonely fourteen year old boys. We may not have been the target demographic for *Larry* when he was conceived by his creator Al Lowe, but it spoke to and reformed the scatological style of humour that all of us still have today.

Gateway 2000 Pentium 60 meets Doom

It was minus thirty-five degrees Celsius outside and my feet were freezing under a thin blanket as I squinted at my Game Boy's spinach-green display.

My father's family had invited us to make the thirteen hour drive to our old home town to spend the Christmas holidays with our many uncles, aunts, cousins and grandparents. As excited as I was about the prospect of seeing my extended family, it meant two whole weeks away from my beloved Amstrad. The wonderful squanderings of the Christmas holidays were second only to the summer break, when it came to the ratio of hours I would spend on the computer to days spent away from school.

Earlier that day we had packed the family minivan full and began the long drive up north. My sister and I sat in two bucket seats behind our parents, passing the Game Boy and a copy of *Bubble Bobble* back and forth, trying to finish the game as a team.

By five o'clock the sun had set and I broke out our Game Boy light and magnifier contraption that kept the un-backlit screen viewable after dark. By ten o'clock we were still hours away from our destination; it became so cold that the van's heater could not keep ice off the window, so we put on our winter jackets to keep the chill off. The batteries on the Game Boy light doohickey were draining fast, and the LCD screen's pixels blurred when in motion from the cold. By the time we pulled into our old home town it was midnight and the Game Boy uttered a sickly death croak; we had gone through four sets of 'AA' batteries and had finished *Bubble Bobble* four times in a row.

The arrival at my uncle Fred's house was exciting for my sister and I. For my sister, this meant endless hours of playing with his Dalmatian dog. For me, this meant endless hours playing *Aces of the Pacific* – a combat flight simulator – on my aunt's AST Advantage! 386 PC. My father had not even pulled the keys from the ignition before I had the van door open and was bolting for my uncle's office.

Years earlier, my uncle had caught the technology bug and became an early adopter of multimedia computing. He had become the Canadian north's first computer graphic designer, and devoted hours showing me all the cool projects he was working on using outrageously expensive software packages like *Corel Draw!* And *Pixar Typestry.*[30] As much as I was impressed by his work, I was more enamoured by his penchant for buying the latest and greatest computers.

This Christmas was no different. When I entered his office that night I saw his familiar figure hunched over a *huge* seventeen-inch *MAG Innovision* monitor that lit up the dark office. Beside him was a man I did not recognize. He was tall, blond, broad shouldered and had a beer in his hand; his hoarse laugh and loud voice shook the room. After a brief flurry of hugs and Merry Christmases and an introduction to his tall friend Jeff, my uncle waved me over to his chair. He put a large pair of headphones over my ears and spun the chair towards his hulking monitor.

It took me a few seconds to blink away the glare from the massive radiation coming out of his *MAG* CRT, and when my eyes adjusted I was staring into a dark, three-dimensional room with stairs leading upward in the distance. The bottom of the screen showed a picture of a grisly, beaten, bloodied man with a "29%" beside his mug. I slid around the mouse experimentally and the perspective changed, revealing other parts of the room – holy smokes! – this really was three-dimensional! I heard, far off

---

[30] This is the same Pixar animation studio later famed for its *Toy Story* film series. *Typestry* used its acclaimed "Renderman" 3D rendering technology to create specialized type effects at high resolutions; this is the same rendering technology underlying *Toy Story*. Pixar was originally a subdivision within George Lucas's Lucasfilm conglomerate, and was sold to Steve Jobs for a pittance years later. Jobs retooled the 3D skunkworks subdivision by dropping its software and hardware projects in favour of creating animated feature films.

in the distance, what I can only describe as a "snarfle" (snarl + gargle). The snarfling sound came closer and I began to panic. I ran around the room trying to find better lighting so I could see what was approaching me. Whatever it was, it was coming closer. When I finally saw it, it began hurling fireballs at me! Jeff reached forward and hammered down the spacebar. The creature exploded in front of me into a pile of goo! The sound of a chain gun winded down and I realized that I had not breathed in almost a minute.

I turned to Fred and said, "Whoa. What is this?"

And then said, "I want it."

Jeff was in mid-swig of his beer and almost spit it out laughing. "Good luck! I heard they're backordered for three months."

The game, of course, was *Doom* by id Software. It turned out that Jeff was the sysop of a local bulletin board system and some generous user had uploaded the shareware version of *Doom* to his BBS.

Three weeks earlier *Doom* had begun spreading like wildfire from its originating point at a UNIX server at the University of Wisconsin. Expertly told in the book *Masters of Doom,* the author describes how one of id Software's employees spent an entire day trying to upload the shareware version of the game to the University's server. Fans were so ravenous for the game that the server was saturated with users for hours, finally requiring the server administrator to boot people off so the id employee could complete the upload and release the game into the wild.

It took three weeks for the software to spread from Wisconsin via telephone lines to BBSs in Western Canada. Eventually, at a cost of over a dollar a minute, the *Doom* files were transferred to Jeff's BBS in the north. Overnight it made his BBS the hottest nerd hangout in town, and now I was among the first in the north to play it.

We spent the next hour playing through the shareware version of the game – *Knee Deep in the Dead* - which included only the first third of the complete game. It was maddening to know that there were two-thirds of the game out there, ready to be explored and imps waiting to be blown into giblets. It was so smooth and responsive and atmospheric! How on earth did this run so fast on a 386 anyway?

I then glanced at the computer tower that hummed noisily beside me, and realized that the old AST Advantage! 386 was no more. In its place was a massive beast: two fans pumped air out of the back, its front had four full-sized drive bays that included a tape drive and a disk drive. It was a behemoth of a machine. The sticker pasted on the front read "Gateway 2000".

Jeff must have saw me making eyes at the shiny new tower because he started enumerating its many qualities: *sixteen* megs of RAM, *two* five-hundred meg hard drives, and the jewel of its crown was Intel's flagship *Pentium* class CPU. The average computer in a family home had a 286 or 386 processor (or a 486 if they were rich) – but the 586 or "Pentium" processor was a leap forward in engineering *and* an astronomical leap upward in price. Four megabytes of RAM was more than enough – sixteen was total hubris! A family would be lucky to have a 250 megabyte hard drive in their PC, but dual hard drives that added up to a gigabyte of file storage? Lunacy. If none of these quantifications impress you, at least the price tag should give you pause.... The entire setup including the hulking *MAG* monitor set my uncle back over five thousand dollars. Even though IBM-compatible computers were relatively expensive in the 1990s, I had no idea it was even possible to spend that kind of money on a computer.[31]

All of a sudden it made sense that this incredible first-person shooter game was running full-screen at lightning speed. At home I was running a XT (or "186") PC – my best friends had a

---

[31] As it turns out, my uncle had bought the computer from Jeff himself, who had recently expanded his business to include computer sales. Although Jeff's presence that Christmas made little impression upon me at the time, this chance meeting was a precursor to my first career job a year later.

486 PC – and this computer had a Pentium or "586" architecture CPU. It was like riding to school on a horse-and-buggy while watching your neighbour back out of the garage with a Porsche 911.

When our eyes finally grew tired (and Fred and Jeff were fairly well toasted from their dozen beers and bottles of wine), we quit *Doom*. The exit screen filled the monitor, advertising the complete or "registered" version of the game. For fifty bucks we could get the full, registered version direct from id Software. Sold!

Despite it being past midnight and during the Christmas holidays, I picked up the phone and dialled id Software's 1-800 ordering hotline. The line echoed touch tones as several long-distance exchanges bounced my call across several provinces and states… seconds later emitting a busy signal. I shrugged and redialled the number. Busy again. In fact, for the next two hours my dialling attempts were met with failure. The game really was as hot as Jeff had promised.

It was now past three o'clock in the morning, Jeff and Fred had moved their conversation into the living room, and I was falling asleep with the telephone in my hand. The next morning I awoke and immediately redialled, getting a busy signal. It was like that for the entire ten days I spent at my uncle's house. I eventually rationalized that the number was not reachable from the north and that I would try again from the acreage when we returned home in the New Year.

When I returned home a couple of weeks later, I took one look at my Amstrad and sighed. There was no way this hunk o' junk was going to play *Doom* anywhere as responsively as my uncle's Gateway 2000 had. I installed the shareware diskettes, copied from Jeff, and tried to run the game. It wouldn't even load on our XT! Forget this! Who on earth wanted a game that needed such a fast computer anyway?

I deleted the game from my hard drive and said 'sour lemons' to *Doom*. Perhaps we weren't meant to be.

1993: Grade Nine

Undersea Adventure

After my exposure to Robert and Trevor's new 486 and my uncle's Pentium, the Amstrad's clean white plastic began to lose its sheen, fading to a sickly yellow from years of sitting in the sun on its old oak desk. Lacking the capabilities to play games that required an Intel 386 or better, my beloved machine was getting long in the tooth. Its days were numbered in my mind but there was no way of getting a new computer in the foreseeable future. I had to come up with a stopgap measure.

Although Robert and Trevor's computer dwarfed mine in every aspect, the one add-on accessory that stuck in my mind was its CD-ROM drive. CD-ROMs were exploding on the home computing market as far as advertisements in computer magazines were concerned. You could watch full-motion videos *on your computer* with a CD-ROM! Real, actual digitized video! Computer stores in malls were displaying demo models of new computers with integrated CD-ROM drives, showing off early versions of programs like *Compton's Interactive Encyclopedia* that bedazzled me: over 650 megs of information could be stored on a CD – that was *twenty* times the total size of our little Amstrad's hard drive. All on a little silver disc.

The idea of video on a computer became an obsession and I hunted computer stores for a solution. In the end I was so hungry for a video experience that I purchased an edutainment title called *Undersea Adventure* from a popular publisher called Knowledge Adventure. The educational game promised digital video crammed onto a half-dozen floppy disks. It would have to do as an intermediate step between my computer's meagre capabilities and a real CD-ROM drive.

In my rush to buy the software I did not notice that the floppy disks were in the new "high-density" format that stored twice as much information as the low-density diskettes the Amstrad used. After a long ride home from the City, once again daydreaming about how great this new piece of software would be, I discovered the disks were incompatible with my computer. *Incompatible.* The worst possible curse in the computing dictionary. I begged my mother to drive me back to the City to exchange it for another title that evening, but she would hear none of it. She suggested writing a formal business letter to the friendly people of Knowledge Adventure, asking them to exchange my disks for low-density versions that were compatible with my Amstrad. The letter was address in the sternest tone I could muster:

```
To Whom It May Concern:
Your "Undersea Adventure" box did not advertise that
the disks inside were 3.5 inch high-density, when my
computer at home uses 3.5 inch low-density disks.
This is clearly false advertising. I require a low-
density version of the software or a full refund per
your customer satisfaction guarantee. Thank you.
```

It was exactly the kind of acrid letter that would earn an eye-roll from a customer service agent, and subsequently get directly deposited into the recycling bin. I received no reply to my righteous demand from Knowledge Adventure, and since I had opened the shrink-wrap, I could not return it to the computer store. *Undersea Adventure* collected dust on my shelf.

It took a few weeks to realize that Robert and Trevor's new 486 had a high-density disk drive. Although clearly aimed at a much younger audience… eight to eleven year olds… *Undersea Adventure* delivered on exactly what it promised: less than a minute of low-resolution video the size of a postage stamp showing a great white shark swimming around. Although the video was grainy and pixelated I was only encouraged by this development to pursue full-frame video on a real CD-ROM. If *this* was what video looked like stored on floppy disks, just imagine how crazy cool it would be on a CD!

If getting a new computer was out of the question, maybe a CD-ROM upgrade for our Amstrad was a possibility? I called Radio Shack, who informed me that my computer would require an external (rather than internal) CD-ROM drive, and unfortunately they did not stock that particular product. I dug through the local Yellow Pages and phoned every shop that had "computer" in the name. By 'every shop' I mean: Every. Single. One. I spent the entire weekend on the phone calling each store asking questions about CD-ROM drives. How did an external drive hook up to the computer? Why couldn't I buy an internal drive? Did I need anything else to make the drive work? How much did an external drive cost? What was the difference between a single-speed and double-speed drive? How much did CD-ROM games cost? Did I need a new computer completely, or could I upgrade the Amstrad? Ad nauseam I asked the same questions to dozens of salespeople, and all of them agreed upon a few facts that troubled me:

1. The Amstrad's 8 MHz Intel 8086 CPU was too slow to play back video from a CD-ROM. I definitely needed a new CPU… an Intel 386 was required, and a 486 was ideal.
2. The computer only had 640 Kb of RAM. CD-ROM software required at least 1 megabyte of RAM. I needed to check if the Amstrad could even be upgraded to 1 megabyte.
3. A single-speed drive was approximately two hundred bucks, but I needed a double-speed drive to play back full-screen video reliably without hiccups; it was going to be $400 to $500.

All these technical limitations might seem like minor inconveniences to most, but I took these as portentous signs that the Amstrad was about to be put to pasture. I could not have been more right but for the wrong reasons.

If I was to persuade my mom and dad to buy a new computer I had to work through each step of a systematic sales psychology I had perfected over the years. The first step involved making a sales pitch they would consider for a tenth of a second and instantly reject.

I brought a magazine article to my mother describing an external CD-ROM drive, showing how amazing the technology was. I raved about the possibilities of "multimedia" software like I was a vendor working the Consumer Electronics Show in Las Vegas. I brought her to the computer store in the mall and showed her how amazing a computerized encyclopedia was – a veritable fountain of information that would no doubt help my sister and I make the grade at school. Just when I thought my enthusiasm for the gadget was persuading her, I pulled the rug out from underneath her feet: the external CD-ROM drive cost over six hundred dollars.

That was an automatic "no sale" in her eyes; our family was in dire financial straits. My father had been out of work for months due to a traumatic brain injury that left him despondent and angry, and my mom was working part-time to make up the difference. Asking my mom and dad for a $600 computer gadget was a dead end.

But this was only the opening round of my complex bargaining strategy. Next I came up with an alternate solution that seemed like a bargain in comparison, and worked out perfectly in my favour. I proposed that "we" buy a whole new 486 computer that *already* came with a CD-ROM drive. Two birds, one stone.

Before I made my pitch I needed documented evidence that the Amstrad was on its way out. I needed to prove that neither the computer's CPU nor RAM could be upgraded; therefore rendering it a fossil. This was a job for Dr. Phillips.

To date I was strictly forbidden from taking apart the computer. From a young age I had earned a reputation for taking a Phillips screwdriver to every single electronic toy I owned, prying it apart to gaze upon the magical parts inside. Usually I extracted the electric motor and Frankensteined small devices that I hooked up to batteries just to see what they'd do. In my head I was a mad scientist creating wonderful inventions. In reality I was a little kid wrecking expensive toys my family bought for my birthday. For that reason my mother had unequivocally forbade me from tearing apart the computer for any reason. Until that day I had complied with her sensible rule without issue.

I opened the back of the computer and gently removed the AdLib music card. The plastic case to the computer seemed to have no convenient snaps or hinges for easy access, and it took a while to find twelve Phillips-head screws that led deeper into the case. An hour later the top half of the case was off and I stared at a sheet of perfectly smooth metal covering the motherboard. A sticker with an exclamation mark was applied to the metal with the words, "ELECTRICAL HAZARD! NO USER SERVICEABLE PARTS INSIDE!"

Hah, don't be coy my little Amstrad. We both know you've got secrets in there, and I want to know them! I removed the metal casing and found what I had suspected: a computer logic board full of silicon chips, but not a single place that allowed for memory expansion. The CPU was soldered into place instead of resting in a replaceable socket. The computer offered no upgrade path whatsoever. I carefully replaced all of the components in place, worried that my parents would come home and catch me in the act of disassembling their three-thousand dollar investment.

I heard a truck rumbling down the driveway and began sweating. The only part left was re-installing the AdLib card. I looked over my shoulder at my parents getting out of the truck and for an instant lost track of what my hands were doing. I felt the card resist a little as I inserted it into the slot and eventually snap into place. I quickly turned on the computer to make sure everything still worked, and heard a loud, metallic *pop!* from the rear of the machine. The computer instantly shut off. A puff of black smoke rose out of the back and I groaned. I opened the plastic ISA slot cover and found the AdLib card half-inserted into the slot, with a black blast zone around it. I had accidentally inserted the music card backwards, causing an electrical short!

I had fried the Amstrad. Fuck. Fuck. Fuck.

I broke into a complete panic and fled downstairs to my bedroom. I cleaned my room feverishly as if this would somehow fix the situation, trying to think of what I would tell my parents. The problem solved itself an hour later when my sister went to use the computer and could not get it to boot. I feigned surprise and went through the motions of "fixing" it. After an hour I told my mother that I could not figure out what was wrong with the computer.

I mumbled, "After all, it's pretty old I guess...", and left the rest to her imagination.

The following Monday my mother took the entire computer – monitor, keyboard and all – back to *The Brick* store where she had purchased it years earlier. I cannot imagine the polite, perplexed smile the customer service representative had when my mom plopped the entire computer on the desk and demanded repairs. The Brick was a furniture store – it didn't sell computers! After my mother produced a faded Brick receipt, the store manager was called in to consult. The manager confirmed that, yes, years earlier the store had experimented with computer sales. The manager shrugged, explaining that they had no way to repair the computer as the store no longer dealt with computers, and that the computer had been out of warranty anyway. To his credit he called a local computer shop that could repair Amstrad computers and pointed my mother there.

A week later the computer shop called and left a message on our answering machine. The repairs would cost between $500 and $1000 and the parts needed to be ordered from the United Kingdom, which would take 6-8 weeks to arrive. My mother was on the verge of completing her university degree, and two months without a computer to write papers on was not going to work. Despite feeling guilty about causing all this strife, excitement was building in my stomach. My mother and father talked in the kitchen that night in hushed tones, running numbers by each other. They could only be talking about finances. They could only be talking about buying a new computer!

Computers at Home

To my great delight, by 1993 the computer craze began to spread through my rural school. Parents were seeing other parents buying computers, and computers became the next hot thing on Christmas wish lists. Brands like Compaq, Packard Bell, AST and IBM became commonplace consumer products sold in big box stores instead of independent computer stores holed away in industrial districts. These computers were not the monochromatic beasts of the 1980s that belonged in elementary school classrooms and college computer labs. These were *real* computers with Super VGA graphics and 16-bit sound cards that could network with one another. The textual environment of MS-DOS was becoming a thing of the past as graphical user interface environments like Windows 3.1 became user-friendly enough that mom and dad could play Solitaire on them. Instead of typing commands like "START.EXE" to run a program, Windows made launching a program a simple case of double-clicking. By 1994 a half-dozen people in my grade had Intel 486 computers, and many of those people were my friends.

The tiny critical mass of new teenaged computer users meant that I had a much better shot at trading games with my friends. Computers were just now catching on, and I had a three-year head start on the rest of my friends! If the Amstrad had been the cozy bedroom of my childhood, our next computer would become the entire house of my adolescence. Almost everything that happened in my life, from 1993 to 1997, somehow emerged from my relationship with this nearly-indestructible beast of a machine: an IBM PS/1.

A New Computer

The next morning, a Sunday, my parents called my sister and I into the kitchen. They told us to get ready for a trip to the City. As we made the 45-minute drive my parents were coquettish about the reason for the sudden shopping trip; everyone was excited about the prospect of blowing a few thousand dollars on a new gadget – even my parents.

We arrived at a new electronics store that had opened a couple of years earlier – *The Future Shop*. At the store my dad patiently listened to the salesman's pitch and explained that he wanted to finance the purchase over a couple of years. The plan to finance the computer over the next two years, so he would have enough time to recover from his brain injury and return to his construction business.

At that the time the store exclusively carried IBM-branded computers. Some were priced at under $2000 but were underpowered for the price, having small hard drives and were without CD-ROM drives. The "MPC" or Multimedia PC-class computers were more expensive but had everything I wanted in a new machine. I quietly guided my parents over to the entry-level "MPC-1" compliant IBM PS/1 computers. I convinced them that this computer would be one we would keep for five years AT LEAST! It would not become obsolete like the Amstrad had, or require its parts to be shipped in from the U.K. This was a true-blue IBM and that meant quality, *and* locally grown, free-range, gluten-free, Made in America, replacement parts. My salesmanship went on and on, which must have amused the salesman standing behind me who remained silent. I was doing his job for him!

In the end my father agreed to buy the IBM PS/1 Model 2133: an entry-level multimedia PC with a 486 SX/33 MHz CPU, a double-speed CD-ROM drive, Sound Blaster 16 sound card, 4 megabytes of ram, a 384 megabyte hard drive, and onboard Super VGA graphics.

My father had grown up in a different era, where bartering and bargaining were a part of the sales dance. He leaned over to the salesman as if he was confiding in him a secret between friends, "Swing me a deal and I'll walk out of here with it right now. Gimme it for Twenty-five hundred." The computer was listed at $2995.

"Uh, I'm sorry sir. I'm not allowed to budge on the price."

I stood by awkwardly as my father tried to wheedle the salesman for a few bucks off of the sales price, my face turning a bright red. He always did this, and each time the sales person apologetically refused to drop the price.

In the end just to get my father out of the store the salesman agreed to "throw in" an array of CD-ROM games that were *clearly* already included with the computer, and a small Canon bubble jet printer. It was a symbolic gesture that pleased my dad's ego and we walked out of the store carrying three huge boxes full of heavy equipment.

It was all happening – we finally had a 486! On the ride home I couldn't contain myself and made little gasping sounds like my lungs were going to explode from my chest. When we got home that night the next phase of my computing life began.

IBM PS/1 Multimedia 486 SX-33

In contrast to the initial setup of the Amstrad, my parents didn't hover around us as my sister and I unpacked the boxes. After a few years we were clearly more adept with computers than they were, and the unpacking ritual was clearly in our wheelhouse and not theirs.

This time we had an entire library of software and games at our disposal. The hard drive was so large – ten times the size of the Amstrad's drive – that every single one of our games could co-exist on the hard drive simultaneously; there was still *tons* of room left for new stuff afterward! As the computer booted I was immediately drawn to the RAM test in the top-left corner of the screen. It began at 128Kb and the numbers blurred as it incremented until it hit its final sum: 4096Kb RAM OK. Four megabytes! I'm rich!

My sister rooted through the new CD-ROM titles we received with the computer. There were a half-dozen titles that all ran in MS-DOS. Our favourite was *Compton's Interactive Encyclopedia* which had grainy, postage stamp-sized, low frame-rate videos that played when we looked up specific encyclopedia entries. *San Diego Zoo Presents: The Animals!* was a series of full-motion videos and photos of animals imprisoned in California, clumsily accessed by navigating through a series of menus.

I was in heaven but I can appreciate how underwhelming this experience is to the average reader after years of access to online streaming services like Youtube, Hulu and Netflix. But back in 1993 the notion of playing back a video on a computer was wild. Computers were underpowered, glorified adding machines that made a lot of beeps and boops; video belonged on VHS tapes and televisions. The two worlds were never meant to co-exist in the same machine.

Seeing pixelated video playing back on our very own computer in our house was mind-blowing, and I became the 1990s equivalent of a YouTube couch potato. I watched and re-watched low-quality historical and zoological reference videos for hours just for the sake of it. And when I was finally sick of watching the same old videos, I began my hunt for affordable CD-ROMs at computer stores. Even though the floppy drive still got use installing my older games, it was becoming a relic of a less civilized age, like 8-track tapes.

Some of my earliest purchases were adventure games that were re-released as "talkie" editions that featured full voiceovers for characters and narrators.[32] LucasArts titles like *Loom, Day of the Tentacle,* and *Sam and Max Hit the Road* got high quality re-releases as CD-ROM talkie editions.

My favourite talkie edition was *King's Quest V*, mostly because I had already played the silent 16 colour EGA edition a year earlier on my Amstrad. The move from 16 colours to 256 colour VGA was a shock. Suddenly the game looked like a *painting*... trees and snowy mountain landscapes made King Graham look like he was wandering through a bucolic fantasy. I had only imagined what the characters' voices were like before, and now I finally could *hear* how they were supposed to sound. King Graham got a surprisingly expressive voice actor who gave him a sense of aristocratic nobility and dignity I had not imagined. Even Cedric the Owl, Graham's sidekick throughout the adventure, got a fun, cartoonish voice suited to the role.

---

[32] Talkie editions of games hearkened back to the history of early cinema. At the height of Charlie Chaplin's popularity, films had no audio tracks and relied purely on the expressivity of actors and simple title cards for dialogue. When audio tracks were added to celluloid film, all of a sudden the audience could hear actors' voices for the first time. In the 1930s when audio was added to films, the choice proved controversial – many filmgoers preferred the silent film era. The same divisive reaction returned in the 1990s when characters were fully voiced for the first time – many gamers still prefer the silent era of adventure games. The particularly vehement hatred of Cedric the Owl's voice in *King's Quest V* by adventure game players today is evidence of that fact.

Star Wars Rebel Assault

In the subsequent months I bought every computer magazine I could find that had the words "CD-ROM" on the cover. Most of the local stores had only a handful of CD-ROM games to choose from at first, and they didn't come cheap. When a new store opened at the mall, *Virtual Reality Megastore,* I was stunned to see that they had a whole *wall* devoted to their CD-ROM game titles! A computer at the entrance to the store had a demo playing in a loop, and it was absolutely incredible. Unlike the CD-ROMs featuring tiny videos we had at home, the video was *full screen* and in brilliant colour. The game was called *Star Wars Rebel Assault* and had everything I wanted in a CD-ROM title: digitized video footage from the films, VGA graphics and John Williams' famous soundtrack. My friends – many of whom were Star Wars devotees themselves – were going to be dumbfounded when they saw this. I *had* to buy it. I spent the remainder of my Christmas cash – sixty-five bucks – and raced back to the family van with my new find.

When I opened the box I was dismayed to find only a CD-ROM in a cardboard sleeve, a flimsy black-and-white manual consisting of a few photocopied pages stapled together, and a thin LucasArts product catalogue. Where was the inch-thick colour manual to pore over on the ride home? Where were the feelies – the maps and trinkets and printed paraphernalia – that made buying the boxed version worthwhile? My stomach churned. What a rip! It was like ordering a greasy pepperoni pizza with double cheese and getting a saltine cracker with peanut butter smeared on it instead.

Thankfully the game proper redeemed itself. *Rebel Assault* differed from all my other CD-ROM titles. Where other games required me to sit back and watch video after video passively, *Rebel Assault* allowed me to "direct" the action of the cinematic story. Videos played back and by making choices at critical junctures in the action – by taking the left path instead of the right path in my ship in Beggar's Canyon for instance – a different scenario played itself out. I invited my friends over and they too were spellbound by the smooth video and rich musical score. This outstripped anything we'd seen on video gaming consoles, which were only now beginning to introduce CD-ROM "multimedia" games. In short: *Rebel Assault* made gaming systems like the Sega CD and its interactive video games look like steaming piles of bantha poodoo.

Willy Beamish

I spent the remainder of the ninth grade blissfully searching for bigger and better CD-ROM games I could try out on my hot new PC. Even though CD-ROMs were cheaper to mass-produce than floppy disks, publishers sold them at even higher prices because of multimedia-hungry kids like me. Like before, acreage chores and odd jobs over the summer added up to just enough to buy me a new game title every few months. Buying heavily discounted or second-run bargain bin games was a better bet, because these usually sold for a fraction of the price of a new release. Nothing in life is free however, and I sometimes paid a high personal price for being a spendthrift. This became apparent when I went school supply shopping a week before the tenth grade began.

Our last stop on the day-long flurry of budget-breaking shopping for jeans, shirts, pencils, pens, White-Out correction fluid, duo-tangs, binders and everything else that made the last weekend of August exciting – was a retailer called London Drugs. As its name suggests London Drugs was a pharmacy chain that had expanded to include all kinds of other goods, like home appliances and stationary. The store was my mom's ace-in-the-hole every year as the store always put packages of lined loose-leaf paper on sale for fifty cents. This was a whole dollar cheaper than anywhere else, and she figured that saving five bucks on paper somehow made up for the hundreds of dollars spent on clothing that day. I resisted the urge to point out the incongruity as we walked into the store, because London Drugs *now carried computers and games.*

My mother made a bee-line for the bins of lined paper, and I made a bee-line for a narrow shelf of games at the back of the store. While London Drugs didn't have a particularly great selection of new game releases – they were more focused on family productivity software – they did have a shelf of bargain-priced games.

I was not disappointed. Sandwiched between ten jewel cases of *Where in the World is Carmen Sandiego?* and fifteen of *The Journeyman Project*, was a case that caught my eye because of its Sierra/Dynamix logo on the spine. The CD cover art depicted a cartoony boy and his frog riding a skateboard. I recognized it immediately from the Sierra catalogue as *The Adventures of Willy Beamish* – an adventure game that had been released a year earlier on floppy disk. This must have been a CD-ROM talkie edition of the same game! And if that was not enough, the price was right too: $19.99! Even though I loved having complete boxes replete with trinkets and manuals, I was willing to settle for a flimsy jewel case today. After the disappointing *Rebel Assault* box contents I became inured to the idea of buying a game simply for the disc. I fished my only twenty dollar bill out of my pocket and met my mother as she walked to the checkout counter.

The cashier was a young woman in her late teens or early twenties; she chatted with my mom as she rang in the stacks of paper my mother had hoarded in her basket like white gold. I hung back a little, trying to conceal the jewel case in my hand. My mother must have saw my reticence.

"What do you have there my son?" she asked, pointing at the CD ostentatiously.

All of my shy, self-conscious, fourteen year old boy nerves went haywire. Here I was caught between a beautiful girl only a few years older than me, my mom, and the CD-ROM in my hand. My instinct was to run: girls should never *ever* find out that I played computer games.

I stammered some kind of reply and the cashier looked up at me and smiled. I caught her eye and for a brief moment I lived out fantasy stereotypical of an average fourteen year old boy: I would come back to the store some day, riding my badass motorcycle and pat the space on the seat behind me, she'd climb on to the bike and we'd ride off into the sunset, her long blonde hair flowing behind us like a million golden rays of sunlight.

My eyes glazed over and I dropped the CD on the counter.

The cashier reached forward and flipped over the disc to type in the UPC code. She frowned quizzically, "Oh cool. What band is this? I didn't know we carried music..."

Gulp.

She flipped over the case once more and gawked at the front cover: a goofy brown-haired cartoony kid and his frog on his shoulder, riding a bright red skateboard. A child's computer game. *A computer game for babies.*

If only I could describe the crooked half-smirk that grew on her face, concealing the uncontrollable guffaws building inside of her. I turned bright red and began pouring buckets of sweat from my pimply face.

If that wasn't enough, my mother then snagged the CD from the counter, rolled her eyes at me and howled to the entire store, "Oh, my son, *you are such a nerd!*"

That was too much. The cashier broke out giggling and flashed a sympathetic smile at me. She put the game inside of a plastic bag and handed it to me. I couldn't bear to look up to her eyes which were still in the throes of laughter. She barely controlled a final giggle and said in the sweetest possible voice, "Have fun with your... computer game!"

Seeing my horrific embarrassment only made my mother laugh harder and as we stepped out of the store I yelled in my most outraged teenage voice, "MOMMMM!"

This purchase marked a transition in my life. Computer games were no longer something worth bragging about to my friends or anyone else for that matter. I was a full-fledged teenager now, expected to live by the values of polite, non-nerdy, society. Computer games had to become a hidden, masturbatory secret in order to survive adolescence, and it marked a symbolic end to my junior high experience.

Thanks for introducing me to adult shame, Willy Beamish.

1994: Grade Ten

The Transition to High School

In many parts of Canada, the school system was neatly divided into three stages: elementary school consisting of kindergarten through grade six, junior high from grades seven through nine, and ending in high school with grades ten through twelve.

The most exciting, often usually stressful, years were the transitions between each type of school. A kid in the sixth grade might be at the top of the food chain in an elementary school, only to find themselves a bottom-feeder the next year in a seventh grade class. The same was true for ninth grade students making the transition into a high school, where many kids were sporting moustaches and driving cars to school instead of taking the bus.

In my school, beginning high school meant suddenly having access to courses that were out of reach for younger students: Shop ("Industrial Education 10"), Computers ("Information Processing 10") and Band ("Music 10") were exciting new opportunities for kids who up to that point only knew a low-sugar diet of core curriculum courses like math, social studies and science.

Taking Information Processing 10 meant reuniting with my favourite teacher, Mr. M, and more importantly getting access to his lab of shiny new Macintosh LCs.

Macintosh LC: The Cross-Canada School Flame War

It was the first week of the tenth grade and academic life suddenly became serious. Going to class now meant actually working for grades that would determine our placement in the educational "stream". Although my grades were always more than sufficient in junior high, the pressure to perform became an ongoing stress for most kids in high school. Our entry to some post-secondary institution years in the future was always hung over our heads like the Sword of Damocles.

One would imagine that these educational demands would have cut down on my computer time, but all the pressure only buried me deeper in my habit. Worse, my family's finances and personal relationships entered a sharper downward spiral; home was no longer a place I wanted to be. My dad's emotions were out of control, my sister was getting in trouble at school, and my mother was working later and later hours. The computer was a safe place to hide from it all.

I found a new means for escape from all the pressures of family and school when I found out our school had a new computer lab. The Apple //e's remained in the "old lab" as reminders of a more barbaric, simpler time, and a whole new classroom was devoted to four banks of Apple Macintosh LC computers.[33] Compared to the monochrome Macintosh computers I was familiar with, these LC versions were a leap

[33] In the early 1990's, Apple had experienced its own downward financial spiral. The Apple // line had finally expended itself and the original black-and-white Macintosh line had all but failed. In this period, Steve Jobs was fired from Apple (subsequently founding a new computer company called NeXT), and replaced by a CEO driven by the bottom line. The Macintosh LC or "Low-Cost" computers targeted educational institutions and families on limited budgets. These new Macintosh computers lost the original, playful, Macintosh aesthetic and were now designed to look more like their boring beige PC counterparts.

forward. They had colour screens, attractive keyboards and mice, and a stylish MacOS operating system that blew away Windows 3.1. Although I was firmly entrenched on the PC side of the computer fanatic boundary, I could appreciate why these new machines were the pride and joy of my beloved computer teacher, Mr. M.

The junior high "Computers" course had graduated to the title of "Information Processing" in the tenth grade. The course was intended to give students a crash course in using computing applications, instead of learning theory and LOGO programming. No more hard core computer logic or nerdy knowledge about silicon chips... the course was aimed at turning 30 kids into future paper pushers. At least, that was the idea until my friends and I hit the keyboards.

The course began, predictably, with two weeks of typing lessons with an infernal typing tutor program. My buddies and I were already proficient typists and broke the 30-word-per-minute goal in the first fifteen minutes of class. That meant we had two whole weeks of dicking around while the rest of the class caught up.

If idle hands do the devil's work, idle time in the hands of teenage boys in a dull computer course is a recipe for mayhem. It didn't take long to figure out how to change all of the operating system notification sounds to a built-in "QUACK!" sound effect. When that got boring, we dragged critical system files to the trash bin rendering the machine inoperable, leaving it with a flashing "?" at boot. Renaming the hard disk drive label with foul language didn't take a genius to figure out either.

By the end of the week Mr. M's hands were full with trying to outmaneuver our ongoing war against his precious Macs. And like most teachers he was smart enough to devise a diversion for us nogoodniks.

"Hey. Guys! Yeah, you comedians!" He pointed at our band of techno-troublemakers: myself, and four boys named Wayne, Andrew, Anthony and David.

"Gotta new job for you guys. I hooked up the computers to a

new network. It's called the Canada SchoolNet. You guys gotta learn how to use it to write messages to others kids across the country."

Network? That sparked some genuine curiosity as I had never used a computer on a network before. The "SchoolNet" turned out to be a messaging network that relied upon point-to-point modem connections between major cities as well as outlying communities such as ours, using bulletin board system software called FirstClass.

SchoolNet also made use of the Internet's "Usenet" newsgroup service. Like most online message boards of today, Usenet allowed users to post messages and reply to one another in a public forum. The Canada SchoolNet secured a number of Usenet groups specifically for Canadian students from Kindergarten to Grade 12 to post and reply to messages from one another, across the country. In theory this was a brilliant implementation of an idea that was years ahead of its time. *In theory.*

We spent the rest of the week learning how to use this new messaging forum. We configured our FirstClass BBS clients to send and receive messages, and learned how to use our unique SchoolNet addresses that operated just like e-mail addresses. Our addresses used our real names, so there was no hiding behind the comforts of anonymity.

Our teacher wrote a post introducing our class to the SchoolNet, encouraging other kids to interact with us:

```
March 24, 1994, 1:00:00 AM
Subject: Exchange?
Mr. M wrote:
I'm looking for an some high school classes to
exchange information with my computer students. We
have a web page and would like to correspond with
students from other parts of the country and the
world. It wouldn't have to be anything formal.
Students have access to internet email or to
accessing another school's web page.
```

* * *

Many of the messages in reply were completely benign in content, as teachers tried to encourage students to use the SchoolNet to post questions and answers about homework, or find penpals across the country. Of course, there were a few gems that classmates posted that had nothing to do with schoolwork:

```
February 6, 1995, 1:00:00 AM
Subject: SCHOOL SUCKS
Tere wrote:
You think school sukkks, come to our own. Its like
stranded on death row!!!!!!!!!!!!
This is a small community, with 454 kids in school.
=borrriiinnnngqggg
```

The complete lack of anonymity should have dissuaded us from what we did next. David, Andrew and I dug through the list of discussion forums. There were some devoted to science and mathematics, mostly filled with messages from students asking for help with their homework. There were a few forums devoted to writing and literature. It wasn't long before we discovered forums specifically about faith and Christianity.

The school and the town it was located in was predominantly Catholic and Eastern Orthodox. While this produced a majority of well-adjusted, God-fearing, church-attending, parent-obeying, law-abiding kids, it also produced a handful of anti-religious, atheistic, Generation X miscreants like myself, Andrew and David. We truly believed, at the time, that the friends, family and students around us were crazy to believe any of the junk they were taught in church. Christianity, to us, was like believing in Santa Claus or the Easter Bunny.

That day we took those beliefs to the Canada SchoolNet and posted them ruthlessly.

We began our jihad with a dozen new topics in the CA.SchoolNet.Religion.Christianity forum, all wildly polemic and heretical. The "Does God Really Exist? (NO!)" and "Jesus is

Lame" topics proved to be particularly inflammatory, and within days had generated replies that were equally vicious. Andrew, David and I delighted in reading the incendiary responses and replied in kind, stirring up the flames of holy war even more with new dismissive, brash and sacrilegious messages. Although we were not familiar with the term at the time, we had generated the SchoolNet's first "flame war".

Unbeknownst to him, Mr. M was glad to see we were no longer playfully trashing his beloved Macs and we appeared to be working diligently at the computers. Information Processing 10 was quickly becoming our favourite class of the day, and we spent entire lunch-hours discussing strategies for launching our next profane assault on the Believers who frequented the SchoolNet.

Of the handful of messages from the flame war that weren't deleted by Mr. M, this is a brief sample of the *most* civil ones:[34]

```
October 31, 1994, 1:00:00 AM
Subject: Atheism
VGA wrote:
To any Atheists out there, I would like to be your
penpal.

----

November 1, 1994, 1:00:00 AM
Jeff wrote:
I wond what atheists have in common that they would b
discussing. I personally have no beliefs in any God
but I find that talking to people with various
DIFFERENT beliefs makes for much more stimulating
conversations. But if you want to hear more about my
lack of belief in an idol, feel free to write to me.
```

[34] You may have noticed that all of the posts are dated 1:00:00 AM. This was because our school's FirstClass BBS server synchronized all of its messages with the City's central server once a day, at precisely 1AM, to minimize the cost of long-distance telephone charges.

* * *

```
November 2, 1994, 1:00:00 AM
Andrew wrote:
It's not conversations with people different religons
I don't like, It's their fanactical defending of them
that I don't like to listen to.
```

```
Craig wrote:
VGA was only saying that he wants to be your penpal
because he is disturbed that I believe in the Lord
and that I was brave enough to speak out and tell the
people of the Lord.
The devil is scared now, and it is good...
```

```
November 3, 1994, 1:00:00 AM
Jeff wrote:
The devil is scared? An you know this because..... I
like haveinig Xtians around because i find that they
bring a certain fantasy edge to this group that keep
it amusing. I hope that that wasn't too offensive the
the devil's not scared anymore
Take er easy
jeff.
```

The daily posts were mean-spirited, no doubt, but to us the flame war was no more harmful than a model U.N. debate: nothing was at stake for anyone on virtual discussion forums. Discussion forums were not "real" places full of real people – they were collections of argumentative e-mails written by people we didn't know personally. Nothing would come of our kicking over sandcastles; that is until Mr. M hauled us into his classroom in the midst of our week-long offensive.

His eyes were ringed with red like he had not slept in days.

"HEY! You guys. Get in here!" He stabbed his finger at

Andrew, David and I, and then into his empty classroom. He slammed the door behind us as we cautiously scooted inside.

"Do you guys want to tell me what this garbage is on the SchoolNet?" He turned a computer monitor towards us and our names weaved through a branching list of messages.

"I got a call last night from the principal from another school in the City. Do you guys know how much… *shit*… you're in?"

We all looked at each other, everyone trying to affect casual ignorance until the charges were read aloud.

"I just spent *three hours* going through those messages you guys wrote and deleted the worst of them. Do you know where our Internet connection to the SchoolNet comes from? From the god damned Catholic School Board in the City! And now they've cut us off because of you guys!"

We had never seen Mr. M so angry in the three years we had pranked him with his own computers. Even Andrew, who was infamous for his clever comebacks to angry adults, chose to remain silent.

"So what are you going to do to us?" David asked sheepishly.

He combed his fingers through his thick black hair and preened his moustache. "I dunno. I don't know. Maybe you guys need to be suspended for a few days. Or maybe I need to have a chat with your parents. I dunno."

He looked at me. "And you. I can't *believe* this was you of all people. Of all people!"

I almost fainted. Although I had been in trouble for messing around with the computers before, I was allergic to getting in trouble at school. Worse, Mr. M was my favourite teacher and I was (admittedly) his pet student. This felt worse than disappointing my own parents.

Thankfully we were saved by the bell. "I'll deal with you guys tomorrow. And don't go into my lab during the lunch hour anymore."

"Jeez. I've never seen MacMan so pissed off," Andrew chirped cheerfully as he tried to alleviate the tension as we all walked morosely down the hallway. 'MacMan' was Andrew's favourite sarcastic jab at M's love for Apple computers.

"Yeah. Geez. It's not like we wrecked MacMan's computers or something," David pouted, afraid his mother would get a phone call from the school over the lunch hour.

I remained silent and spent the rest of the day angry with myself. I had disappointed my mentor, my favourite teacher, my friend. I had abused the small amount of trust I had developed with him over the years, and there was no easy fix. At the end of the day I took a deep breath and knocked on the door of his computer lab. He was inside grading exams at his desk.

"Hey. Come in." His eyes were still tinged an angry red but he had cooled off. He continued, "Siddown. Y'know, I don't know what got into you guys. It's kinda funny, y'know, but it's not."

He smiled despite himself. "This stuff's all new and there aren't any rules yet, but you guys gotta stop acting like jerks right? You're my best student. I can't let you get into this crap with these jokers yer hangin' out with."

I nodded and mumbled a few words of an apology before my throat closed and my eyes filled with tears. I felt ashamed for all the compassion the man was giving me, in spite of all my misbehaviour. I had been a complete dick, and worse, had cost the school its only connection to the Internet.

"Do you think you'll get SchoolNet back?" I asked, hopeful that the damage wasn't permanent.

"Nah. Probably not. But I'm looking into getting us our own Internet service anyway."

A week later things returned to a semblance of normal in Information Processing 10. There was no SchoolNet for anyone anymore, but at least Mr. M had forgiven us for our childish holy war. Our posts had been removed permanently, and Usenet to this day carries only a few brief exchanges of the Canada SchoolNet's first flame war that Mr. M deemed civil enough for public consumption.

It took weeks for Mr. M to overlook my misdeeds in his class, so I spent that time diligently working on my computing assignments. My brief adolescent flirtation with being a black hat troublemaker was over and I was ready to prove myself as the A-student he thought I was.

One day he decided to let my friends and I back into the computer lab at lunch to play games on the Mac LC's. This little footstep into his circle of trust wasn't something we were going to abuse again – games like *Lunatic Fringe* and *MacBolo* kept us entertained over the boring lunch hours. *Lunatic Fringe* was a cute variant of the classic game *Continuum* in which a small spaceship explores an expansive space, shooting enemy ships and upgrading its weapons.

MacBolo was a networked top-down tank shooting game, which was at its heart a multiplayer capture-the-flag experience. Mr. M took advantage of the Mac LC's "AppleTalk" protocol to set up a token-ring network that allowed us to play *MacBolo* with up to *sixteen* simultaneous players. Only the most complex arcade cabinets like *Gauntlet* allowed up to four players, so the idea of a sixteen-player game was insane. Embarrassingly there were only a handful of geeky students that we could convince to play games with us in the computer lab, so the most we ever tried was eight players. Not even my old gang – Trevor, Robert and Donny – would join in. A clutch of pasty, overfed computer nerds trash talking each other as we drove pixelated tanks around on a CRT was the epitome of loserdom in high school. And we loved every minute of it.

During one of the *MacBolo* matches Mr. M tapped me on the shoulder and nodded at his own Macintosh, which sat in the corner of the lab. It was an "A/V Mac" – a Macintosh equipped with specialized hardware that allowed it to do audiovisual work using non-linear video editing software. He walked over and clicked a few times, and I heard the metallic sound of a phone dialling. There were some screeching noises a half minute later that sounded a little bit like a fax machine.

He grinned, "Gotta new modem. Check it out!"

He monkeyed around with a program that I didn't recognize, containing lists of messages and file folders. Eventually he dragged one of the files in the program to his desktop and a dialog box appeared:

```
Downloading…
Estimated Time: 29 minutes 18 seconds.
```

I didn't understand much of what I was seeing. What exactly did "downloading" mean, and why was it going to take the rest of the lunch hour to complete?

Mr. M explained – the computer was transferring a file from a remote computer *over the telephone lines* using the modem.[35] It was connected to a computer running "BBS" or "Bulletin Board System" software on the other end. This was the technology that made our Canada SchoolNet possible, using plain old telephone lines and computers.

* * *

[35] Modem: Modulator/Demodulator. If you did not grow up with a modem you will recognize the sound whenever a fax machine (if those still exist when you read this) or a debit banking card machine dials a remote phone number and tries to connect. The unforgettable 'SCREEEEEERRRRNNNGGGGGG…' modem connection sound, called "handshaking" is the sound of two modems making a connection with one another. Binary data from the computer is transformed or modulated into sound waves that travel over the telephone line, before they are demodulated by the receiving modem back into binary data. In the broadband era, few people now use sound waves or copper telephone lines to carry data.

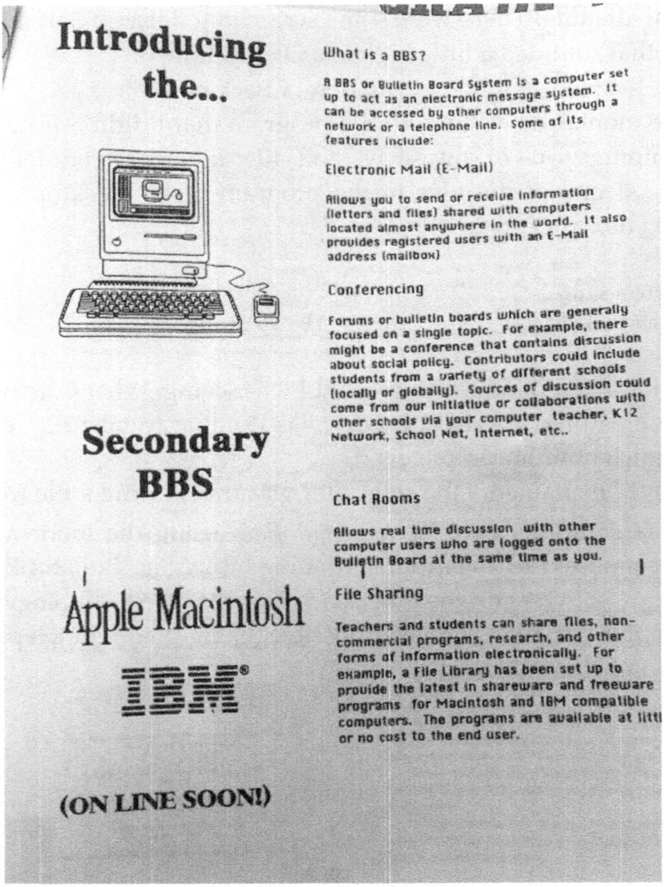

Introducing the...

Secondary BBS

Apple Macintosh

IBM®

(ON LINE SOON!)

What is a BBS?

A BBS or Bulletin Board System is a computer set up to act as an electronic message system. It can be accessed by other computers through a network or a telephone line. Some of its features include:

Electronic Mail (E-Mail)

Allows you to send or receive information (letters and files) shared with computers located almost anywhere in the world. It also provides registered users with an E-Mail address (mailbox)

Conferencing

Forums or bulletin boards which are generally focused on a single topic. For example, there might be a conference that contains discussion about social policy. Contributors could include students from a variety of different schools (locally or globally). Sources of discussion could come from our initiative or collaborations with other schools via your computer teacher, K12 Network, School Net, Internet, etc..

Chat Rooms

Allows real time discussion with other computer users who are logged onto the Bulletin Board at the same time as you.

File Sharing

Teachers and students can share files, non-commercial programs, research, and other forms of information electronically. For example, a File Library has been set up to provide the latest in shareware and freeware programs for Macintosh and IBM compatible computers. The programs are available at littl or no cost to the end user.

A school newsletter from 1995 advertising Mr. M's school Bulletin Board System, Co-SysOp'd by classmate Craig, which we used to connect to Canada SchoolNet.

I sat there stunned for a minute. How on earth did a computer transfer a file *over a phone line*? Phone lines were for people talking with other *people*, not computers talking to computers!

I had a million, billion, and gazillion questions for him. How *exactly* did the computer send files over the phone line? What computer was he connected to right now? Was this even legal?

Did you have to ask the government for permission before you used a phone line with your computer? And most importantly: how do *I* connect my family's computer up to the phone?

He answered the last question first. He told me that I'd need to buy a modem for my computer if it didn't have one already. He pointed at a small plastic box beside the A/V Mac which had a half-dozen LED lights blinking on the front. My family's IBM didn't have anything like that, but maybe I could convince my mother to buy me one.

Before I began a new sales pitch I had to gather some information first, by making a much more thorough inspection of our IBM PS/1. After my disastrous experience disassembling the Amstrad I was very hesitant to fry a machine that was only a few months old.

I inspected the rear of the machine first. There was the usual array of ISA expansion slots – all were empty with the exception of two. One was the Sound Blaster 16 – the veritable champion of the OPL-3 music world. The other was a small, strange looking card. I had ignored it previously because it had no name nor obvious purpose – it only had two black ports that, months earlier, I had assumed were for a special peripheral like a joystick or printer. Upon closer inspection they appeared to be phone jacks!

I vibrated in place. This must have been *some* kind of modem even though it looked nothing like the black plastic box Mr. M used on the Mac. I removed the card from the slot and checked it over carefully. There were a set of tiny switches called "DIPs" that were used to modify settings in the computer; there was not much else on the card that betrayed its use. How the heck could I use this thing in Windows 3.1?

I thought back to the program Mr. M used on his Mac. He mentioned something about a "terminal program". My mind raced through the different pieces of software I had on my IBM, and it didn't take long to remember the strange telephone icon in Windows 3.1. I scrounged up a spare phone cord and hooked up the computer to the phone line. I launched *Terminal* in Windows

– and it showed me the same blank white screen it always had in the past. It took a few hours of experimenting with the rather terse software before I managed to get a dial tone out of it, and by the end of the evening I managed to dial up my neighbour and heard her voice coming out of the modem speaker.

My computer was talking on the phone line!

The moment felt like it came from the film *WarGames,* except that David Lightman's computer was a crude pile of circuits compared to my shiny new 486. I couldn't even imagine all the crazy stuff I could do with a modem.

The Brown Mushroom BBS

The next morning I popped my head into Mr. M's lab before class started, and yelled, "I've got a modem!" He smiled and gave me a thumbs-up, "Good! Come see me at lunch!"

A few hours later I walked back into the lab and the dot matrix printer was scree-screeing pages upon pages of line-feed paper into a wobbly pile. "Here, check this out. I gotta BBS list printed out for ya. Pretty cool huh?"

I looked at the long list of names and phone numbers. The vast majority were City numbers, and many of them had cool and futuristic sounding names. "The Wizard's Castle" and "Dark Dungeons" and "Cyber Dreams" caught my eye. There were over a hundred names and numbers. I jammed the stack of paper into my backpack and spent the rest of the day marking down the BBSs I would try, and the order I would try them in. When I got home I called the first one on the list: "Brown Mushroom BBS".

I typed the phone number into the Terminal program and listened to the clicks of the modem as it emulated a rotary phone dialling. After a few rings the line clicked and I heard the piercing sounds of the modem handshaking with the remote computer system: *screeeer-erererérr-rscree-shhhh-nnggggg*… and then, unbelievably, letters began to rain down my screen:

```
CONNECT 2400
BROWN MUSHROOM BBS
DO YOU HAVE AN ANSI-COMPATIBLE TERMINAL? [Y/N]
```

The cursor blinked as the computer waited for me to respond, so I hit "Y" on instinct. The window scrolled down as if possessed and strange ASCII text appeared:

```
ÁÁÁÓÓÓÓÁÁÁÓÓÓÓÓÓÓÓÁÁÁÁÓÓÓÓ
ÓÓ WELCOME TO THE BROWN ÓÓ
ÓÓ      MUSHROOM BBS    ÓÓ
ÓÓ 9600BAUD/SINGLE NODE ÓÓ
ÓÓ       FILE AREAS     ÓÓ
ÁÁÁÓÓÓÓÁÁÁÓÓÓÓÓÓÓÓÁÁÁÁÓÓÓÓ
```

I grinned and bounced around in my office chair, my legs shaking with excitement. The black-and-white Terminal text flowed down line-by-line in a waterfall of strange accented characters. I could make out most of the information by skipping past the indecipherable characters, but there was definitely something wrong with my Terminal program. This BBS was nothing at all like the Macintosh FirstClass BBS Mr. M had shown me, with its slick user interface that looked like MacOS. This was more like an MS-DOS command prompt, except all happening over the phone lines which made it exciting anyway.

Why was I so excited about watching ASCII characters appear on the screen, at one line per second? To answer this we have to think back to the early 90s, when data only really existed on a diskette or CD-ROM: putting information on a computer meant installing something, or loading a document or a saved game. The idea of data *streaming* onto my computer from a computer at a remote location – in my case, over fifty kilometres away – was alien and delightful. And not only was that information streaming live from the other end via modem, but I was able to *direct the remote computer* by typing commands from my end. Today, the idea of remote data streaming – say, from Netflix or YouTube – holds no magic for the average person.

Back in the 1990s, live interactivity over phone lines was even better than the canned interactive experience computer games offered. It really felt like I was hardwired to a computer very far away. Think: do you feel like you're interacting with a remote computer when you're watching YouTube videos? Probably not. The visceral, interactive feeling that comes from computer-to-computer modeming has vanished thanks to "cloud" computing, bit torrents and wide area networking.

So when The Brown Mushroom BBS sent the following line of text all I could think was: YES, YES, YES!

```
ÁÁÁÁÁÁÁÁÁÁÁÁÓÓÓÓÓÓÓÓÓÓÓÓÓÓÓÓÓÓÓÓÓÓÓÓÓÓÓÓÓÓÓÓÓÓÓÓÁÁÁÁÁÁ
Enter Alias or type "NEW" to create a new account:
ÁÁÁÁÁÁÁÁÁÁÁÁÓÓÓÓÓÓÓÓÓÓÓÓÓÓÓÓÓÓÓÓÓÓÓÓÓÓÓÓÓÓÓÓÓÓÓÓÁÁÁÁÁÁ
```

Whatever an "Alias" was, it was obvious that I needed to create an account to use the system. I answered a few questions about my identity, age, location and phone number – and I was welcome as user #54 of The Brown Mushroom.

I spent the next hour exploring the BBS and tried to understand how it worked. From what I could gather, Bulletin Board Systems were a weird hybrid of community message boards, the classifieds section of the newspaper, and a library. I could post messages for other users to read and reply to, advertise my own BBS (if I somehow created one), and transfer files between my computer and the BBS. There was even a place called "The Wall" that allowed people to scrawl anonymous messages on it, not unlike the graffiti found in a bathroom stall. It felt like a little electronic village that I could explore on my own, at my own pace, leaving notes and files for others to discover after I departed.

```
ÓÓÁÁÁÁÁÁThe Brown MushroomÁÁÁÁÁÁÓÓ
[F]ile Areas [M]essage Bases
[P]age Sysop [D]oor Games
[R]ead Mail  [W]rite Mail
[H]ang Up    [W]all
ÓÓÁÁÁÁÁÁÁÁÁÁÁÁÁÁÁÁÁÁÁÁÁÁÁÁÁÁÁÁÁÁÓÓ
```

Everything was communicated through text and yet it delivered a very visceral, spatial experience. It felt like I was traipsing through a village in the Old West, with signposts and buildings; some buildings were full of small rooms, and some were huge warehouses full of documents and programs.

I understood what a message base was after my (disastrous) experience with the Canada SchoolNet, and knew to keep my nose out of there. Most of the messages were about boring stuff an adolescent wasn't very interested in anyway. The file areas on the other hand piqued my interest immediately. The BBS had a few hundred files available for "download", and each came with a brief description of the file's purpose.

Many of the files I recognized as "utilities" – programs used to do very specific jobs like Zipping or UnZipping (compressing/ decompressing) files. Although I had no idea what I was doing, I hit a few keystrokes to download a familiar program to my computer: PKUNZIP.EXE. I waited and a second later the BBS asked me what "protocol" I wanted to use for the file transfer. Ah, now this was getting tricky! Some supplementary reading on the BBS explained that a protocol was a program used to transfer files between computers – and that there were many types of these programs, some with specific benefits that others did not have. I picked the simplest of these protocols – one supported by my Terminal program – and successfully downloaded the file. It didn't take long to realize that Windows Terminal was not designed for serious BBSing. It did not support any of the most popular file transfer protocols.

Users in the message bases argued over which terminal program was the best, and all agreed that the MS-DOS based programs like *Terminate!* were far superior to any Windows 3.1 programs. Downloading *Terminate!* took one very painful hour: I watched the single file transfer across the telephone lines one byte at a time. I had been on the phone line for over two hours and hadn't even noticed the sun had set.

My parents arrived home from work later that evening and I immediately showed my mother the discoveries I had made with the modem and phone line. After the *Police Quest II* incident she was understandably concerned that I was going to run up phone bills using the modem, and said so in no uncertain terms. I reassured her many times that the calls were all local and she would never receive a bill from the phone company for them. (A month later when the phone bill arrived, clear of any suspicious long distance calls, she finally believed me.)

The next morning I loaded up *Terminate!* eager to determine if it was truly superior to Windows Terminal. When I installed the program I felt a little overwhelmed by the sheer complexity of the interface – it had dozens of options for baud rates, flow control, protocols, file compression, and so on. Instead of messing around with the default settings I dialled The Brown Mushroom. This time I was greeted with bright, colourful shapes and characters instead of the strange black-on-white jumbled ASCII text I had gotten with Terminal. The BBS had fancy 16 colour graphics and text using what was called the "ANSI" character set. It was like watching a Technicolor movie after a decade of black-and-white films – the *Wizard of Oz* effect once again. Everything was so bright and colourful. I wandered over to the board's file areas, intent on starting a download before having to take the bus to school. I dug through the "Shareware Games" file area and found a few dozen games that looked mildly interesting.[36]

I had played shareware games that I had purchased at the grocery store once before but found them all wanting. I wanted

---

[36] Shareware: a term for a software marketing and distribution practice that emerged in the 1980s and became ubiquitous in the 1990s. Big-budget software like database programs, computer games and operating systems were usually sold through computer stores in big fancy boxes. Shareware was a marketing tool that allowed software creators to sell their software through a less formal process. It encouraged everyday people to exchange (share) programs and games with one another, and if someone liked the program they could send a cheque to the creator to pay for the program. Paying for the program provided a user with an official "registered" copy that usually came with extra features, like additional levels in a game or removing "unregistered" watermarks in productivity software. Games like *Doom* came in two versions: the shareware version that had only one level, and the registered version that came with all of the levels and the ending to the game. In the late 1980s and early 1990s, shareware was primarily distributed through BBSs.

to download something I could sink my teeth into. I wanted the *full* version of a game. I wanted to pirate something.

There was about an hour before the bus arrived to cart me off to school, which meant I could download about one megabyte over my PS/1's anemic 2400 baud modem.[37] The vast majority of games under a 'meg were shareware titles, with the exception of one conspicuously inconspicuous file named TIM.ZIP.

Where all the other shareware titles had extensive file descriptions, TIM.ZIP had a suspiciously blank file description. Why would all the other games have proper names and descriptions but this one didn't? Besides, this file was shy of a megabyte and could be transferred in under an hour. I put my money on the mystery file.

I spent the next hour pacing around the den and watching the XMODEM transfer crawl forward.[38] I went to the kitchen and prepared a bacon and toast sandwich for breakfast and gave the clock a sidelong glance. If the transfer didn't complete before I had to run for the bus I would have to turn off the computer and try again later that day. I couldn't risk leaving the modem on the

[37] At the time, 9600 baud and 14400 baud modems were available and popular. The 2400 baud modem that came with my model of IBM PS/1 was an entry-level modem installed by IBM to justify the ridiculously high cost of the computer package. At 2400 baud the modem could transfer information at approximately 0.3 kilobytes per second. One "baud" is *roughly* equivalent to one bit-per-second of information (although, due to modem design and phone line noise, it is often much less efficient). In comparison the average cable modem or DSL line currently transfers around 20 megabytes per second; this is approximately 50,000 times faster than my old 2400 baud modem.

[38] XMODEM is a protocol used to transfer files between computers. Unlike newer protocols it did not support batch file transfers, error correction or resuming botched transfers. Years later protocols like YMODEM, ZMODEM, HS/LINK, iCEMODEM and so on added many fancy features. Some bi-directional protocols like HS/LINK even included a chat interface which allowed the user to text chat with the Sysop during a file transfer – this was the only true multi-tasking possible on a BBS that I am aware of.

phone line and tie it up for the entire day. My folks would have kittens.

I heard a double-honk from the far side of the large pond across the street. The bus was at our neighbour's house picking up their kids. That meant I had about three minutes before the bus arrived. Please, God! Stall the bus! Give it a flat tire! I just need a few more minutes!

The bus honked again. Yes! The neighbours were going to be late which gave me another minute or two. I checked the computer: 4 minutes left. My sister announced that she was leaving – "Come on! You're gonna be late!"

I clawed my fingernails into the oak desk for the last thirty seconds of the download. I heard the bus roll down the road getting nearer to our house. My father walked into the den and said, "What are you still doin' here? Get movin' or you're gonna miss the bus!"

Just as he barked out the last few words the file download completed and the hard drive grinded noisily, saving the file. DONE! I hit the power switch and ran out the side-door of our house onto the lawn. Like a kindergarten child I ran with my backpack dragging behind me as I tried to pull my arms through my jacket, legs crazy and feet pounding the dirt driveway. When I got to the bus, the driver – who was also our village mayor – burst out laughing in a deep, bass voice, "Hoooo! I never seen anyone run like that! Ha ha ha!" I grinned as I climbed up the bus stairs. I panted out breathlessly, "Sorry I'm late. I just downloaded a game."

Those words, spoken to a middle-aged bus driver in the early 90's must have come out like poorly accented Klingon. I might as well have said, 'I just fnork'd a bejoozle', and he would have had the same blank expression on his face. He shook his head and laughed as I found my seat. *He* might not have known how important my little achievement was, but *I* did: I had a file to experiment with when I got home later that day.

Nine hours and two bus rides later I rushed back to my computer and ran the PKUNZIP command on TIM.ZIP to decompress it, revealing its goodies. To my great surprise the file decompressed into an entire directory of files! Two executable files immediately caught my eye: INSTALL.EXE and TIM.EXE. Out of habit I ran the installer first and my jaw fell off its hinges – the installer program was made by Sierra/Dynamix just like *The Adventures of Willy Beamish*. I let out a choked gasp like a strange bellow made by sea lions at the zoo.

I wrung my hands in a caricature of Dr. Fred Edison from the game *Day of the Tentacle* as the game loaded. The screen went black and to my delight the familiar Sierra logo, rendered in high resolution appeared. I beamed as I watched an animated blue horned trollish character walk from the right side of the screen to the middle of the screen where it stopped and said, "Phew!", producing a cute digitized voice from my computer speakers.

The mystery game I had downloaded from the BBS turned out to be a foundational puzzle game called *The Incredible Machine*. The brainchild of programmer Jeff Tunnell, the game had the player create Rube Goldbergesque inventions in order to satisfy a win condition: a rat running in a wheel, powers a conveyer belt, which sends a bowling ball flying into the air, which lands on a light switch, which turns on a light. You get the idea.

The game was designed in an intuitive manner, requiring no instruction manual. I played the game voraciously and waited for the game to exit prematurely, with a "Call 1-800-555-5555 to buy a full version of this shareware product" screen. But, nothing happened. The game kept going. *This was the full version of the game!* I had pirated a computer game and it was *glorious*.

That day marked my baptism into the seedy, luxurious world of BBS piracy. If The Brown Mushroom had one pirated computer game, it meant that other BBSs had similar hidden treasures – it was just a matter of dialling them up and finding them.

'Yo ho ho, and a backpack of games!' I giggled to myself as I rode the bus to school. My friend Andrew was not going to believe his eyes.

A night earlier I had tied up the phone line for hours, downloading every game I could find on a handful of BBSs that had pirated software or "warez" hidden in their file areas.[39] Users were actively trading files with one another using the file areas of BBSs. Part of me knew there was something unseemly about the practice but it never occurred to me that there was anything illegal about it. After all, how was downloading files any different from the time I traded *King's Quest IV* for *Police Quest II* with Carl at school? Weren't games meant to be shared?

If you're rolling your eyes at these desperate rationalizations it's likely because the cultural mores of piracy have changed since the 80s and 90s. With few exceptions, in those days copying a program was not seen as a serious immoral or illegal act. The vast majority of my family's Tandy TRS-80 CoCo II software on cassette were copies of originals owned by someone else. Software existed in a grey zone – it was not like stealing a computer from a shop. To the average person copying a computer game was about as controversial as recording a radio song on a cassette tape.

At the same time, even as a teenager, I knew better. I knew that people like 'The Two Guys From Andromeda' and Roberta

[39] Warez: pronounced 'wares' (not 'where-ez'!) is a computer buccaneer's term for pirated software. Unlike games that are traded between friends face-to-face, warez is intended for mass consumption among anonymous sharers. Warez is usually 'cracked', meaning that copy protection measures are disabled so that players can freely exchange the software without needing its original documentation or diskettes. BBSs were a critical medium for the spread of warez in the 1980s and early 1990s.

Williams, pictured on the backs of Sierra On-Line game boxes, worked hard to make these games. These were real people making real things, and not paying for their creations seemed pretty chintzy. But I was fourteen years old and honestly, the appeal of getting a game for free that would have cost me sixty bucks was an offer I could not refuse.

When I realized that I could pirate games from BBSs with no consequences whatsoever, boy did I go to town. At 2400 baud the average game took 2-3 hours to download, so I had to be strategic about my download choices.

Pirated software came from a variety of sources on BBSs. The vast majority of bulletin boards on the printed list of BBSs I had consisted of file areas full of completely legal shareware. A handful among them, like The Brown Mushroom, had a couple of pirated games snuck in to their shareware file areas. These pirated files were often uploaded by users, and the System Operator or Sysop turned a blind eye to their existence on the BBS.[40] (And why not? Sysops were getting free software from users who took the risk of uploading it.) Unfortunately there were few pirated files found on the BBSs I frequented.

I hit the jackpot a few days later when I downloaded a game called *Stunts* from a BBS called The Lily Pad. It was 1AM, well past my bedtime on a school night, and I was digging around The Lily Pad's file areas. The BBS had a small message area and a file area, and neither appeared untoward. I was about to hang up

---

[40] Sysop: 'pronounced sis-awp', short for "system operator". This is the person who owns and controls the Bulletin Board System software and the computer it resides on. The sysop is generally treated by users as a jealous, fickle deity that can giveth and taketh away. Sysops were exulted by their users for at least two reasons: (1) the sysop had voluntarily sacrificed an entire PC as the server for the BBS software, and (2) paid for the phone line the system was attached to. Sysops can do whatever they want to users – disconnect them at a whim, initiate chat sessions, increase or decrease their security level and access, read their 'private' mail... mere mortal users dared not cross a power-crazed sysop.

when my screen suddenly blanked. I watched as words began to appear, one character at a time, across the top of the screen.

`> hey whats up. you look lost.`

My heart stopped for a few beats before I realized what was happening. A living, breathing sysop was typing messages to me in real-time! It was an interactive chat session! I wrote back that I was just looking around his BBS, and that I was new.

`> kewl. where are you calling from?`

I told him that I was calling from an acreage about forty-five minutes away from The City, where he and his board were located. He was surprised as he had never received callers from that distance before. After an hour the conversation became more intimate – he discussed his personal and familial problems, going into detail about a degrading relationship with his father. I gave him a compassionate ear, and related my own dissatisfied family life and my father's spiralling mental health.

The feeling was incredible. I was conversing with a *complete stranger* about our deepest personal problems. Who could imagine that people could connect their computers over a phone line and then talk about their personal lives using a keyboard?

Today, interactive chat isn't seen as a special or exceptional human experience. In fact, interactive chat has all but disappeared in favour of asynchronous messaging like SMS/ Texting, Facebook and Twitter. But in the 1990s, typing messages to each other over a phone line was absolutely magical. There was a rich, earthy, interactive quality to it that is all but lost today. You could watch the letters appear on the screen one at a time, knowing that somewhere very far away, a flesh-and-blood human being was sitting in front of a glowing screen typing them on a keyboard. I could watch the sysop make spelling mistakes as he typed and corrected them with the backspace key. Although Facebook, iPhones and Android devices have chat capabilities, none of them approximate the instantaneity of BBS chats.

I peeked outside the curtains: the sky was a deep violet. It was going to be sunrise soon! The clock in the corner of my *Terminate!*

software showed it was almost five o'clock in the morning. We had been chatting for over four hours. I promised the sysop I would come back as his board had instantly become my favourite hangout. He thanked me for letting him share his personal crises with me and I told him that I'd be happy to lend an ear any time. Just before I was about to disconnect he stopped me:

> hey so wanna be co-sys?

My eyes lit up despite my drowsiness. Seriously? Yes!

> sure watch this

The chat session suddenly exited and the screen went back to the BBS's main menu. With the blinding speed of a console jockey in a 1980s cyberpunk novel, I watched him execute a series of commands and menu selections that blurred my display. My modem could not keep up with his keystrokes and my screen became a cacophony of ANSI graphics and letters spilling down the monitor. I squinted at a few of the screens that passed before my eyes and realized that he had upgraded my security access level.

> there its done call back later try it out

I beamed. I had no idea what role or responsibilities a "co-sysop" had but I knew this was a promotion rarely doled out to newbies like myself. I had not told him that I had only been modeming for less than a week, but I intended not to let him down. Whatever he wanted me to do as his co-sysop, I promised myself I would be the loyal Friday to his Robinson Crusoe. And of course I wondered: what extra permissions did this give me?

I went to bed and dreamt of pirating the high seas as co-sysop and master of modulated bits.

I soon discovered what becoming a co-sysop of The Lily Pad meant: it gave me unparalleled access to secret file and messaging areas that were not visible to the average user. I found out that, contrary to the image of a publicly-facing benign and lifeless shareware BBS, The Lily Pad was a tight band of software pirates who swapped games with one another in a hidden back room. The file areas were full of registered versions of shareware games, cracked commercial titles and even tantalizing "HPVAC" files.[41]

Best of all, as co-sysop I had unrestricted access to all of it. No "upload/download ratios" or "download credits" to worry about, no mandatory message base posts, just free warez. I had run across credit-system BBSs before. A credit-based system gave the BBS user a number of virtual "credits" that could be spent on downloading files. When the user ran out of credits, they could no longer download any more files. In order to get more credits, users would have to upload new files, post messages in the message areas, or sometimes win credits by playing online games called "door games".[42] The credit system was created to control "leeching" – the tendency of users to download all of a

---

[41] HPVAC: Abbreviation for "hacking, phreaking, virii, anarchy, and cracking" – basically every illicit activity one could accomplish with the help of a computer. A few HPVAC text files were ubiquitous, like *The Anarchist's Cookbook* which detailed how to pick locks, build pipe bombs and get away with various criminal activities. I printed off a copy of the *Cookbook* to impress my friends at school, but disposed of it a few days later when I was overwhelmed by paranoia that one of my teachers would find it in my locker and tell my folks I was the next Unabomber.

[42] Door games were textual games delivered live during a BBS session. There was no need to download a piece of software to play the game, as it was delivered purely over the telephone lines as text. Many of these games were simple trivia or gambling games and some earned the player download credits if they won.

BBS's files without returning anything to the community. Credit systems worked fairly well, but I avoided them because my slower-than-molasses 2400 baud modem made it impossible to get new credits by uploading files in a reasonable amount of time.

My recent knighthood bypassed all that stuff. I was free to download as many games as I wanted. But with great power came greater responsibility: I dared not download excessively and get a bad rap as a leech. Just like my family who was struggling through the economic recession, I had to be bit-frugal at 2400 baud.

The majority of The Lily Pad's games were three, four and five megabytes. That meant three or more hours of tying up not only my family's phone line, but the board's single "node" or phone line too.[43] In the end I restricted myself to one of the only one-meg files the board had: a game called *Stunts*.[44] I had no idea what the game was about but the file description mentioned that it was a three-dimensional driving simulator. What did I have to lose, besides one hour of phone time?

Stunts became the second pirated title under my belt and a local sensation among my PC-using friends at school.

When I got to school I tracked down my friend Andrew on his way to class. As a technical writer for a software company, his mother had recently caught on to the computer craze and bought

---

[43] The majority of Bulletin Board Systems were "single node" or single phone line systems. That meant: one computer and one phone line supported a single person dialling in at a time. Later versions of BBS software would add multi-line, multi-user support, like the popular *Wildcat!* software that became popular years later. Articles in *2600 Magazine* discuss popular multi-user pirate BBSs in the 1990s that had over 128 nodes, supporting 128 simultaneous users! The ubiquity of pornography on the Internet is partly owed to the massive multi-node BBSs that sprung up in the 1990s, illicitly selling scans of pornographic magazines for a monthly fee. Legal multi-node systems typically allowed users to play multi-player MS-DOS games like *Doom*.

[44] Published as *4-D Sports Driving* in Europe.

him a dream machine: a 486 DX2-50 with 8 megabytes of RAM. I secretly envied his raging powerhouse of a machine compared to my comparatively anemic 486 SX-33, and had a scheme to try his out.

I showed Andrew a diskette clumsily labeled with my chicken scrawl. "I downloaded it last night… *over the phone line.*"

He raised an eyebrow ostentatiously as we walked into English class, "Sounds interesting…"

During our lunch break over a game of *MacBolo* Andrew asked me about the game I had pirated. I told him it was called *Stunts* but I hadn't had a chance to try it out yet – it was hot off my floppy drive. Apparently that was enough to pique his interest, and he pushed away the Macintosh keyboard and stood up. "Let's go to my place. If we run we can make it back in time."

So we ran to his house, the floppy disk in my sweaty little hand. The plan was to copy of the game as quickly as we could, grab Pillsbury pizza pops from the freezer, microwave them, install the game, then run back to school in time for class – all in under thirty minutes.

Copying the disk only took a minute and we sat down to *Stunts*. As promised by its file description it was a 3D driving simulation with race cars and a track. But much more surprising to us was that it appeared to be a clone of the extremely popular and technically impressive arcade game *Hard Drivin'*.[45]

Set on a race track the player drives a low-polygon race car around, through loop-de-loops and over fantastically large jumps. The game even had a hilarious "instant replay" feature that allowed us to watch car accidents and cackle as the car exploded in a fiery wreck. With its appeal to our boyish love for driving cars at high speed and watching stuff blow up, *Stunts* became a hit with my friends.

Best of all, I now had a trustworthy friend to swap games

---

[45] Also known as *Race Drivin'*.

with. Andrew offered to give me copies of his purchased games in addition to unlimited lunches at his house, and in return I supplied him with games downloaded from BBSs. It was the beginning of a long friendship mediated by computer piracy.

For the next few months I "worked" evenings as a co-sysop for The Lily Pad. My pirating career involved doing light housekeeping in the file areas and helping the sysop delete nuisance posts in the message bases. The sysop and I chatted occasionally but any delusions of grandeur I had about my position as co-sysop were soon thwarted when I realized that there were ten other co-sysops on the board. He was using the co-sysop security level as a means for controlling access to the pirate areas!

By promoting so many users to co-sysop, he kept the warez flowing over the lines. I kept my downloads limited to one diskette per day, minimizing the amount of time I was spending on his board; over a few months I managed to accrue a sizeable directory of pirated software. The majority of my downloads turned out to be registered versions of shareware titles like *Jill of the Jungle*, *Crystal Caves*, *Epic Pinball*, *One Must Fall 2097* and *Jazz Jackrabbit*. Every week without fail, Andrew and I spent lunch hours making copies of diskettes, drinking pop while eating pizza pops and nervously watching the clock, until we made a sweaty race back to school in time for the bell.

One day without warning The Lily Pad disappeared. The modem rang and rang without answer, and a few days later the phone number went out of service. For a week I was terrified that the BBS owner had been apprehended by Interpol, had his pirate BBS hardware confiscated, and I would soon be scooped by the police for my role as a sub-lieutenant in a den of thieves.

I wish I could say that I lost a good friend that day, but beyond the initial conversation I had with the sysop, I barely knew the guy. He just disappeared – a common ending to many BBSs that were run from the bedrooms of family homes. And with the loss of the board I lost my only pipeline to warez.

The loss meant once again seeking through the phone line for another sleazy BBS that could feed my insatiable appetite for new games. I pulled out my BBS list, earned months earlier from Mr. M, and resumed my systematic search for software.

CompuServe and Prodigy

After the initial glut of modeming to local BBSs and the disappearance of The Lily Pad, I became bored with dialling up the same old places. I wanted something new, and the answer was right under my nose the whole time. Brochures for two online services were tucked away inside of my adventure game boxes. One service called Prodigy offered five free hours online. The brochure included a 1-800 number that allowed me to download Prodigy's custom terminal software, free of charge.

After dialling the number I was prompted to download a new terminal program purpose-built to access Prodigy. The surprisingly small Prodigy graphical terminal dialling program turned out to have a graphical user interface not unlike the kind I had seen on Mr. M's Macintosh FirstClass BBS. I dialled the 1-800 number again, this time using the special graphical Prodigy client, and was greeted by a set of icons that reminded me of my bank's ATM interface. Each icon had text below explaining the area of Prodigy you could navigate to: Finance, Stock Markets, Mail... it looked like the kind of online service I imagined businessmen in suits and ties and suspenders used in the 1980s. A few years earlier I would have been impressed by the high-res EGA graphics and user interface but none of these business applications appealed much to a broke high school kid. Finding few game-related topics, when my five hours were up I deleted the client software from my computer and moved on.

The next day I remembered the second brochure I had found called "CompuServe". Unlike Prodigy which ran in MS-DOS, CompuServe was a Windows 3.1 program. The program queried me about my location, and a few seconds later began dialling a phone number in the City. The program came with only three free hours of use – I had to use my time carefully.

CompuServe turned out to be similar to Prodigy, except that it appeared to be more geared towards home users instead of business moguls. There were chat rooms, computer support and knowledge bases, downloads and electronic mail. In the message areas I found an impressive array of information relevant to computer users like anti-virus reviews and PC maintenance tips. The file area had a large collection of shareware software similar to the kind I'd found on my local BBSs. But it was the chat rooms that caught my teenage eye. I clicked on the chat room icon and was greeted with a large list of rooms, all with names like "Houston" and "402" and a dozen chat rooms devoted to teens. I entered the room with the largest number of people in it: "Teenchat".

It was exciting. I had never been inside of a live multi-user chat before. Messages blurred down the screen and my eyes could barely keep up to the pace of the lively room. Very few of the messages made sense to me, replete with acronyms like "A/S/L?" or "NE1 from 403"?[46] I eventually caught on to some of the colourful language and began joking around with the other teenagers.

An hour into the chat a fellow teen addressed me directly and said, "Hey, you're in 403 too?"

"Yes, I am!"

"Want 2 chat private?"

Woo. Sounds like fun. "Sure!"

The prospect of talking with someone from my own province over a world-wide network was strangely exciting, like setting up a tin-can telephone between your treehouse and your neighbour's bedroom.

A private chat window popped up and I began chatting with "mikey" who introduced himself as a thirteen year old boy from the City. I told him that I was from a farm a half hour away and that I was fourteen going on fifteen.

Mikey was glad he had someone local to talk to and proposed an idea. "so, wanna j/o?"

---

[46] A/S/L: short for "Age/Sex/Location?". "403" referred to my telephone area code at the time.

"Sure!" I replied immediately, worried I might look uncool if I asked him what the acronym meant.

"ok awesome," mikey replied.

I waited for a couple of minutes. Nothing was happening. I prompted him to say something.

"So what now?" I asked surreptitiously.

"haha. u know dude."

I frowned at the screen. How would I know what we were supposed to be doing?

Mikey kept the game going and said, "u start yet?"

Now the conversation was becoming very abstract. I was convinced he was playing mind games with me on purpose, and it was time to lay my cards on the table.

"Ok I give up. What does j/o mean?"

"haha u serious?"

"Yes, I don't know what it means."

"j/o. jack off."

Ah.

Um.

Let me get this straight. I had been propositioned to masturbate with someone describing themselves as a young male online, had accepted, and had now humiliated both him and me with my cyber-naiveté. He closed the chat window a few seconds later, and I hung up on CompuServe right then and there. I had not even used my three free hours.

As much as I was excited by the prospect of chatting with other people around the world, the idea of having anonymous imaginary sex with them wasn't in my wheelhouse. And I certainly was not about to pay $3.99 an hour for the privilege of doing so. I resigned myself to resume my search for new BBSs in my local calling area which were free, and more importantly, a little more focused on what I wanted at fourteen years old: warez.

Texas Instruments TI-85 Graphing Calculator

It was January and the tenth grade was half over, and when my time wasn't poured into acquiring warez it was invested in playing the games I had acquired. Final exams for the first half of the school year were done and I was free to dally in that sweet first month of a course where we reviewed concepts from the previous year, before the real work started.

Our Mathematics 10 teacher, Mrs. H, told the class that newfangled "graphing" calculators were now a required part of her class. Like all governments gripped by a collective sense of boundless hope for (and fear of) new technology, our province's education ministry was convinced that all high school students should all learn how to use them in the classroom.

Hell, you didn't need to convince *me*. I was sold on graphing calculators the second she slipped hers out of its navy blue plastic case, punched a few buttons and let it plot an exponential function graph before my eyes. It was a computer the size of a Game Boy!

Acquiring one of these little babies meant at least a $150 investment from my parents. One can imagine the looks on dozens of farmers' faces as their kids came home with a note from their math teacher recommending a calculator that cost over a hundred bucks. Even today that's a lot of money for a plastic device that adds and subtracts things. When I brought the note home to my parents they looked at each other dubiously, like I was trying to pull a fast one on them with a forged document.

With a wry frown on his face my dad looked at my puny solar calculator and started punching keys. "See? What's wrong with this one? It adds, multiplies… divides just fine!"

In vain I tried to explain that these new calculators were superior in every way. I promised that with a graphing calculator, my math grade was finally going to climb over a "B". Heck I'd pay for half of it if they really wanted me to, and…

My dad laughed as he watched me do oratorical gymnastics. "Go ask your mother," he nodded. YES! In our house that phrase was code for "fine, just leave me alone because I'm trying to watch the hockey game."

Sure enough, my mother and I drove to the City that weekend and shopped for a graphing calculator.

It turned out that there were a couple of different models and brands of graphing calculators. My mathematics teacher had a Texas Instruments TI-81, which was the entry-level model that got you in the door for about $150.

But, as my mother would remind me many times over, I could never quite live within my means; I always had to have something just *slightly* out of my financial reach. I usually funded my greediness by borrowing money from her or some other gullible relative. In my mind if a toy was five dollars and I had a fiver with me, the seven dollar toy on the shelf just above it must be infinitely better. My predilection for sparing no expense happened again when I spotted a sleek, black Texas Instruments calculator on the shelf: the TI-85. It had more memory than the TI-81, an extended character set that included lower and upper-case characters, and most importantly a TI-LINK port that allowed me to connect it to other calculators. The networking capability alone was the instant selling point for me; in seconds I had a million plans for that glorified adding machine.

And, of course, the price tag exaggerated the admittedly minor technical differences between the TI-81 and TI-85. The TI-85 was over two hundred bucks – this was an unbelievable amount of money to spend given my family's financial straits. I pleaded, I begged, I swore oaths upon my own grave. Finally my mother took me up on an offer I had made earlier during my pitch to my parents: I would pay for half of the purchase from my own pocket. That meant $100 – my entire Christmas and New Year's cash haul! I gnawed on my knuckle thinking about all the purchases I would forego – at least two brand new Sega Genesis or computer games were going out the window! After years of tactical miscarriages in negotiating over technology purchases, my mother had finally gotten wise to my wheedling and called my bluff.

A minute of emotional calculus revealed no other avenues – her brilliant gambit had won. I'd have to pony up the cash. I handed over the entirety of my wallet and snatched the TI-85 off the shelf. My hands and feet and face were on fire as I walked toward the cashier – it was a victory bought with blood, but a victory nonetheless. As I watched the cashier ring in the shocking sticker price I felt a bloom of pride: it was the first time I had contributed towards a major technology purchase for myself. My parents were not going to be thrown in a Dickensian debtor's prison because of my insatiable need for the next cool computer thingy.

On the ride home I pored over the rich technical contents of the TI-85's inch-thick manual. The calculator was replete with dozens of built-in functions, many of which described by abstruse mathematical terms. I fingered the tiny keys on the calculator, squinted at the labels above each key, spying one titled "PRGRM". Program? This thing had programs?

I thumbed through the manual and found an entry discussing "Programming in TI-BASIC". The calculator even had the BASIC programming language?! What *couldn't* this thing do? The BASIC syntax was slightly different than I was used to thanks to my experience with Microsoft GW-BASIC and Apple BASIC but the premise was the same.

There is a nameless BASIC program that every single kid on the planet writes and giggles at their own brilliance:

```
:LBL A
:DISP "HELLO I AM AWESOME"
:GOTO A
```

I ran the program, and in turn the calculator spewed output in an endless loop:

* * *

```
HELLO I AM AWESOME
HELLO I AM AWESOME
HELLO I AM AWESOME
HELLO I AM AWESOME
HELLO I AM AWESOME
```

I broke out in a goofy smile as I sat quietly in the passenger seat. My mother glanced sideways at me, smiling too.

"You are too easy to make happy kiddo," she chuckled.

The next day I went to school and showed off my new gear to my friends like I was a recently engaged 1950s fiancée showing off her sparkly diamond ring to her clucking co-workers in accounts receivable. My old gang – Donny, Trevor and Robert – had bought TI-81's and were nonplussed by my black beast. But a few of the science geek friends of mine, like Wayne, David and Anthony, appreciated the additional technical capabilities the TI-85 had. And of course that meant *they* needed one too – a few days later there was an elite cluster of students in my Math class that had TI-85s.

The remainder of the first month of Mathematics 10 was overshadowed by the TI-85. While our teacher wrote formulae on the board and expected me to take notes, I was hammering away at the calculator, trying to discover wild tricks I could pull off with it and demo for my friends. My BASIC programs became increasingly complex as I learned how to wrangle the calculator into doing neat graphical stuff. Like modeming, programming the TI-85 quickly became an addiction.

Legend of the Red Dragon

During my BBSing I became infatuated with a door game called *Legend of the Red Dragon*, known to most BBSers as *LORD*. Set in a fantastic world that was a blend of *The Lord of the Rings* and *Grimm's Fairy Tales*, *LORD* was everything I wanted out of an adventure game and role-playing game fused into one. The premise, like many other RPGs, was simple: kill monsters, get loot, and advance to the next battle. But unlike most other computer RPGs, the experience of playing the game over the phone line gave the game a persistent and unpredictable quality – like I was walking into a living world that continued to exist after I hung up the phone. And in the truest sense the game did continue to exist after I hung up, because other players would then dial the BBS and take their own character for a tour around the fantasy world we shared.

The game is played through a simple menu system driven by individual keystrokes:

```
[G]o to the Forest.
[V]isit the Tavern.
[C]heck balance at the Bank.
[X]Log off.
```

Visiting the forest triggers a random encounter, like battling witches, monsters, wild animals, or discovering treasure. In most situations the player can beat the monster up, receive gold and treasure, and haul their loot back to town to hoard in their bank account or spend on armour and weapons. Like other RPGs, as the character wins battles he or she gains levels of advancement and power. The "Tavern" allows the player to flirt with the voluptuous barmaid Violet, with the pathetic nerdly hope of someday engaging her to be married.

But it was not the combat that made the game exciting for me. Rather, the asynchronous interaction with other players made *LORD* special. Even though the game was designed so only one player could be in the world at a time, it still allowed players to interact with one another indirectly. One could challenge another player to a duel, scrawl a message into a wooden bar table with a dagger so all other players could see their witty remark, or even murder another player's character in their sleep. I delighted in these adolescent mischiefs, and more often than not got my butt handed to me by other more powerful players in the process.

LORD was lighthearted and full of sardonic humour, all written by a single programmer under the pen-name Seth Able the Bard. It didn't take long for me to become engrossed in Seth Able's silly fantasy world and spend all my BBS online time killing monsters and seducing Violet. It was the kind of repetitive, simple enjoyment without end that made it terribly addictive game for any modemer.

After a month of getting myself acquainted with TI-BASIC programming I felt an itch for a grandiose coding feat that would impress everyone in my class. As Mrs. H lectured on trigonometry, the idea came to me in a flash: I would remake *Legend of the Red Dragon* as a single-player game on the TI-85.

I spent the rest of the second month of Math 10 painstakingly coding my own version of *LORD* into the calculator. I copied every single line of text, every key command, and every random encounter I had seen on the BBS game to the calculator. I tried to make it look as identical as I could to its MS-DOS progenitor, and after a few weeks the game was shaping into something playable; it even included character level advancement and banking. It was going to knock everyone's socks off.

We were half-way through the semester when development on *LORD* came to a grinding halt. The mighty TI-85 proved to have more limitations that I had expected – the calculator had less than 32 kilobytes of internal memory and I had used all of it with the hundreds of lines of BASIC code I had entered. I had run out of space and no amount of programming gymnastics would solve the issue. My final version of "LORD85" as I titled the program was a wispy fart in the wind compared to Seth Able's BBS masterpiece.

That fact became evident when I smugly showed off my feat

of coding genius to my buddies. In the middle of a particularly boring math lesson on probability, I handed my calculator to the people in the row behind me and let them play LORD85. A few minutes later someone handed the calculator back to me. I had expected them to play it for at least an hour.

After class I approached my friends Wayne and Anthony for a quick review. They gave me ambivalent shrugs with a much less ambivalent reply – "It's kinda cool I guess. Did you really waste half the semester making that?"

"... yes."

Yes, I wasted half the semester making the greatest BBS game on earth for you philistines! I was crushed and resolved to improve the game by squeezing more out of the tiny memory the calculator had. But any hope for enhancements came to an end when Mrs. H clued in to the nature of my feverish typing sessions during class. The sharp decline in my math marks, expressed in my inability to calculate factorials, was a not-so-subtle indicator that my time wasn't being spent usefully in class. In one fell swoop she seized my calculator and locked it up in her classroom closet. "You can have it back at the end of the semester. You don't need a graphing calculator for the last few units anyway."

And with that the TI-85 was MIA for the remainder of the tenth grade. Although *LORD85* received no programming accolades from my classmates, I was still proud of what I had managed on the tiny computer. I felt like I had invented the modern aircraft and flew it over a gaggle of undeserving spectators, shrugging before they returned to shovelling shit in the hayfields. Oh well - next time I'd wow 'em. My experience with TI-BASIC proved far more useful to my classmates a year later, in an eleventh grade physics course, which is a story for a later date...

386 SX-20 IBM Clone and the World Wide Web

While I wrestled with the realities of high school academic life, my mother had managed to complete her university degree and was already working on a Master's program. This new program was even more demanding than before. Instead of leaving my sister and I alone at home this time, however, she brought us along to her new graduate student office on campus.

If you have never seen a graduate student's office, imagine a modern jail cell with three to four steel desks crammed along the walls, a battleship-grey metal bookshelf along the wall full of books and ungraded papers, and three unhappy serfs slaving away in exchange for food and lodging. The only thing missing in the cell was a communal toilet.

The cramped space forced my sister and I out into the common areas of the building where we would kill time until my mother was ready to leave at the end of the day. Sensing our boredom my mother shooed us over to a room across the hall from her office; she keyed a number combination into a keypad mounted on the door and quietly snuck us inside.

I looked around the dim room and took a mental inventory: Two very large and impressive black computers sat in the corner with "DO NOT TOUCH WITHOUT PERMISSION FROM COMPUTING AND NETWORK SERVICES" signs taped to the sides of the jet black monitors. Beside them was a large wood and Plexiglas cabinet with a dot-matrix printer humming away inside, its line-feed paper curling up in an endless loop of students' blood, sweat and tears. Nearer to me were two banks of ten nameless beige mid-tower IBM clones with students working at a few of them. My mother pointed us to two computers in the corner and told us to keep ourselves busy, trying not to arouse the attention of the undergraduates hammering away at their term papers.

She whispered hoarsely, "Just work there. Here is my user ID and password. Don't leave unless you need to go to the bathroom… you're not supposed to be in here."

My mother handed me a slip of paper with her quick, elegant script detailing her login credentials. The computer in front of me was running Windows for Workgroups (3.11), and had a few obscure icons on the desktop that I didn't recognize. Most of the programs appeared to be geared to official college student work but I was happy to poke around anyway.

Before I could begin spelunking I had to find a way to keep my sister occupied. I opened the Games folder on her computer and found a small trove of kid-friendly games there. The first one I ran proved to be an instant hit: *Jezzball*. *Jezzball* appeared to be a faithful adaptation of several popular arcade titles in which the goal was to gradually enclose a bouncing ball within expanding walls. The player's goal is to drop new walls around the ball to squeeze it into a tighter space, forcing the ball to bounce more often and quickly, making setting up new walls incredibly tricky. My sister had uncanny dexterity and a minute into playing it was far better than I at trapping the ball, and began setting high scores.

I left her to it and returned to my own computer, inspecting the LED readout on the front which said "20". Based on my experience with Robert and Trevor's computer which had a similar LED readout, I guessed that this meant I was working on a 386-based 20 MHz computer. This was slightly anemic compared to my PS/1 but after looking around at the types of people in the lab I suspected that college students weren't supposed to be playing games in the computer lab anyway. I ran every program on the desktop trying to discover their purposes.

A few minutes of systematic snooping paid off: one program launched a window with a black background and bright green text – the kind I'd seen in movies about hackers:

```
WELCOME TO THE COMPUTING AND NETWORK SERVICES
DEPARTMENT NETWORK. ALL USE IS MONITORED AND FOR USE
BY STUDENTS AND STAFF ONLY. PLEASE CONSULT YOUR CNS
GUIDE FOR MORE INFORMATION. ANDREW FILE SYSTEM (AFS)
```

```
USERS PLEASE NOTE NEW STORAGE LIMITS.

USERNAME:
```

Whatever this program was, it was very similar to the Terminal programs I had at home for modeming. This program must have established a link with some remote computer! And strangely, unlike my computer at home, there was no modem *screeeeeech* that heralded the connection – this must be one of those computer networks that Mr. M had talked about in class. Aside from the flimsy AppleTalk network set up in his classroom between the Macintosh computers, I had no experiences with networks to speak of. Fantastic!

I entered my mother's login credentials and was welcomed to a cursor dumbly blinking at me:

```
\~dptcns%2231\>_
```

The blinking prompt reminded me of MS-DOS so I naturally began entering MS-DOS commands that allowed me to see the contents of directories. None of them worked. What the heck?

I looked around at the other students working diligently, suddenly feeling self-conscious. Was I allowed to be messing around with this network program? It was one thing if I broke our family computer, but my mom would be in serious crap if I messed up her department's lab computer. Leaning back in my chair I spied that one other student was slowly pecking in commands into the same terminal program. I squinted and made out the word "pine" and watched as her screen transformed into a complete text interface that reminded me of a Bulletin Board System user interface.

When in Rome…

```
\~dptcns%2231\>pine_
```

I hit the enter key and watched as my screen instantly sprung up with green text. It was so fast and responsive compared to a modem! Exploring a BBS at 2400 baud meant that the screen loaded line-by-line, and often I could read messages on the screen while it was still loading. But here, the text blinked into existence almost instantaneously.

It didn't take me long to understand what *PINE* was: a program that let people send and receive electronic messages, just like on a BBS. It was an interface to access this "e-mail" stuff that a few users on BBSs were beginning to talk about. Like I had done with every pirated game that had no instruction manual, I began exploring every nook and cranny of the program. I correctly guessed that my mother's user ID was her e-mail address, and successfully sent myself an e-mail. *PINE* was incredibly simple to use – it was not unlike the Canada SchoolNet mail program that Mr. M had taught us how to use a year earlier.

Of course, e-mail was a little superfluous when I had nobody to send mail to. More poking around revealed a program called "FTP" that allowed me to explore remote file systems and download and upload files.[47] I made a mental note of the program as it would undoubtedly become useful if I managed to find a source for warez within the network.

I hit the real jackpot when I found a program called *Lynx*, which allowed me to view text resources called "web pages". These reams of text were full of interesting, random tidbits of information; they reminded me of the *HyperCard* stacks found on Macintosh computers at my school.[48] Unlike *HyperCard*, which only existed on one computer, these web pages were accessible from any computer on the network and resided on some remote system far away. To my delight there appeared to be no end to

---

[47] FTP is short for "file transfer protocol", and allows a user to transfer files between computers over a network.

[48] *HyperCard* was a program that allowed Macintosh users to create their own webpage-like information resources and link them together, an early precursor to the World Wide Web's Hypertext.

this resource. There were thousands upon thousands of web pages to read, mostly concerned with scientific and technical research at universities. Although I hardly understood the technical information on each web page, the exploration alone was exhilarating. Navigating these early web pages felt like exploring deep underground caves in a role-playing game with only a torch, making notes on a map as I traversed the depths.

I stumbled across one web page – a Frequently Asked Questions document about web pages – and finally understood where I was. I was surfing what the document called "The World Wide Web" which was a service provided on "The Internet".

Web. Internet. The words reverberated in me as my mind tried to grow large enough to envelope the ideas. I strained to digest the glut of information I had incorporated and my mind bulged at the seams.

I felt a tap on my shoulder and looked around, my eyes straining to adjust to the dark room around me. I was the only person in the computer lab.

"It's eleven. Let's go home. Your sister fell asleep in my office."

I stumbled out into the brightly lit hallway and realized that I had spent the last *five hours* learning how to use the Internet! The ride home that night was spent in silence as I ran over in my head all of the different programs and keystrokes I had used to explore with. My mother, intrigued by my silence, asked me what I had been up to in the computer lab. I lied, afraid she'd get into trouble if I had been using the Internet without her permission. "Oh, nothing. Just playing games."

Over the next couple of months I made every trip I could with my mother to her university office and spent countless hours in the computing lab. My mother asked no questions about what I was doing in there, likely happy to *not* know what was keeping me busy for an entire afternoon.

During those months I learned that the university's server used the VAX/VMS operating system, which used UNIX commands. I learned how to search public FTP sites for hidden warez directories, a few basic UNIX commands for storing files on my mother's student account, and searched the Internet using tools like *Gopher* and *Archie* to find games and walkthroughs for games. I learned how to write basic HTML and build my own little web pages[49]. I was developing a whole new set of skills on a different computer architecture, all in the darkened secrecy of a college computer lab. This was real hacking I reckoned, at blazing network speeds!

Coming home to the 2400 baud modem began to feel like wading through lakes of Jello. File transfers on the college network were 1000 to 3000 times faster than my modem at home. The Internet made finding information and warez so much easier than on BBSs. I was already beginning to buckle under the constraints of our IBM PS/1, after less than a year of ownership.

---

[49] HyperText Markup Language: the programming language consisting of tags like <italic>this</italic> that are used to create a web page which browsers can display as formatted text and graphics.

A New Modem

It was Valentine's Day and I felt alone. It was another one of those excruciatingly awkward high school experiences replete with a mandatory Valentine's Day school dance and honeymooning teenaged couples and prospecting dates roaming the hallways for other lonely people. I wanted none of it and was happy when the school day was over and I could return to the loving arms of my PS/1.

I was deep into a game of *Dune II* when I heard my mother's van rolling down the driveway. After helping her unload the weekly supply of groceries, she handed me a large, brown paper bag stencilled with the college's logo on the side. "Here! Happy Valentine's Day my son!" She gave me the excited smile she always did at Christmas as she watched me open a gift, rushing me to tear the wrapping off instead of surgically removing the tape bit by bit.

I peeked inside of the bag and found a stack of Valentine's Day-themed chocolate and candy. "Aw, mom. Thanks." I gave her a hug. My mother never neglected to buy my sister and I something sweet and chocolatey on any given holiday.

"No! Open it up! There's something at the bottom."

I frowned and dug deeper into the bag, which was disproportionately larger than the candy would imply…

Alongside the wads of junk food was a half-inch thick book that looked like a magazine. I pulled it out and arched my brows. It had the university's logo printed on the cover: "General Purpose UNIX (GPU) User Guide".

I did a Wile E. Coyote double-take, and thumbed through the pages. It sure did look a lot like the UNIX operating system I had been learning to use in the preceding weeks at the computer lab. Fantastic! I could finally learn some new commands to try out in the computer lab whenever I got to visit it next.

I gave her a second hug and thanked her, beaming. "Thanks mom, this is really cool, I didn't…"

"Oh GODDD! Here!" she groaned and dug deep into the bag, and fished out the contents from the very bottom.

Out of the top of the bag emerged a pink and white cardboard box, about the size of a shoebox, with *U.S. Robotics* printed on the side. I hadn't heard of this company before and flipped the box over to look at the product pictured on the front. A robot?

Words poured out of my mom as I gazed at the box with a truly baffled look on my face. "I wasn't sure which one to buy. There are sure some expensive ones, more than this, but the guy at the campus computer store said this would be good enough for you and..."

"Oh my god mom! OH MY GOD!" I almost swooned like a damsel in distress from a trashy Harlequin romance novel. The side of the box pictured a squat, rectangular ISA computer card with a small black speaker mounted on its face. I clearly saw two phone line jacks exposed on its spine. The top of the box read *U.S. Robotics Sportster 14.4K Modem* in soft pink lettering.

In my life I have been fortunate enough to receive some extraordinarily thoughtful birthday and Christmas gifts from friends and family; there are many that still bring me to tears when I remember how generous these people were to me. But no gift, before or after the day I got the USR Sportster 14.4, penetrated my heart in quite the same way.

I had no idea my mother had even noticed all the time I was spending on BBSs or in the campus computer lab, or that I had been learning UNIX commands. I had no idea she knew that our 2400 baud modem was painfully slow. I had no idea that she knew I was sad, dateless and lonely on Valentine's Day. After years of familial and financial turmoil I had begun to wonder if my mother still knew if I existed. The confluence of all these thoughts weakened my knees and rang in my ears. I almost fainted when I first saw that box.

Despite myself I began jumping around like a little kid and hugged my mom several times. She laughed and appeared to be relieved that I was happy about the modem she chose. "Maybe now you won't tie up the phone all day now!" she joked.

That statement could not have been further from the truth. I had the IBM's case off a minute later and replaced the feeble generic 2400 baud modem with its beefy, super-hunk cousin. My mother handed me a box of diskettes that I had missed at the bottom of the bag, each with strange names like *MS-KERMIT, SLIP* and *WINSOCK.* She told me that I would need each of these programs to access the university's lab from home.

The words bounced around in my head: I could access the campus network from home?! I spent the rest of that afternoon installing new, strange Windows 3.1 software: *Trumpet Winsock, SLIP* and *NCSA Mosaic* were nothing like my MS-DOS terminal programs. There was apparently more to the Internet than I could see using the text-based terminal I had been using for months in the lab. That evening I got the software configured and made my first dialling attempt to the campus Internet server using *Trumpet Winsock…* I launched the *NCSA Mosaic* "web browser" program, and as I watched my first graphical web page load, my world changed forever.

Doom, Revisited

Since the day I had played it on my uncle's computer a year earlier, *Doom* became like an old ex-girlfriend or boyfriend to me. Sure, you've had a few passionate nights together but due to bad timing or bad luck, in the end the chemistry wasn't there. After a few unreturned phone calls, you shelve your feelings for a few weeks. The weeks become months, and eventually you run into them at the mall and have to make a split-second decision: do I say hi or do I keep walking and pretend I didn't see them?

It was another one of my many weekend trips to the City, and I was wandering around the mall in a daze. There were now *three* computer stores to peruse games at, each in opposite corners of the mall. As I walked from one store to the next, I saw a huge metal and plastic kiosk surrounded by parents and kids set up in the middle of the hall.

The ring of people gave way to a boy who stood in the centre, wearing a heavy plastic helmet on his head. The helmet dangled from a flimsy metal gantry on wires; cables ran from the helmet to a large computer and TV monitor nearby. People gawked at the television screen as the boy wandered through a dark room. A shotgun blast echoed through the mall, and I realized that he was playing *Doom* hooked up to a Virtual Reality visor. The VR phenomenon was sweeping through North America and enterprising mall kiosk owners were looking to make a quick buck, selling VR-Doom to kids at a vicious rate of ten dollars for five minutes of play.

Even though I knew I could play *Doom* at home in the comfort of my computer chair on my IBM PS/1, there was something irrevocably cool about the same game in VR. But I refused to drop ten bucks on a game I could pirate for free at home, and resolved to come back after I had done my computer game shopping. If I had ten bucks left to spare, I'd give it a shot.

I came back an hour later and the kiosk had just closed. I thought: no big deal, I'll just come back next week!

For one reason or another my family did not return to the same mall for over a month. When I walked my habitual circuit between the computer stores, the kiosk was no longer there. In its place was an elderly couple giving away Christian bibles at a folding table. I had lost my chance to rekindle a fling with my hot yet nasty ex.

The *Doom* craze had not only spread to malls – it also had spawned numerous BBSs devoted specifically to playing multiplayer "deathmatches". These multi-node or multi-line BBSs allowed *Doom* players to compete with one another for the most kills using specialized software and expensive computer setups that most kids couldn't afford. Although I was keen on playing my first graphical multiplayer game over the phone line, I was gutted when I found out that the *Doom*-specific BBSs charged hourly fees for the service! Some of the boards were making thousands of dollars every month by letting players to call in, blow one another up into giblets, and brag about their kills. Being a teenager without a credit card, and wise enough not to try pilfering my mother's credit card, I gave up on playing *Doom* over the phone lines.

There was one last place I thought I might be able to play a multiplayer networked game of *Doom;* it was the only place that I knew had a network of PCs: the campus computer lab. I recruited Robert and Trevor to join me on campus, so we might play a deathmatch together. My plans were thwarted almost immediately when my mother dropped us off at the lab… there was a new sign taped to the door: "NO DOOM ON LAB COMPUTERS!" Apparently hundreds of other students had the same idea too, and campus administrators had summarily banned it from all campus labs. A decade later, the author of *Masters of Doom* described similar scenes happening at several universities throughout the United States; networked multiplayer was so popular that it had brought campus computer networks to a grinding halt. Some universities and colleges had even installed programs that searched for *Doom* installation folders on the computer and deleted them on sight.

My mother's university was one of them.

The timing was never right for *Doom* and I, and it eluded me for years. I didn't bother to pirate the registered version from any of the BBSes I frequented, electing to try other newer games with my download credits instead. When *Doom 2* came out a year later and my friend Andrew regaled me with tales about his gory adventures, I dumbly listened to him and realized that I had lost interest in the franchise altogether. I wouldn't play the second and third chapters of the game until I was in my twenties, and my first multiplayer deathmatch was when I was 34. By then, it was too late – the ship had sailed.

I'm sorry, *Doom*. It wasn't you; it wasn't me. It was just bad luck.

Hard Lessons At Play Me

I was broke and there was no Christmas money on the horizon for quite some time. My mother and father had their own financial problems to deal with and were sick of hearing about computers and computer games; the last thing they wanted to hear was my latest micro-loan pitch for a new game.

There were new games out there and my weekend visits to the mall were making me mighty itchy for the latest and greatest game. The two-diskette affairs of late-1980's games were now over, and most games now had eight, ten and twelve high-density disks jammed inside of the boxes. CD-ROMs were cracking open the game market, but most developers were busy trying to lure new buyers with full-motion video and Redbook audio music tracks. CD-ROM re-releases of floppy disk games were the current fad. This created problems for the average software pirate with a 14.4Kbaud modem – it took hours to transfer a ten-diskette game over the phone lines at 1.3 Kilobytes per second. The file sizes dissuaded few hardcore pirates of course, but for someone who shared a phone line with an adolescent sister and two working parents, it made downloading tricky.

I was pressed for options and fell back to my only source of potential income: trading in some of my older PC games for cash. There were several computer stores that took trade-ins, but most of them did this on a consignment basis. Consignment meant that I would have to give them the game, wait for them to sell it – and *if* it sold I would receive 30-50% of the final selling price. In theory this was a great way to recoup some of my initial investment on computer games, but I was desperate for cash and the prospect of waiting weeks or months for my used game to sell was excruciating. I wanted something to play *today*.

I brought nine of my PC games I was prepared to part with, and went to my least favourite store in the mall: *Play Me*. The store always seemed to be devoid of customers despite its gargantuan walls of computer games, always manned by the same clerk who eyeballed customers from the safety of his till. The lanky, bulgy-eyed clerk with greasy uncombed hair was in his mid-forties, and he looked like the slimy alien shopkeeper "Fester Blatz" from *Space Quest III*. I despised going into his store, and he was always scrutinizing his customers as if they were going to rob him blind. But I had little choice that day as *Play Me* was the only store I knew of that didn't do consignments. Fester gave straight cash or trade-in value for computer games.

I walked over with my two heavy bags of computer games, which represented the bulk of my computer game purchases for the Amstrad from day one. Among them were my prized *Carmen Sandiego* games and *Out of This World*. I was loath to part with any of them because not only did they represent my only worldly assets, but they were also the games my sister and I had played together

"Hi… can I sell these here?"

The man jutted his chin at my bags. "Yeah. Lemme see whatcha got."

I gingerly removed the treasures from my plastic grocery bags and placed them in a neat two-foot high stack in front of him. He glanced at each game in turn, casually tossing them to the side like playing cards. I winced at the dents and creases he was no doubt making on the corners of my pristine game boxes as they landed on the glass counter top. He grimaced and wiped his hand against his stubbled face. "Could prolly give twenny bucks for 'em. Cash."

I thought I had misheard him. "I mean, how much for *all* of them?"

"Twenny bucks I said!"

I had spent years working all kinds of miserable farm jobs to earn enough money to buy each of these games. There was at least four hundred dollars sitting on the counter, and he was offering me twenty dollars for *all* of them? He must have seen the disbelief on my face because he quickly added, "Or I could give ya more fer store credit… I guess."

I wanted to throw them back into the bag and stomp out of the store and tell him where to stick his twenty dollar bill. I wanted to grab him by the collar of his stained white tee shirt and say in my best Clint Eastwood impression, 'Do you *know* what I had to *do* to get these buddy?' But I saw my mom standing outside of the store staring at me and impatiently tapping her watch. It was time to go. I had no money, and the idea of coming home with nothing from a trip to the City was unimaginable.

I choked back my ire and tried to bargain as best I could. "Fine, I'll take store credit. But I want to keep these two." I rescued *Where in Europe is Carmen Sandiego?* and *Out of this World* from the pile.

"Awright that works. Well, take yer pick," he flicked his finger absently at a wall of games behind me, "any game off that shelf over there."

I walked over and skimmed the titles on the shelf. They were all budget-priced games of a much lower quality than the games I was used to buying. The Sierra On-Line, LucasArts and Origin Systems games were nowhere to be found, and lame Accolade and Activision titles dotted the landscape. I had just been screwed and I couldn't do anything about it. My heart was pounding. I didn't want to do this anymore. I hated the clerk for exploiting me. I hated myself for being too sheepish to argue. I wished my mom wasn't standing at the entrance waiting to leave. I grabbed the only game on the shelf that had the MicroProse logo on it and appeared to be an adventure game. The rest were all arcade titles and lame budget re-releases of games from the 1980s.

I examined the box cover: it depicted a man being chased by women on a desolate landscape. The protagonist looked a little like Han Solo met Roger Wilco and made a bastard man-baby together, yielding a child that had neither of their good looks nor taste in fashion. The box art title blazed in a pseudo-holographic foil clearly meant to draw one's eyes away from the substandard artwork: *Rex Nebular and the Cosmic Gender Bender*.

I stewed in my seat the entire ride home. My mother prodded me a couple of times about the new game inside of my bag, but I did not want to admit to her that I had just gotten fleeced by an alien scumbag. Her reaction would have been worse than mine and I feared she would drive us back to the mall and embarrass me in a confrontation with the slimy Fester Blatz.

The box was heavy and I rifled through the contents – the manual was reasonably large and it came with a free hint book. It was a MicroProse game, published by the wizards who made *Railroad Tycoon* and *Pirates!*, so there was an outside chance this game might actually be fun. But MicroProse was more known for its strategy titles and I had never heard of them making adventure games. As we drove I found my anger giving way to sadness: I had just lost games I had treasured for years, all because I was a little desperate for something new.

Rex Nebular proved to be quite different than I had expected. It was obviously a spoof of *Space Quest* (which itself was a spoof of pop culture sci-fi) or at least paid serious homage to it with its intrepid and bumbling protagonist, Rex. *Rex Nebular* played much like a point-and-click Sierra or LucasArts adventure game involving logic puzzles and inventory items. The game's twisted sense of humour grew on me, likely because it appealed to immature adults more than mature adolescents. I had been ripped off trading seven games for this one, but at least the game was funnier than it deserved to be.

Aside from the adventure-style gaming and warped humour, *Rex Nebular* had a single moment of payoff that genuinely surprised me. Early in the game, Rex finds himself marooned on an island. He spies from a distance a beautiful Hawaiian-looking woman emerge from the ocean in the nude. Her large breasts undulate as she walks onto the beach.

That is to say, a brownish collection of pixels roughly in the shape of a human being moves frame-by-frame from the blue area of the screen to the yellow area of the screen. Two darker points of brown-black imply the existence of nipples on the animated character's body.

But that was enough to make my teenaged eyes pop into pie plates, Looney Tunes-style. I snapped up the telephone handset and called a few of my friends and bragged to them that I saw a naked woman in a computer game. And this time, unlike *Leisure Suit Larry* which only teased the player with the promise of digital nudity, *Rex Nebular* delivered the real deal for three whole seconds!

Hint book in hand, I cheated my way through the entire game with the hope that this scene was only a taste of the glut of smut hidden within. A couple of hours later I finished the game and was bummed to find out that it had no more naked ladies. Still, nudity in a mass-market computer game in the 1990s was nearly unheard of and I had the bits to prove it.

The following week, during school lunch hour, I brought the diskettes to Andrew's house and endured a half hour of frenzied copying. Andrew told me he'd play it that night and get back to me, disbelieving my bragging about cartoon nudity.

The next morning in Math class I leaned over my desk and gave Andrew a 'So? Did you see it?' look. He replied, one eyebrow raised, lips parted in a half-smile with a thumbs-up. Anthony and David, two desks over, smiled and gave the thumbs up. Apparently all of them had gotten together at Andrew's house to collectively gawk at the nude scene. Mission accomplished.

A month later I walked past *Play Me* and saw my seven used games on the shelf, priced at forty-dollars each. Blatz caught my eye and smirked, "Come trade more games here any time guy."

Bastard.

Zero Day Warez

I had finagled a phone number to what was obviously an "elite" or pirate Bulletin Board System. The custom ANSI art drawn by one of the sysops, the gigabyte of "live philez", the weekly rotating CD-ROM archive of even more warez, the daily flow of "0day" files, together made *DARK ViSiONZ* the first real elite BBS I frequented.[50]

Getting an account involved surviving a gauntlet. The first step was passing a New User Password or "NUP" check . Unlike public access BBSs which encouraged visitors to create new accounts, elite boards required a guest to enter a password *before* they were allowed to create a new account. Think of it as a secret knock on the treehouse door before entrance is allowed. This "security through obscurity" approach was a simple and effective to deter law enforcement officials from cracking down on pirate boards: if you knew the NUP, it probably meant you were a friend of a fellow buccaneer or at least frequented other elite boards. I fell into the latter category – I had read a conversation between two bragging buccaneers swapping war stories on another board and wrote down the phone number and NUP before the sysop (wisely) intervened and deleted their

---

[50] 0Day (pronounced "zero-day") warez was pirated software that had been released by the cracking group the very same day. The distribution process over phone lines meant that warez often took days or weeks and even months to flow from the original source – a cracking group – to the end user. The further away the destination BBS from the source, the longer it took for the freshest warez to arrive. There was an exception: the most elite boards had sysops that dialled long-distance to WHQs (World Headquarters) of cracking groups and downloaded the files directly from the origin. Large cracking groups even had National and Regional HQ's that acted as waystations and distribution nodes for local BBSs. This ingeniously decentralized distribution model was completely informal and relied upon cooperation and trust between sysops and cracking groups. It was also massively illegal.

messages.

I tried to get an account on *DARK ViSiONZ* as quickly as I could. Many elite boards with the hottest 0day files rotated or changed their NUP once a week, and sometimes once a day. I entered the NUP and was invited to create a new account. I breathed a sigh of relief and was surprised by a barrage of questions. "Are you a law enforcement official? (You are required by law to tell me!)", "What is the area code of the FLT USHQ?", "List three users that recommended you for this board." It was less like an interview and more like a fraternity pledge ritual.

It took me a minute to dig up the area code of the *Fairlight* cracking group's United States' Headquarters – it was buried in a ".NFO" file I had found a week earlier. I only had the two handles of the pirates that were bragging about their exploits on the other board, so I entered their handles as personal references. My heart was pounding. Surely the sysop would see through my pathetic attempt to pass as "31337" (elite)… and out me as a "lamer".

When the Q&A was done I was invited to enter a handle and password. I could only think of the game I had been playing the most recently: *Wing Commander: Privateer.* I needed a handle that was dark and edgy, that would blend in with the other pirates on the board. My mind raced through the quadrants of space in *Privateer*, thinking of their various systems, agricultural planets, military bases, pleasure bases, mining bases and pirate bases. Oxford. Helen. New Constantinople. Magdalene. Padre. Pentonville. None of my usual haunts on pirate runs had much venom to their names. My mind wandered to the far corners of quadrants I rarely ventured due to the danger of lack of fuel. Burton. Speke. War. Famine. Ah ha! *Pestilence.* I loved the dark apocalyptic tone of the name cribbed from the Old Testament of the Bible. But the name was lacking something... something that would identify me as a booty-haulin'-warezin'-modemer-4-life. The inspiration came to me in a flash and I hit the caps-lock key to engage super-elite-speak:

```
Enter a Handle: PESTiLENCE

Thank you. The sysop will verify your information.
```

I hit enter and the line suddenly hung up. What if the sysop found out I was just some farm kid poking his nose into places he had no right to be? What if this was a sting operation and the cops were collecting information so they could send in a SWAT team that evening? What if I made a mistake on the application form and the sysop thought I was a cop? Would the sysop call all his buddies and blacklist me from every pirate board in the area code?

I waited a week before daring to dial *DARK ViSiONZ* again. When it connected I tried my username and password........ which now worked! When I got past the austere black login screen, I broke out in a mischievous grin. The board had customized ANSI art that scrolled past my eyes for two or three pages like an enormous rolling tapestry. I had grown used to rather bland text menus on other BBSs, and the contrast blew me away. This one had gorgeously drawn menus with an overhanging skeleton with a scythe in its hand. The board ran on a new BBS software package called *Iniquity*, and the grey-on-black colour scheme was the nightmarish dream of a death metal guitarist. I was granted the lowest possible security level, which gave me a handful of credits to spend on a few megs of downloads, and gave me access to a few of the message bases.

DARK ViSiONZ became my first online home away from home. I learned how to blend in with the regulars by pretending I was just as elite as they were, riffing in "l33tsp33k" and dropping cracking group acronyms as if I was active in the "scene". As far as the members of this board were concerned, "phr34kz" were "k-rad" and law enforcement officials were lamerz, "l33chz" should be banned from all boards and "c0urierz" were always welcome. Life on *DARK ViSiONZ* involved the kind of linguistic membership politics seen in high school hockey team dressing rooms and prison yards.

It took more than a week to burn up my paltry download credits. Over a ten day period I downloaded a copy of *Command and Conquer* one diskette at a time. This ten megabyte game introduced me to the idea of a "rip". The game was originally released on CD-ROM, making downloading it over a 14.4 KBaud connection impossible. Cracking groups came up with a clever solution that pleased some and irritated many: they stripped or "ripped" out the large volumes of data dedicated to full-motion video and music from the CD.[51]

At the time I had no idea what a "rip" was and assumed the version of *Command and Conquer* I was downloading was the complete game. I only found out two years later, after buying the game on CD-ROM, that I had missed out on all of the video cutscenes that explained the game's story and mission objectives!

The stripped-down version of the game made little difference to my friends at school, though. *Command and Conquer* proved to be even more popular than *Stunts* and spread through my friends like wildfire. It did not take long before the conversation at school shifted away from *MacBolo* to squad-based combat strategies and the best ways of nuking the enemy. Although I was clearly being used by my friends for my software connections, I enjoyed the inflated ego I got from pretending I was an elite data courier like *Johnny Mnemonic*. Besides, bringing new warez to school meant that I now could talk with my friends about the new games I was playing.

Despite my ability to blend in with the locals on *DARK ViSiONS*, my tenure only lasted a couple of months. I had no fresh source of warez to upload to the board, which meant I had zero credits to spend on downloads. I could only drool over the hundreds of megabytes of games that were at my fingertips, yet just out of reach. I needed zero-day warez that I could upload to

---

[51] In many cases cracking groups released add-on packs that allowed the user to add the stripped data back into the game. A "music pack", for instance, restored the game's CD audio tracks (instead of the dead silence found in the original rip).

the board to build my reputation, and credz.

Elite BBSs were like treehouses hidden off in the woods, full of cliquey kids who only lowered the ladder if you knew the super-secret pirate's pass-code. Internet piracy was more like a dense jungle full of tiny villages, each with hidden paths interconnecting them. For the average Internet user in those days, finding warez on the Internet involved grabbing your best machete and hacking your way through a dense jungle of files and directories... searching village-by-village until you found a hidden pirate cache.

My weekend travails in the university computer lab were beginning to pay off: the Internet was becoming my chief source for warez, surpassing what I could find on local BBSs. I had gradually learned how to spelunk the dark corners of the World Wide Web and FTP sites for the good stuff, through exhaustive directory-by-directory searches for files.

Today, people who are looking for pirated software are one Google or Duck Duck Go search away from a downloadable file. But in the 1980s and 1990s there were no convenient search engines for tracking down warez – searchable directories like *Yahoo!* did not knowingly catalogue pirated software, and public FTP sites were advertised only as repositories of public domain software.

In the mid-1990's pirated software came from a variety of sources on the Internet: Usenet (an online discussion group service that allowed users to share files), private and public FTP sites, Internet Relay Chat (IRC), and even via e-mail. Many of these sources involved the configuration of complicated Windows software like Usenet news readers and IRC clients. I was an Internet newbie, and FTP proved to be the most efficient means for getting my hands on pirated files.

The most time intensive, yet fruitful, sources were public or "anonymous" FTP sites. These computer servers, often located at universities around the world, were repositories of free device drivers, programming tools, operating systems, shareware and freeware games, text files and more. Public FTPs were intended to be used by university students and staff who needed a centralized location where their daily free software needs could be met by the university server's administrator. Public FTPs followed an honourable ethic that had developed in the 1990s on the Internet: the free exchange of information.

Of course there is "free" as in "free beer" and "free" as in "freefalling off the back of a commercial delivery truck into my hands and copied to every computer in a 500 kilometre radius". Software pirates follow this second sense of free, and treated public FTP sites as repositories for their warez... a secret cave on an island where they could bury their treasure for others to find.

University FTP sites were targeted by pirates for several reasons. Compared to home PC's, university FTP servers had comparatively huge file storage – gigabytes of free space were available on most servers in in the mid-1990s. University FTP sites also tended to have laissez-faire administrators who rarely bothered to check the system's bandwidth use or security logs. Universities also had a very large, very receptive crowd of frugal users that were only too happy to download and upload warez, possessing more brains and free time than money: undergraduate students.

A public FTP server like *wuarchive.wustl.edu* (Washington University in St. Louis Public FTP) began its conversion into a hidden pirate base in a typical manner. First, an enterprising pirate would create a subdirectory on the server called ".warez" or ".philez" in the "/pub" (public) directory. (The period before the name is important, as this prevented the directory from being visibly shown when browsed by the average person.) In effect this created a hidden folder where files could be stashed.

The second step was simpler: generously uploading pirated software into the hidden folder. In the third and final step, the pirate advertised their hidden booty location on online services like Internet Relay Chat rooms, Web message boards, and Usenet discussion groups, where greedy leechers like me waited hungrily.

Within minutes of the announcement, the FTP server was hammered by users trying to leech files from the hidden folder, to the bafflement of the system administrator (if he or she was paying attention at all). If an administrator *was* watching the FTP server's bandwidth usage, he or she would sometimes "kill" or reset the FTP server and boot off the glut of greedy leeches. An especially cagey admin might dig through each subdirectory of the /pub directory, looking for hidden names like ".warez" nested within. On rare occasions the hidden folder was deleted, but let's face it: university IT jobs were often staffed by students, and that was too much work for the average, slovenly, Dennis Nedry-type admin.

It was likely a combination of those factors that led to my first strike on a repository of pirate booty. It was past midnight and I had spent an hour digging through subdirectories of the wuarchive.wustl.edu FTP site. Just as the search was beginning to feel futile, I struck gold when I found a stash of files hidden away in a nest of directories: /pub/drivers/3com/ms-dos/.d0nt/.l00k/.h3r3/.l0s3r

Inside the directory were sixteen 1.5 megabyte files named WIN95B1.ZIP, WIN95B2.ZIP and so on... in total there were twenty megs of software in the directory. Incredibly, the files appeared to be a "beta" or pre-release set of diskettes for the upcoming Windows 95 operating system. Windows 95 was Microsoft's new flagship operating system that was going to knock the socks off both Windows 3.11 and MS-DOS 6.22.

But twenty megabytes! The idea of downloading that much data over a phone line made my head swim. It was like trying to load a galleon worth of gold one coin at a time into a birch bark canoe. It would take over four hours to download all of the files over my 14.4 Kbaud modem. Worse, the campus dial-up Internet connection had a two-hour time limit, and would sharply hang up on me at exactly two hours even if I was in the midst of a download.

After a half hour I had managed to download two of the disks and began feeling desperate. If the system admin caught on to the pirate folder, it would be deleted within hours or days and I might not ever get the complete set of disks to install Windows 95 on my computer.

The solution to my time problem came a few minutes later while I was messing around with the server's UNIX command shell. My mother's account gave me access to five megabytes of personal storage in her student directory on the campus server. I could use her personal storage folder as a temporary holding place by transferring the files from Washington to the university server, then copy each file from the server to one of the PC's in the college computer lab, and *then* copy the file from the PC to a 3.5″ diskette. It was a convoluted process, and involved a trip to campus and a big pile of floppy disks, but it sure was better than trying to download twenty megs over a sketchy phone line at 14.4 Kbaud.

That weekend I had a pile of twenty one blank diskettes stashed in my backpack, ready for my clandestine operation in the campus computer lab. When we arrived at the university I went straight to the lab where it was full of students fulfilling their roles in the grand paper mill. I logged in to a computer and loaded up a graphical FTP program called WS-FTP, connecting the computer to the wuarchive.wustl.edu server thousands of kilometres away. When I began downloading the files over the campus's massive data pipe, I gasped. I had never *imagined* speeds like this were possible: 100.. 200.. 300 kilobytes per second! The download speed crept up incrementally, finally hovering at 450 kilobytes per second… the equivalent of one high-density floppy disk every three seconds. At this rate I would have all of the files downloaded to the lab computer in under one minute. Incredible!

Copying the files from the computer to the floppy drive was another story. Each diskette took over a minute to write the 1.44 meg file – a painful, laborious process of disk swapping. The neighbouring students gave me sidelong glances at the huge stack of 3.5-inch floppies on the desk, making me even more nervous as I swapped each disk for a half hour. I was worried that at any minute some computer department administrator dressed in a Schutzstaffel uniform was going to show up and yell 'Halt Schweinhunde!'

But that didn't happen. By lunch I had copied the entire contents of the hidden pirate cache onto floppy disks, and had them stored safely away in my backpack. I scooted out of the lab and buzzed around my mother's office, prodding her to wrap up her work so we could leave early. I *had* to know what Windows 95 was going to look like on my PS/1. Windows for Workgroups (3.11) was only a handful of disks – just imagine how amazing Windows 95 had to be if it took up over thirty megs of space!

At home I unpacked each ZIP file to my hard drive, one floppy disk at a time, then copied the files back to the disk. Rinse and repeat, sixteen times. Unzipping the files from floppy was painfully slow – it took two hours just to get all of the files properly unpacked.

I began the installation process, which had a slick automated installation program… far better than any installer I had seen in a computer game. But like every other installation program, it required a lot of manual labour: every five minutes it prompted me to insert the next disk in the set. With over sixteen diskettes, this was going to take the entire evening.

By ten o'clock at night I had finally inserted the last diskette and waited for the installation program to complete. I felt excitement building in my stomach and shivered at the prospect of using an entire new operating system… months ahead of the release date!

That was until the computer beeped and I got an unexpected prompt:

```
Copying files….
Insert Disk #17.
```

Disk #17? What the hell?

I counted my pile of floppy disks twice: there were sixteen. I began to sweat and thought back to my frenzied file copying in the college lab earlier that morning. Had I missed a file somehow? Impossible. There only had been files in the folder up to WIN95B16.ZIP and nothing else.

I dialled the college Internet server to double-check, and when I finally connected my FTP program to wuarchive.wustl.edu I gasped. The pirate directory was *gone!* Some Washington University server administrator must have noticed the little cache of booty and wiped it from existence.

I spent the next month searching in vain for the rest of the missing files from the Windows 95 beta diskette set. FTP searches on the Internet turned up nothing – it seemed that Washington University had run its well bone dry. The only place that had the files was my local warez BBS, DARK ViSiONS. But I had no download credits available to download the missing files. It was excruciating seeing the files *just* out of reach, but begging the sysop for download credz was tantamount to labeling myself a leech or lamer.

In the end I gave up on being an illicit tester of Windows 95 beta, frustrated by my own lack of elite connections and Internet savvy. This would have never happened if I had a faster modem, personal phone line, or both.

From Party Line to Private Line

The neighbours were complaining. Every night around nine o'clock, our nearest neighbour picked up the telephone to call her sister and was greeted by a screeching whine on the line. Not knowing the anthropogenic source of these alien transmissions, she had even called the telephone company to complain about noise on the line.

It didn't take long for word to spread to my parents, and they knew right away that my modem was the cause of all the fuss. Until the early 1990s, many of Canada's rural communities did not have private telephone lines running to a residence, and instead used a shared or "party" line system. A Party Line was a single telephone line that was spliced at a junction point in a neighbourhood so the line could be shared among two or three neighbouring homes. Each house had its own special telephone ring that signalled whom the incoming call was meant for. House #1 had a single long ring, house #2 had a quick double-ring, and house #3 had an impressively staccato triple-ring. Our house, beyond the second, had the short and sweet "ring-ring!"

Party Lines were mischievous delights for kids like me. Because three houses shared the same line, one could pick up the phone handset and listen in on the latest neighbourly gossip and naughty romantic talk.

Between the three houses in our acreage development there were nine adolescents and five adults, all competing for a scarce analog service. Everyone wanted to talk to their friends and family after school, my father wanted to talk with his construction business clients, and I wanted to ride the line on a wave of bits for as long as possible.

Like all other technical problems we faced in the 1990s, the solution was simple: spend more money. The phone company had recently upgraded its local exchange circuits and was offering farmers a deal: for the low, low price of $800 the company would run a new "private line" to the residence.

The prospect of buying a private telephone line generated more argument at our house than the purchase of the Amstrad and IBM PS/1 put together. My mother was dead-set against it, reminding us that none of us had the money to pay for it; the private line was only a want and not a need. My sister and I changed strategies and appealed to my father's ability to rationalize any purchase: we told him that he could use the private line for his construction business. That single rationalization made the sale, and a week later the telephone company sent out a linesman. We eagerly watched him hook up the new telephone box on the power pole outside of the house. Even my dad was excited.

The new line came with a catch: I could only use the modem after 9pm when no one else needed to make a phone call and/or when my father's business clients were asleep. That suited me just fine: the BBSs I frequented and the campus dial-up modem pool was busy earlier in the evening anyway.

A private line meant no more random disconnections because one of the dozen people who had access to the party line picked up the phone in midst of a transmission. I still had my own family's phone habits to contend with, but the implicit agreement was that no one else wanted to use the phone after 9PM anyway.

1995: Grade Eleven

Return to the Mac Lab

The eleventh grade was that uncomfortable place between life as a pimply tenth grade guppy and the end of over twelve years in the public education system. Students were expected to have started making plans for their post-secondary lives; leaving behind the trappings of childhood like *Star Trek: The Next Generation,* Saturday morning cartoons and lunch hour *MacBolo* tournaments.

Firmly entrenched in all of those things, I wanted none of what adulthood had to offer. Even in high school, I was already homesick for the simple pleasures of elementary school life like lunch boxes and hockey trading cards.

So when I had a chance to get my hands on computer games at school, I leapt at every opportunity. In the eleventh grade, this meant taking Information Processing 20 and returning to Mr. M's Macintosh lab.

Ultima VIII: Pagan

I had finally found a small but solid community of PC players that were happy to trade games with me. My friend Andrew did not relent in torturing me with stories about his most recent purchase: a computer role-playing game set in a dark, murderous world where he had the power to summon demons and cruelly manipulate gods to do his bidding. One day he brought the box to school and teased me with the cover art which consisted of a large, flaming, pentagram. This kind of "satanic" symbol was forbidden in our prairie hick school full of Catholic believers, and we both knew it. The game was called *Ultima VIII: Pagan* and the second I saw it I knew I had to have it for myself. The next day we made a swap: his copy of *Pagan* for my copy of *Wing Commander: Privateer*.

Computer role-playing games were new to me. Aside from *Legend of the Red Dragon* which was a completely textual affair, I had never played a graphical RPG before. In fact, until that day my experiences on a PC were limited to Sierra and LucasArts adventure games, strategy titles from Microprose like *Railroad Tycoon* and *X-COM*, and shareware arcade games like *One Must Fall 2097, Crystal Caves* and *Skunny Kart*. Each genre equipped me with a different set of gaming skills. Adventure games were dialogue-driven stories that required logical problem solving. Strategy games were more about managing and balancing complex rules and reasoning through combat scenarios. Arcade games exercised the parts of me that loved white-knuckled action and quick reflexes. There seemed to be no single genre that knitted all of these genres together into one experience. That was, until I played *Ultima VIII: Pagan*.

Pagan had me on the edge of my seat in the first five minutes of the game. It began with a grisly execution on the end of a pier; I watched helplessly as a man was beheaded by an executioner and the man's wife howled in horror. As the executioner's axe chopped off the head there was a *splort!*, and his head rolled off the dock leaving behind a trail of gore. The head fell into the sea with a *sploosh!,* and into the maw of an antediluvian fish that looked like an alligator crossed with a coelacanth. The fish chomped down and roared as it disappeared back into the watery depths.

Even in 1994, computer game violence was nothing new. *Doom* had been out for over a year and its raw, atmospheric gore had become a part of the gamer collective unconscious. But *Doom*'s visceral gore was inherently different than the gore in *Ultima VIII*. *Pagan* had a more psychologically engaging tone, reminiscent of tolling funerary bells than *Doom*'s comically violent chainsaw massacres. *Pagan*'s isometric perspective pulled in tightly around the protagonist, making movement and exploration an anxiety-provoking experience… I never knew if an evil spirit or skeleton or giant spider was waiting for me just around the corner. *Doom* relied far more upon "boo scares" and adrenaline-pumping terror like a 1980s horror B-movie. *Pagan* creeped me out in subtler ways, reminding me of films like *The Shining* and *The Exorcist*.

Musically, *Pagan* was the first time I had heard a fully orchestrated MIDI soundtrack that painted each scene of the game with a sonic brush. Some music compositions expressed the wondrousness and supernatural power of *Pagan*, while others were dirges for a dying world. For the first time in my life I felt truly rooted in the fantasy world I was charged with saving… or in this case, exploiting.

The next day at school, Andrew and I excitedly swapped notes.

"Man! Did you see that dude's head pop off and his wife bawling after? Crazy!"

"Ha ha! Yeah! Did you try walking up to the Tempest lady and pissing her off? It's hilarious!"

"What about *Privateer*? Did you find the Retros yet? Or make it to New Detroit?"

"Ha ha ha! Yeah!" Andrew affected the tone of a street-side fire and brimstone fundamentalist preacher and howled out,

"HEATHEN! Taste the purifying fire of the lorrrrrrrd!"

I croaked back at him in my best Kilrathi, "Monkey-boy, you make me laughhhh!"

We spent the rest of the week putting one another in stitches, exchanging witty bits of dialogue from each game. It was the first time I had even spoken openly in the kind of annoying for-fans-only nerdspeak that was more appropriate at a Star Trek convention than a public place. And I was loving it.

While we geeked out on *Ultima* and *Wing Commander*, the academic pressures of the eleventh grade ramped up. Our teachers made it clear to us that the tenth grade was only an "easing-in" experience, meant to ready us for the "real work" this year. Instead of having a single class devoted to Science, now there were three separate courses: Chemistry, Physics and Biology. Our homework load was expected to at least triple.

More homework was only the tip of the iceberg. What drove an icicle into our hearts was the teacher we were assigned for our Physics and Chemistry classes. For years the scuttlebutt on the school bus was that "Mr. G" was the toughest and strictest teacher in the school, and God help you if you got him for Chemistry or Physics. Andrew and I had him for both. *Gulp*.

Our first day with Mr. G confirmed every rumour I had heard. He was the only teacher in the entire hillbilly school district to wear a three-piece suit to work every day, cycling through a different suit for each day of the week. I could have set my watch to his perfectly coiffed hair, perfectly square half-Windsor knot on his tie, and polished penny-loafers. His writing on the overhead projector was rigidly font-like, as if his hand was a laser printer. He spoke by enunciating each syllable of a word, and corrected the lazy farmer-slur that all of his students used in class. In other words, Mr. G had a stick up his butt that had a stick up *its* butt.

The wisecrackery and clever comebacks that had earned Andrew a place in the hearts of my friends and I throughout junior high were turned to dust in G's class. Not only did he not tolerate any "funny business" in his class, but he absolutely detested anyone who spoke out of turn. Our job as students was to quietly enter the room, sit down with our backs in an erect posture ("no slouching!"), listen to his lecture and take notes diligently, then depart silently. "And do not, under any circumstances, track mud into my class room with your *dir-ty* shoes," he warned.

All of us withered in fear under the overwatch and tutelage of this rigid sentry who could have taught East Berlin police proper discipline.

Andrew and I needed an outlet from the intense pressure of the eleventh grade, and it came out in weird ways. Andrew discovered that outlet when he found a particularly evil demonic god with twisted goat horns in *Ultima VIII* called "Pyros" (pronounced 'pie-roas'). Pyros was a god of pain and fire, whose only joy was in tormenting the denizens of Pagan with his powers. Andrew whispered as he described the god to me during Chemistry class, and G turned to us barking, "Boys. Is there something more important than redox reactions you'd like to share with us?"

I turned red and quickly muttered, "Um. No, Mr. G."

As Mr. G resumed writing equations on his overhead projector transparency, Andrew leaned over and quietly whispered, "I bow to your will, *Gar-gos!*"

It was a cruel mockery of our teacher's last name. I bit my lip trying to stifle a giggle.

Again he whispered, this time with a growl to his voice and shook his fist in a parody of Pyros, "Foolish mortal! Your flesh will *burn* in my chemistry class!"

This was too much. I guffawed like a choking horse and Mr. G' head shot up from looking down at his transparency. I covered my mouth and tried to stifle the laugh with an exaggerated cough.

"Um. Sorry Gargo… Mr. G. I had something in my throat."

The demonic academic god "Gargos" became a private joke that only Andrew and I enjoyed, and because of that we had an intimacy only known among the nerdiest nerds who share a common language. We had a pet name for our archenemy and it relieved the tension of the academic pressure cooker we were living in – all thanks to a computer role-playing game.

Only a few years earlier, computer games were a casual entertainment shared between friends alongside soccer and hockey and Saturday morning cartoons. Now, for myself and for Andrew, computer games were eclipsing all other forms of entertainment and my friendships began to reflect that reality. These adolescent jabs at our Chemistry and Physics teacher served to cement a friendship that had once been solely based on a common love for computer games.

As the eleventh grade wore on, my friendships became differentiated. My old gang of friends from elementary school became my weekend friendships for outdoor sports and trips to the City to watch movies at the theatre. The friends who played computer games were a separate clan, speaking in the geekily cyphered languages of *Wing Commander* and *Ultima*. There was a huge emotional and interpersonal gap between these friend groups, and inevitably as my interest in computers eclipsed all else I became more distant from my old gang. The slow disintegration of our elementary school group was another step towards a different way of life solely organized around the computer.

My First Home Page

In the 1990s, Information Processing 20 was considered a "terminal" high school course, because there were no courses that followed it in the twelfth grade. This meant that our teacher had to try packing as many advanced modules into it as possible, making it hell for computer illiterates and heaven for dorks like me.

By 1995, the World Wide Web had finally entered the public consciousness in Canada and our curriculum had finally caught up to the idea of students using the Internet for education.

In the wake of the SchoolNet Flame War fiasco, Mr. M wasn't overly excited about the prospect of his class getting involved in online forums again. He turned his attention to learning how to browse the web using *Netscape* instead, and handed out assignments that amounted to easter egg hunts using popular indexing websites like *Yahoo!* and *Infoseek*.

It was old hat to a grizzled cyberspace explorer like me, and I begged him for an alternate assignment.

"Awright. How about you make a web page?"

I perked up and beamed at him. Now *that* was something in my wheelhouse!

"Sure! I even have five megs of web space on my mom's university account and I already know how to write HTML and-"

"-Alright, alright! Get at it!" he chuckled.

Finding images to use on WWW servers and writing the HTML code was the easy part. The problem was that I didn't know what to *say* on the page, because it wasn't clear to me what a homepage was supposed to be about. I browsed around a bunch of *GeoCities* homepages, and noticed that most of them were simple one-page biographies of the author, and a handful of links to web sites they enjoyed.

An uncredited photograph of a young boy in a straw hat and eating a watermelon, circa 1940s-1950s.

It began innocently. I began building a homepage about myself, with some… ahem, poetic license. Uncomfortable with my looks, I found the idea of showing a photo of myself on the Internet unnerving, so I downloaded a scanned black-and-white photograph of a young boy wearing a straw hat eating a hunk of watermelon. To this day, I have no idea why I thought this photo expressed the idea of *me* at all. I was not fair-skinned, freckled or redheaded. I didn't own a straw hat. I was a teenager; not a ten-year-old. And I certainly wasn't the subject of an American prize-winning photographer.

I got about three lines into the biography when I ran out of things to say about myself, and began to fabricate full-tilt lies in the biography. Captain of the high school volleyball team? Sure. Straight-A student? Why not. Coolest kid in the eleventh grade? Who could prove otherwise.

It took about three days to finish an assignment that was supposed to have taken me the entire month, and I was looking forward to pissing away the rest of the semester playing *MacBolo* while the rest of the students feverishly clicked on school-approved links in *Netscape Navigator*.

I uploaded the single *index.html* file and photograph to my mother's university server, and grinned as the page slowly loaded in the browser. The class of twenty-five students shared a single 28.8Kbaud line, and the image slowly loaded one line at a time.

"I'm done, Mr. M!"

He walked over and glanced over my shoulder. I expected him to give me a thumbs-up, write a "10/10" in the assignment checkbox, and send me on my way to *MacBolo* nirvana.

Instead, he barked out to the class, "Hey, everyone. Come check this web page made by one of your own classmates!"

I was feeling pretty smug about it until I realized that my fellow classmates were going to read what I had written on the page.

Shit.

I lurched to the monitor's power button to turn it off, but it was too late. The page had finished loading.

Wayne stood behind me and yelped incredulously, "Volleyteam team? You got cut at try-outs!"

Then David chimed in, "Yeah, that's bullcrap Mr. M. That's not even a real photo of him!"

I turned a deep shade of wine red as twenty five kids crowded around the monitor, pointing out the various falsifications of my character.

When the feeding frenzy finally dispersed, I quickly deleted the files from my mom's university server and hoped no one would ever remember it.

A week passed, and the homepage incident faded into the

background radiation of high school drama like fist fights, alcohol binging and dating rumours. I mentally locked away the embarrassment and never heard from nor spoke a word of it again to anyone.

Until ten years later.

A handful of my friends and frenemies from the school got together for a beer, rehashing old times. Halfway through the night Wayne turned to me and said, with a demonic curl of his lip, "Hey, remember that time you told the whole school you were the captain of the volleyball team?"

A RAM Upgrade for the PS/1

The IBM PS/1 was only a year old and I was already feeling trapped by the constraints of its hardware. Andrew had a 486 DX-2/50 MHz and *eight* megabytes of RAM. *Ultima VIII* and *Wing Commander: Privateer* ran flawlessly on his computer, making saving and loading times almost imperceptible. Everything ran just a bit smoother on his machine compared to mine which "only" had a 486 SX/33 MHz processor with four megs of RAM. And of course Andrew did not let me forget that fact with weekly reminders that my IBM was the "inbred step-cousin" of his far superior PC.

The jabs at my PC were grating on me. The days when LucasArts and Sierra On-Line's adventure games pushed the limits of computing hardware were long over. Now, Origin Systems was the new leader in processor and memory-crushing technologies. The *Wing Commander* series was renowned for forcing gamers to upgrade their computers just to max out the audiovisual capabilities of the games.

I had a few hundred bucks in my bank account when I stumbled upon a brand new Origin Systems game that had been positively reviewed in a computer gaming magazine. At the computer store, the box cover immediately leapt out at me on the shelf: a monochromatic green X-ray image of a biomechanical three-fingered hand clawing upward. A small image in the corner of the box advertised the game as an "Interactive Movie".

At $74.99, *BioForge* was more expensive than any game I had bought to date – computer game or otherwise. I was already looking for excuses *not* to buy it when I found out that my computer didn't meet the minimum system requirements. The game recommended at least a 486 CPU with eight megs of RAM, which was just out of my reach.

Then, in fine print, I spotted a note that the game *could* play at a limited speed on a computer with only four megabytes of

RAM.

Alongside *BioForge* was another new release that caught my eye immediately. Its box was strangely V-shaped and the art on the front cover immediately rapt my attention. *Star Trek: A Final Unity* was a new adventure game entry in the Star Trek universe that had escaped my notice in the gaming magazines. Unlike prior Star Trek adventure games, this one was set in the *The Next Generation* universe that I had grown to love over the past five seasons of the television series. The TV series was at its peak in my life and going home *without* a CD-ROM adventure game that featured the voices of the cast was unimaginable. At $79.99 it would require me to boldly spend as I had never spent before.

I picked up both the *BioForge* and *Star Trek* boxes and compared them side by side, as if I was choosing between two VHS movies at a video rental store. The deciding vote arrived when I saw the system requirements for *Star Trek* which demanded a 486 DX processor. My 486 SX wouldn't cut it.[52] As far as I was concerned the system requirements made the decision for me, and I bought *BioForge* on the spot though my heart was set on *Star Trek*.

Later that evening the *BioForge* install program predictably

---

[52] In the 1990s, DX processor designation indicated that the processor was hardware-capable of "floating point" mathematics. The SX CPU lacked this capability, making it much slower at crunching complex numbers. The DX's built-in floating point support meant that the CPU could calculate mathematical instructions using real numbers much quicker than the usual method (e.g. adding 1.445 and 95.38548238). An SX-level processor used the usual "carry" method for addition, requiring many more steps to complete addition or subtraction than a floating-point method. The end result was that for specific games, especially those using complex three-dimensional visuals, the DX processor was far faster than the SX. Moreover, the SX processor was identical to the DX processor in every way *except* for the difference of floating point calculations... the manufacturer Intel had purposely disabled the floating point function on the SX processors in order to create an artificial market for DX processors, allowing the company to price DX processors much higher.

complained that the computer was dangerously starved of RAM. Thankfully, Origin Systems' programmers had anticipated there would be poor saps like me who did not have over two hundred bucks to drop on another four megs of RAM. They had composed an elegant solution: the game created a "paging file" on my hard drive that simulated RAM.[53] The game would perform a little slower than it would have with real RAM, but it'd work in a pinch.

And that it did. Sort of. Well, kind of. Not really. The game *did* run, which was a feat in itself on my RAM-poor PS/1. The opening cinematic was breathtaking and the first scene of the game promised that an exciting mystery was going to unfold before me. The problem was that the game – thanks to the RAM simulation hack – was accessing the hard drive every second, thus causing the game to constantly stutter and lag. The cinematic "Interactive Movie" experience promised on the cover of the box was being ruined by a welterweight computer that couldn't handle the load. The effect was not unlike watching a film reel slowed down to the point where a movie is a series of still frames in sequence – the illusion of smooth motion was broken. I couldn't follow the story this way, and the gameplay was unbearably slow. I needed more RAM, period.

That weekend my mother and I went to the mall for our yearly Christmas gift shopping expedition. I had just over two hundred dollars left in my wallet, and – shamefully I must admit – I bought my family all the cheapest gifts so there'd be enough left over for my RAM upgrade. I walked over to *Virtual Reality Megastore* to look for an upgrade, and in a glass display cabinet normally found in a museum or art gallery, was a neat row of six-inch green and black silicon RAM sticks. Although the sticks were the same size and shape, each had a different number of

---

[53] Paging files allowed the computer to use a portion of the hard drive as RAM space, fooling the CPU into thinking that the computer had more RAM. This allowed the user to run larger, more complex programs and games, without investing in more expensive RAM chips.

silicon chips on it, and the price tags reflected that. My IBM PS/1 User's Guide recommended 72-pin SIMM RAM along with a bunch of technical specifications that I didn't understand.[54]

I must have been standing there gawking at the RAM for quite a while because my mother wandered into the store and stood beside me.

She sighed, "I thought I might find you here. What are you buying now?"

"Oh... um, I need some RAM for the computer. It's running too slow."

You can imagine how my mother rolled her eyes at hearing my latest want for an obscure-sounding computer gadget. She had a less than subtle reaction to the price tag: a four megabyte module was $199.99.

"Don't worry mom. I have enough here with me. I'll pay for it."

That barely placated her. Although I knew my family was having money problems, I didn't realize how deep the problems were. The financial strain on my parents had worsened to the point where two hundred bucks wasn't just a lot of money to *me*, it was a lot of money to *them*.

After ten minutes of rocking back and forth on my heels, I went to the salesperson and asked to see the RAM. He unlocked the case and reached inside, saying apologetically, "We don't sell a lot of these to be honest. We're more of a game store."

The RAM module was clouded by a grey baggie of anti-static plastic, and I slipped it out to read the tiny letters and numbers printed on its surface, pretending to know what they meant. (After all, I was a computer whiz as far as my mother was concerned – I had to keep up appearances!)

The salesman must have sensed my hesitation, "Are you sure this is the one you need? We don't allow returns on these things.

---

[54] SIMM: Single in-line Memory Module. 72 pins referred to the number of gold-plated electrical contacts on the bottom of the module.

We don't have a computer to test 'em with."

I looked at the stick again. It sure looked an awful lot like the RAM stick in my computer. When I spied the letters "72-pin 70NS" printed on the label I smiled. "Yeah, I'm sure!"

Two hundred dollars later I felt like a rich man. Like the hacker/dealer Henry Dorsett Case of the cyberpunk novel *Neuromancer*, I was on my way home riding high with a stick of RAM and a few yen left in my pocket. *BioForge* was going to be incredible, and *Ultima VIII* was going to fly with this much memory!

I quickly de-cased the PS/1 and peered into the box, angling a desk lamp overtop to help me see the motherboard. There were three empty RAM slots. I fitted the new stick of RAM gingerly into the slot and pushed backwards on it gently, snapping it into place. I booted the computer and watched it engage in the RAM verification sequence... boy this was going to be great! 1024 KB... 2048 KB... 4096 KB....

And then the computer booted into MS-DOS as usual. What the? I checked the current available memory with an MS-DOS command called CHKDSK and my heart sunk. 4096KB RAM total. The computer had not recognized the new stick of RAM at all.

I spent the next hour moving around each stick of RAM between the two empty slots on the motherboard, each time hoping that the problem was caused by the order they were placed together. No matter what I did, the computer didn't recognize the new RAM. I re-read the IBM PS/1 User's Guide and frantically flipped through the hardware installation guide, praying for a solution. On a page with technical errata was the cold, hard, answer: the computer specifically needed *"60 NS"* RAM. The new stick of RAM was clearly marked "70 NS" on its label. I flipped the stick over and read another label: "NO RETURNS/EXCHANGES".

I felt like vomiting. I just spent my last $200 on a piece of computer hardware that was absolutely useless to me, and probably useless to anyone else I knew. I couldn't return it. I couldn't sell it. It wasn't even heavy enough to be a paper weight.

My mother came into the den and saw the computer case removed and the wounded look on my face.

"What's wrong now?"

"The RAM I bought… it doesn't work."

"What do you mean it doesn't work?"

I worried that she would blame me for wasting my money, "It doesn't work. I put it in, and the computer doesn't recognize it." A half-truth.

She tried to soothe me. "Well, we'll just take it back tomorrow and get a new one."

Now I was on the edge of tears. "They said no exchanges or returns. I'm screwed, mom."

Her eyes narrowed and face soured as if she had bitten into a lemon. "We'll see about that!" She stomped into the kitchen and snatched her keys from the table.

"Grab your things and the receipt. WE are going back to that store!"

She drove the van furiously back to the City. It was past eight o'clock and the store closed at nine. When we got to the store the same salespeople were on the floor, chatting around the checkout counter and waiting for the dull night to come to an end. My mother stomped in with the stick of RAM in her hand, and jabbed it into the air like a knife at the group of young men. My stomach was tied up in knots – the salesmen were stunned.

Her words hissed through her teeth, "You are going to return this. Or exchange this. Whatever! It doesn't work and my son just spent all of his money on it!"

One of the salesmen looked at the RAM module dubiously and said, "But it's clearly marked: no returns. We can't—"

"Enough! You exchange this piece of shit right now."

I had never heard my mother swear at another adult before, and I began to sob. It was my fault that I had picked out the wrong RAM module, and these poor guys were getting hell from my mom instead of me. I felt like crawling into a deep hole, and

I escaped to the corner of the store and blindly gazed at a wall of used computer games and pretended it wasn't happening.

I could still hear the salesman weakly trying to defend himself from my mother's full-on attack. He was losing ground. I heard the glass display case open behind me and the salesman muttered, "THIS sale is final, okay?"

My mother called me over to the display case and I wiped my tears onto my jacket sleeve. She must have saw my reddened eyes because her voice softened a bit, "Show him the one you need." I pointed at a RAM module marked "60 NS" in the display case. As we walked out of the store with the RAM in hand, the salesman called out to us, reminding us that – once again – there could be no returns.

My mother spun around and barked acridly, "If *this* one doesn't work, you better fuck-ing believe I will be back here. And you will not be happy to see *me*!"

When we left the mall my mother's footsteps lightened a bit and she chuckled to herself. "I think I scared that boy."

I worked up a half smile, "Yeah mom. You were pretty mad."

"Well, they deserved it. No one rips off my son like that."

A large lump formed in my throat and left me speechless for the rest of the ride home. When we got home I took a deep breath and booted the machine – the new RAM worked perfectly. A heavy weight lifted from my shoulders and I walked to the kitchen and gave my mother a big hug. Even though I so badly wanted to be a self-sufficient adult at the age of fifteen, nothing could replace my mother's fearlessness.

The upgrade to eight megabytes of RAM could not have come at a better time. New releases like *BioForge, Star Trek: A Final Unity* and *Wing Commander III: Heart of the Tiger* had all jacked up the minimum system requirements to play them. In those days, failing to meet the minimum requirements did not mean the game would play poorly – it often meant that the game would not play *at all*. The RAM upgrade rescued me from the red zone and placed me in a yellow zone where my underpowered PC would *just barely* play the latest and greatest games. Games just on the horizon were going to require a Pentium processor… keeping computer hardware current has always been a Sisyphean task.

At the time I didn't linger too much on my mother's extreme, yet helpful, reaction to the RAM exchange fiasco. It seemed like she was being good ol' mother bear, defending her cubs from predatory salespeople. A few weeks later, though, I began to realize why she had been so angry over her son potentially losing two hundred bucks.

My father had spent the past two years trying to recover from a traumatic brain injury and his progress was very gradual. Although he was now working long days on various construction projects for customers, he was barely earning enough to pay the labourers he had hired. Worse, more than once clients waited for his crew to complete a project and then refused to pay him altogether. Whether out of a misguided sense of workmanship or pride, my father chose not to sue these deadbeat clients and suffered financial ruin. He was going broke and so was our family.

One very windy day in the autumn far after the leaves had left the poplar trees, my parents had an argument. I was busy exploring a new quadrant of space in *Wing Commander: Privateer* when shouts broke out between my mother and father. I put a pair of headphones on and tried to drown out the commotion.

The argument deteriorated into a shouting match, and then devolved into personal attacks on one another. It was, as many couple fights are, about money. My mom accused my dad of mismanaging the family finances and evading his taxes. My father accused her of wasting her days as a university student instead of working and contributing more to the bottom line. These kinds of fights became more frequent and my sister and I walked on eggshells around our dad, afraid of triggering another one of his bouts of rage.

Until that day, computer games enjoyed a presence alongside all the other entertainments availed to me: cartoons, sports, drawing, reading and exploring the outdoors. After the family fighting began, the quadrants of deep space in *Wing Commander* and the catacombs of *Ultima VIII: Pagan* became places to escape into. Games had become my escape from reality into fantasy, from a farmhouse on the edge of collapse into a safe imaginary world.

Later that night, my mother left. Her keys and purse were gone and my father had isolated himself in his bedroom with the television turned up loudly. I went back to bed with a dull stone in my stomach the shape of a seagull's egg. When I awoke the next morning expecting to hear my mother rushing away to school, there was only a deathly silent house. The kitchen was devoid of her accoutrements and her smell, and her car was still gone.

My sister and I walked silently up the driveway to the bus. When we got halfway to the bus stop her voice grated the air, "I wish he'd just die."

I replied, angrily, "Don't say that! Don't ever say that!"

I wanted to slap her and make her take it back, mostly because deep down, I secretly wished he was dead too.

A day later my father stopped me in the mudroom of the house. His face was flushed and his eyes were underslept. He touched me on the shoulder lightly and his voice rumbled with a gentleness I had not heard in many years, "Don't worry. Your mom just needs to cool off. She'll come back soon."

I choked back tears and nodded. He didn't sound very confident.

My mother did not return for five days. She never told us where she had gone and what would happen to our family next. Over the failing weeks of the autumn, life at our acreage returned to a semblance of normality again. No one spoke of what had happened and the cloud of the fight and my mother's disappearance loomed over all of us. I compulsively explored the furthest reaches of space in *Privateer* and deepest caverns of *Pagan*, pretending that none of this had happened. I fled to these places more and more as I tried to disencumber myself from the weight of my family problems. But no matter how obsessively I played my games, a single feeling penetrated my heart: guilt.

I felt guilty. It was the kind of egocentric guilt that kids feel when something bad happens and they blame themselves for it. It was *my* fault that my father had financial problems. It was my fault that the financial problems had led to fights between my parents and were on the road to a divorce. If I had not demanded an AdLib or a TI-85, if I had not wrecked the Amstrad, if I had not spent all of my money on games and hardware, if I had helped my dad with his company instead of playing games all day, if I had not deleted my mother's college paper, if I had not tied up the phone line all day with my modeming… If I had not existed in the first place my family would not be in ruins and everyone would have been happier.

I poured all of that guilt into the imaginary worlds of *Privateer* and *Pagan*. They became places where I could choose to save the world or follow my own selfish desires. They were places completely under my control in the context of a family life that was spinning out of control. Failure in these games meant reloading a saved game – failure in my family life meant poverty or divorce.

I no longer desired to spend time with my father, mother and sister; my relationships with my closest friends disintegrated. I felt like none of those people could deliver me from my personal instability and suffering, but computer games which let me play the role of a saviour in a fantasy world sure felt like they could. Computer games had become my hideout, and having fun with them was completely secondary to the sense of safety they gave me.

This was a serious change in how I used the computer and played games, and it had a ripple effect. BBSing, programming and exploring the World Wide Web also began to fall under the shadow of repression. Hacking, warez, phreaking and other illicit activities became just as attractive as playing computer fantasy role-playing games.

Computers were no longer about having fun. They were about surviving.

Ultima VII: The Black Gate

Spring fever had hit our high school as it does any place in Canada when the snow is melting and the sun is out for more than six hours a day. Despite the clumps of wet snow still on the yellowed lawns and filthy asphalt, macho guys were wearing their basketball shorts and girls were wearing knee-baring skirts, and that meant hormones were running on high. The jocks in every grade were on the prowl for new girlfriends and many of the girls were looking for a chance to climb up the social hierarchy by dating one of them. Our Math class that day was charged with teen spirit and our teacher had given up trying to keep people from chatting during her lesson.

One of the guys in our class by the name of Willy had recently undergone a social image facelift by dumping his identity as a math and science geek, and joining the boys' basketball team. He sat near the front of the class, close to Andrew and I who were recently moved to the front where we'd be forced to pay attention (and not play with my TI-85). But once again, Andrew and I were talking *Ultima* and *Wing Commander* instead of paying attention to what was happening on the chalkboard. Willy must have overheard our dorky conversation and turned around; I expected him to tell us to cut it out.

Willy partly covered his mouth as he whispered, "Are you guys talking about Ultima?" He was obviously embarrassed by the question.

"Yup. Ever played it? We –"

He cut me off with a hoarse whisper. "Y-yeah. My dad bought it for me last year. But it's not my thing. Too complicated."

I was genuinely surprised. Willy had never once mentioned he had any interest in computer games. I tried to sound cool, or what I imagined was cool, "Yeah it's pretty tough. Magic and junk like that. Maybe um, we can trade games some time."

He shook his head and said, "Naw that's okay. Do you want it? It's yours if you want it."

Our math teacher, Mrs. H, turned around and gave us an icy glare. We clammed up instantly but I nodded emphatically at Willy when her back was turned. Wow, an *Ultima* game for absolutely free! I gave Andrew a sidelong look – he was stewing with envy; when we left the classroom later he shook his head with an annoyed smirk on his face.

"You dirty bastard. He's only giving it to you because you sit right behind him."

It *was* kind of strange – why did Willy want to give me a game for free anyway? We were hardly friends.

As it turned out, there was a social drama playing out behind the scenes that I wasn't aware of. Spring fever and the limited pool of eligible high school girls meant that the jocks began to dip into the well of younger junior high girls. Yes, they *were* younger, but to a jock a hot young date was better than no date at all, and would earn him almost as much respect from his fellow basketball teammates as any girl from his own grade. Willy had apparently set his sights on my sister who was in the ninth grade at the time, two grades below us mature eleventh graders. While there was nothing particularly questionable about dating younger people in my school, Willy was worried that *I* would object to his plans. Instead of asking me directly (as if my opinion would have mattered anyway!), he tried to butter me up with computer games. What can I say? One mouthy teenaged sister for an *Ultima* game? Sold!

The next morning I anxiously waited in Math class to see if Willy had brought the goods. As we sat in class he covertly slipped his hand into his backpack while Mrs. H' generous backside was facing us. He gingerly slid a black box out of the pack and passed it under the desk to me. I hid the box under a textbook under my desk. My heart was racing. It was like we had just pulled off a drug deal at the front desk of a police station. I couldn't help but turn around and give Andrew a shit-eating grin; his face turned bright red as he shook his head. I had won this round of meaningless battle of gamer supremacy and I wanted him to know it.

It was lunch time and even before I had examined the box Andrew and I were racing towards his house so we could make copies of the diskettes. When I finally looked at the monolithic black box in my backpack I was shocked: it was the very coveted Origin Systems title *Ultima VII: The Black Gate*. The black box was simple and featureless aside from its title, and the back of the box only showed three screenshots of the game. The box contained a black, bible-like tome called "The Book of the Fellowship", a cotton map of the land of Britannia covered in runic script, and a small aluminum medallion. These were clearly the best "feelies" we had ever seen come with a computer game and they only whetted our imaginations. We copied the diskettes without saying much to one another.

For the last two years Andrew and I had surreptitiously participated in a Cold War of computer game fandom, each trying to build a more impressive game collection than the other. Like the European explorers who came to the New World, we each tried to stake our claim on new territory and defended it with our lives. In other words – if I bought a computer game series that was new to both Andrew and I, I got to crown myself as "King" of the game series. Andrew had purchased *Crusader: No Remorse* and *Wing Commander III* so naturally he was king of the *Crusader* and *Wing Commander* series. I had grown up playing *King's Quest* and *Monkey Island* so naturally these game series were colonies of *my* empire. Loyalty to king and country was at stake in every single purchase. In all honesty each of us wanted *everyone* around us to bow to us as king of all games.

Until that point there was an uneasy yet friendly understanding between Andrew and I. School was a neutral zone where we could meet daily to exchange games and swap stories about games, and neither of us dared to tread upon one another's territories. I ceremonially asked Andrew questions about *Wing Commander* and in kind he asked me for help with *Sam and Max Hit the Road*. I laugh now thinking how silly this all was, but for two guys who didn't have a hope in hell of having real girlfriends or cars or popularity or happy families, this fandom competition was a place where we could earn some cred with each other.

The day that I took *Ultima VII: The Black Gate* home with me bent that friendly competition to the breaking point. Until that day the *Ultima* series had clearly been in Andrew's wheelhouse: he had bought *Ultima VIII: Pagan* and knew everything about its world and its denizens. I was merely a serf who toiled in the fantasy world that was *his* dominion.

Where *Ultima VIII: Pagan* took place in a grisly, volcanic world of warring gods and power mad mortals, *Ultima VII: The Black Gate* – its predecessor – took place in a quasi-medieval world of bright colours and friendly bakers who quibbled over the price of a loaf of bread. *The Black Gate* was so bright and cheery that it seemed that the protagonist of the series had taken a summer vacation in a smarmy fairy land of unicorns and friendly churchgoers.

There was such a disconnection between the tones of the two games that I wondered if they even belonged within the same storyline. It was like being told that before Emperor Palpatine in *Star Wars* had become such an evil bastard, he had been a kindly school teacher for handicapped kindergarteners. This perplexing contrast between the games only deepened my curiosity about the *Ultima* game series.

Playing the games concurrently brought them into sharper contrast. It turned out that *Ultima VIII* was only a foggy shadow of its predecessor, which had a far more detailed world and complex gameplay. In *Ultima VII* computer characters (NPCs) lived according to daily schedules. For instance, a baker in the city of Britain would awake from his bed at 6 o'clock in the morning and slowly make his way from his home to his bakery. Seeing that it was still dark outside he would light the streetlamp outside of his business, saying, "Ah! T'is better!", then unlock and open the door to his business. For hours he'd mix a bag of flour with water he had drawn from a nearby well, into a dough placed on his baking table. He would place the raw dough on the hearth of his burning fireplace until it browned into a crispy loaf of bread. Talking with the baker triggered a jolly conversation about baking, where he'd invite the player to bake bread for him and pay for any baked loaves. Further conversation with the baker exposed romantic intrigues he was pursuing with two other female characters in the Britannian city.

This was just *one* NPC out of the hundreds in *Ultima VII*, each of which having daily schedules and personal intrigues and secrets and wanton desires and guilts. Most games developed in the 1990s had "levels" or "maps" the player traversed, until they made it to the next stage of game play. Britannia felt like a complete, living, *world* that you, as the protagonist, could become wrapped up in. Unlike *Pagan* which was about the protagonist amassing magical powers and elevating himself to a demigod, *The Black Gate* cast the player as a mild-mannered saviour whose charge was nothing less than saving the world from ruin using his or her smarts and a boatload of charm. Sure, the game involved a dark plot about an evil entity that conspired to destroy the pleasant world of Britannia, but the tone of the game was primarily jaunty and colourful. The bulk of the protagonist's quests while touring Britannia involved solving the niggling problems of the relatively tranquil Britannians, and not clawing ones way to the top.

The Black Gate appealed to me even more than *Pagan* did for one reason in particular: it was about helping and saving people from their problems. For a kid who wanted to be rescued from his troubled home life it was a hopeful and happy world to escape into. Although I had been persuaded into a pessimistic view of human nature by *Pagan, The Black Gate* was a bastion of hope.

For the rest of the year I played *Ultima VII* like it was going out of style. I completed every quest no matter how menial. I explored every basement and dungeon and island and cave; I talked with every character I met and assisted them with their problems no matter how trivial. I made the entire fantasy world of Britannia into my little cabin in the woods.

The fantasy worlds of Britannia and Pagan in the *Ultima* series had become my prime means for escape, and had now eclipsed the library of games behind me on the shelf. Non-player characters from the series like Iolo, Dupre, Shamino and Spark had become as familiar to me as the friends I had grown up with since we had moved south to the acreage.

That being said, I wasn't becoming the delusional psychotic boy featured in the awful 1980s film "Mazes and Monsters" who could not distinguish between fantasy and reality. It was more that I had become emotionally committed to these fantasy worlds which were acting as powerful counterbalances to the pressures and chaos of school and family. I wanted to live and breathe Britannia, even if I knew it was all make-believe.

It was almost Christmas and I set my sights on completing *Ultima VII* so I could find out what happened to the protagonist in the moments before he was exiled to the world of *Pagan* in *Ultima VIII*. I had become hopelessly stuck late in the game and Andrew had no idea how to progress further in the story either. Both of us were at a standstill for weeks. Andrew had mentioned that he had purchased a strategy guide for *Ultima VIII* but as far as we knew, no such guide existed for *Ultima VII*.[55]

The solution to our mental roadblock came as a confluence of my improved Internet access from home over the private phone line, and the emerging popularity of search indexing sites like *Yahoo!* on the World Wide Web. Unlike Google which is a search *engine* that crawls the web robotically finding information and cataloguing it, a search *index* works more like your typical

[55] Little did we know that for years Origin Systems – the developer of the *Ultima* series – had been publishing their own excellent and beautifully illustrated strategy guides for their games. *Ultima VII* did have an official guide title "Key to the Black Gate" available for purchase by mail-order.

Yellow Pages phone book. Businesses and individuals and organizations submitted their information to *Yahoo!* under the subject heading it applied to. For instance, have a personal web page about your love of World War II airplanes? Submit it to *Yahoo!'s* index under: Hobbies -> Aviation -> World War II. After a few days or weeks your web site could be found by hobbyists browsing *Yahoo!'s* hierarchy of websites about Aviation; they might also come across your page by searching *Yahoo!'s* listings for 'world war 2 planes'.

One particular day I searched for the word 'Ultima' on *Yahoo!* which at that time advertised itself as having over *100,000* web pages linked to it. (This number is laughably tiny compared to the billions of web pages Google now indexes.) A handful of web pages came up, and one in particular stood out to me: HappyPuppy.com. *Happy Puppy* turned out to be a gigantic repository of text files full of hint guides and walkthroughs for computer and video games. I spent hours downloading and printing out hint books for each game I owned, then carefully hole-punching them and cataloguing them in a binder. Among the printed guides was a fifty page walkthrough for *Ultima VII: The Black Gate*.

The printed walkthrough was a godsend. At the time the only hint books for computer games that I was aware of were the ones officially published and sold for ten to twenty dollars by companies like Sierra On-Line and LucasArts. The idea that an everyday *person* could write their own guide for a game and then distribute it to others over the Internet – for free! – was utterly enchanting. It turned out that walkthroughs had been around for years, circulated on Usenet and BBSs. But it was the World Wide Web that made homebrewed hint guides and cheat codes ubiquitous for the average gamer.

The next day, after smugly letting Andrew take a gander at my half-inch-thick printed walkthrough for *The Black Gate*, I got to work completing the game. It took only a few minutes of skimming to find the portion of the game that I was stuck at. It turned out that I needed to visit a particular island and speak to a particular character in order to trigger advancement of the plot. I quickly completed the task and felt a rush of excitement finally seeing the next part of the story emerge.

But, like many other readers of hint guides know, I did not close the guide when I had solved that one tiny problem. Instead of traipsing along and discovering the next part of the story on my own, I began reading the walkthrough more like a novel. After all, why should I take weeks or months just to see the damned ending to the game when I could see it *tonight*?

Worse, I discovered in the guide that there was a "cheat mode" that I could trigger with a few keystrokes. The cheat mode enabled instant teleportation between places on the map instead of having to sail the seas on a ship, walking there, or flying on a carpet. The cheat allowed me to arbitrarily make myself filthy rich with gold and weapons and armour that would have taken months to find on my own. The cheat even made my character and his party of companions impervious to damage from enemies. In other words: the cheat mode allowed me to complete the game without having to *play* it.

I used every cheat that night and fast-forwarded myself to the ending, and completed the game. I finally had closure on the protagonist's story and now understood how he or she ended up in the devastated world of Pagan in its sequel. I wanted to feel like it was the end of months of hard work, but my rampant cheating had weakened the punch of the climax. Despite the game's powerful conclusion I felt emptied by the experience, like I had snuck into a full marathon in the last mile and sprinted past all the other fatigued runners for the photo finish. Worse, I felt like I had binged on my entire hoard of Halloween candy in a single night and now had nothing left for the rest of the year. No one else I knew owned the previous games in the *Ultima* series and due to their relative age these games never appeared on pirate-friendly BBSs. I was a junkie going through hard withdrawal symptoms and was tracking my next big hit.

I wouldn't get my next taste of *Ultima* for over a year.

Summer at SSI Micro

It was the end of June and I had survived the eleventh grade. This meant a precious two months to compress as much time into the computer as I could before September came along and swept me back into the turbulence of the public education system. But as much as I wanted to play some new games for a whole languid summer I was flat broke and so were my parents.

My first opportunity to refill my coffers came a week into summer vacation. A local honeybee farmer named Gerard approached my mother and asked her if she knew of anyone looking for work. The job paid eight bucks an hour – far above the minimum wage at the time; an unbeatable deal for a money-hungry teen. I was deathly afraid of bees after a swarming incident years earlier, but my greed easily overcame my sense of self-preservation. Gerard hired me and a couple other local boys on a weekly basis for ten hours a day of work.

I lasted two whole days at the apiary. The constant humming of the bees around my head tortured my paranoid fear of being stung, and when I finally *was* stung I ran screaming out of the building and walked five kilometres back to my house. Gerard sympathetically left a hundred dollars with my mother a few days later and wished me well.

When my father asked me if I wanted to drive up north with him for work a week later, I happily accepted. *Any* job I could find in my old home town was better than risking life and limb in the honey factory.

My father and I arrived in our old home town late one evening and I set up camp at my aunt's house. The next morning I began calling my relatives asking if they knew of any open positions in the town, and a day later I had secured a job as a "barge cleaner" with one of my aunts. She warned me that it was hard work, but this fell on ears deafened by the sweet sonnets of the $12.50 per hour wage the boss offered me. I woke up at five o'clock the next morning while the midnight sun was already above the horizon and was slowly baking away the chilly July air, and climbed into my aunt's truck.

The barge floated alongside the docks near the mouth of a large river. It turned out to be an oil barge, the kind used to float millions of litres of fuel stored in its hold to distant polar destinations like Tuktoyaktuk and Aklavik. If you're struggling to imagine this particular barge, think of a massive, black, rusty sardine can floating heavily in the water.

After a quick 5 AM coffee with the motley crew of barge cleaners we donned paper-thin white Tyvek suits with HEPA breathing apparatuses around our faces, and climbed down a narrow chute into the depths of the barge. We looked like scientists in an alien autopsy episode of *The X-Files,* descending into the canals of some vast extra-terrestrial hive. Like the great husk of an old hive, the hull was separated into a series of steel beam arcades meant to prevent sloshing of its oily contents. But deprived of petroleum for years the barge was now dry, rusty and dusty inside. A crew of welders had recently welded weak points in the steel beams, and our cleaning job was to knock off welding slag with a little pickaxe, sweep it into buckets, and transport the buckets to the surface.

By noon the rusty black tanker had been boiling in the blistering northern sun for six hours. The outside air was 33 degrees Celsius (about 91°F) and it was ten degrees hotter inside of the tank. The plastic suits we wore stuck to our skin and our HEPA masks began to suffocate us as long beads of sweat ran down our faces and pooled inside. It was the damp, hot, miserable work that public education was supposed to have prevented kids like me from doing in the first place. After my twelve hour shift I limped to my aunt's home, miserable and cranky, like a 19th century coal pony. My face and hair were covered in black ferric soot; tears ran down from my eyes with an unforgettable look: I absolutely despised this job.

I lasted a week as a barge cleaner. On payday I received a surprisingly large cheque from the foreman, and later that night

I called my other aunt and told her that I wouldn't be coming in for any more shifts. If Roger Wilco worked even *half* this hard as an interplanetary space janitor, he was damn well justified in blasting off in the nearest escape pod and dooming the rest of his crew!

I now had a few hundred dollars in my pocket – more than I had made in all my previous summer jobs combined. But I felt restless after a few idle days and felt ashamed for quitting two lucrative jobs in under a month, and I badly needed to prove to myself (and to my parents) that I could hack it as a blue-collared worker.

My chance came a week later when I was out for a walk with my uncle Fred and his Dalmatian dog on the beach. He reminded me that his friend Jeff – the same man who had showed me *Doom* two years earlier – was always looking for people to staff his computer business which had finally taken off in the north. Computers? Sure!

Later that day Jeff called me at my aunt's home and asked me a few simple questions about my computer – which operating system it ran (IBM PC-DOS 6), which CPU it had (a 486 SX-33) and how large my hard drive was (384 megabytes). He must have been satisfied because he invited me to "Take a spin up to Prov with your uncle Freddy, and we'll go from there." Although he made no promises that I'd get a job at his company, my foot was already in the door.

"Going for a spin" with my uncle Fred to "Prov" meant making a two hour drive to the village of Fort Providence, which was along the highway to the city of Yellowknife. We woke up early in the morning, armed with a backpack full of sandwiches his wife had made, and called his dog into the van where she sat wiggling and sneezing from the excitement of a car ride.

The drive to Prov was a three-sandwich affair, to be eaten while listening to the science news program "Quirks and Quarks" on CBC Radio. When we arrived in Fort Providence hours later, a new large building stood near the centre of the village, across from the only restaurant and hotel. The building, clad in aluminum siding was the size and shape of a large hockey arena.

I pointed and asked Fred what we were looking at and when he told me, I gaped.

"*That's* the computer store?!"

The Snowshoe Inn Micro computer store's front entrance, ca. Winter 1998.

My knees and ankles felt like they were going to give out on me as we stepped into the double doors of the building. Inside I found a huge but strangely empty retail space. The room had a wall with a narrow shelf of computer software and games, and there were a few desks strewn around the edges of the room with shiny new computers on them.

Jeff yelled from across the room, "Freddy! Right on time!", and greeted us both warmly. He walked us around the store, introducing us to his sales and repair staff, whose names I forgot as my attention was more drawn to the computer software on the wall behind them.

* * *

The front entrance and customer retail area of the store, circa 1998. Gateway 2000 brand swag hangs from a clothing rack, with software and hardware racks along the walls. Photo courtesy of Jeremy Childs.

Jeff walked us through a swinging door that exited the retail space into the "service area". At a waist-high workbench stood a large Polish man named "Mac" whose fingers were currently plunged into the guts of a mini-tower PC doing some kind of emergency surgery. A Gateway 2000 monitor was mounted on the wall above the bench like an EEG display, giving all kinds of readouts on the patient's health. *Damn this was cool.*

I turned around and surveyed a rack of computer towers stacked ten feet high on top of one another. Each tower had a label on its faceplate – "LIVINGSTON", "SeQueL", "BIG DADDY" – cryptic names that did little to explain their function to me. Stranger still was that none of the towers were hooked up to a monitor of any kind; they only sat quietly humming and chirping.

Excitement kept building in my stomach until I thought I would barf. A large docking bay in the service area had a half dozen Gateway 2000 cardboard boxes neatly stacked upon one another – brand new computers! A flight of stairs led to a twenty-thousand foot warehouse space in the basement, fed by a conveyer belt, full of spare parts and skeletons of computers. This was not just a computer retail store like Radio Shack – this was almost like a computer manufacturing plant. I had already sold my soul to Jeff the second I stepped into this place. He need only ask me to do his bidding.

We had a brief lunch at the restaurant across the street owned by Jeff's family. It turned out that his family owned half of the businesses in town, and the computer store of course. My uncle excused himself to visit a friend and left me with Jeff for the rest of the day.

Jeff took me back to the computer service area of the store after lunch and pointed at a small white box with a few serial ports on the back.

"Think you can take that thing apart and fix it?"

I nodded happily and got to work with a Phillips screwdriver. A few minutes later the box sprung open with wires hanging everywhere, and I began replacing a fan that had gone dead inside. Although I had no idea what the box was for at the time, Jeff was impressed that I was fearless in tearing it apart and putting it back together.[56] He hired me on the spot.

Although the comparison is awful to make, I looked like I was about to have a grand mal seizure, hyperventilating, shaking and foaming at the mouth. Jeff and Mac laughed and detailed how I'd spend the rest of the day in the service area. Mac proved to have a wonderful, dark sense of humour and loved computer games just as much as I did. I was in nerd heaven and felt like I was going to float off into the sky.

Jeff, Fred and I sat down for dinner later that day. He promised Fred that I would not get into any trouble living in Fort Providence, and that he'd let me phone my mother whenever I wanted to. And then Jeff named a figure that I agreed to immediately: I would make six dollars an hour, and my salary would include food and lodging for the summer. If he had told me that I would have had to pay *him* for the pleasure of working in his store, I still would have taken the job. Fred gave me a hug and promised me he would let my father know that I would be staying in Prov for the rest of the summer.

Jeff led me to the hotel where he introduced me to his wife

---

[56] The box turned out to be an Uninterruptible Power Supply – loaded with live electrical current that could have easily fried me if I had cut the wrong wires.

who graciously gave me a room for the night.

"We'll work out where you're staying next week. Just crash here for now."

The next morning I awoke early and ate a large breakfast at the restaurant. I felt a mixture of excitement and discomfort as I ate: it was the first time I had to be completely self-reliant and was living among adults doing adult work. My mother, as it turns out, was mortified when she found out her fifteen-year-old son was living alone in a dusty northern town she feared was brimming with family violence, alcoholism and abject poverty. What if I was shot or stabbed or run over by a car or abducted or drowned in the Mackenzie River?

When I arrived at work, Jeff was already on the phone with her assuring her that I would be safe and supervised at all times. He handed me the phone. After a brief conversation with her, promising that I wouldn't hang out with strange men or stay out after dark, she sighed and gave me her leave to stay in Prov for the rest of the summer. YES!

Jeff laughed, seeing my relief. "Geez, your mom sure was worked up about you staying here. Gave me and Freddy shit for not asking her first."

He walked me over to the service area where Mac was slaving away on one of his computer patients. "Buddyyyyyy!" he exclaimed, greeting me with his light Polish accent, waving me over to check out the computer he was diagnosing with Norton PC Tools. The program was busily checking every aspect of the computer's health and Mac explained every step. Jeff appeared satisfied with the progress I was making and headed back to his own office.

The rest of the day was gleefully spent learning how to "prep" a computer. SSI Micro resold Gateway 2000 computers to the north, and Jeff had learned that his customers bought a lot more "extras" like speakers and software and sound cards if the computer came pre-installed with them. It was my job to run the gauntlet of pre-installing Windows 3.11-compatible drivers and testing the equipment beforehand. This also involved installing any RAM or hard drive upgrades, games or utilities, joysticks or mice or modems or sound cards or video cards, and making minor tweaks to the Windows 3.11 interface to make it more user-friendly. After that, the final prep was a matter of re-packing the computers in their official Gateway 2000 boxes so they appeared to be new-in-the-box for the customer. Once a week a large freight truck backed up to the loading dock and whisked away a few new computers to our customers.

This kind of assembly-line work might sound boring to the average person, but for a fifteen-year-old who had just escaped the filthy innards of an oil barge days earlier, this was paradise. Each day I got out of bed early and ordered the same bacon'eggs'n'toast ('over-easy please!') at the company restaurant and sauntered into the service area at ten-to-eight. I prepped computers all day, and Mac handled customer calls on our tech support hotline which was a black phone on the corner of the workbench. At noon I ate the same clubhouse'n'fries ('yes, extra gravy please!') until the cook had my order memorized and just gave me "the usual, with a side of gravy."

The only problem was that I had nothing at all to do in the evenings. I was living out of the black garbage bag of clothing I had arrived with, and the hotel room had no television nor laundry. I did not even have a telephone to call home with and was too shy to ask Jeff if I could place a long-distance call at his expense. When boredom made the hotel room feel as if it were shrinking around me and suffocating me, I wandered around the village for some fresh air.

The village was comprised of less than a dozen dusty roads that converged upon Jeff's family's businesses. The air hung thick with the sickly-sweet scent of woodsmoke from a wildfire burning a hundred kilometres away; the smoke did nothing to discourage the swarms of mosquitoes and sand-flies that followed me around as I walked.

There were ugly mutts everywhere, tied to chains hanging from teetering doghouses, barking at anything that moved. Occasionally a cluster of kids pedalled by on their bikes, their knees and faces covered in silty dust and crusty snot hung from their noses, staring at me as they cruised past. I sat on a large rock by the Mackenzie riverbank and felt tiny, alone and frightened. I was by myself for the first time and I resolved to find something to do with my evenings.

The answer came a few days later. After work one day Jeff drove me over to a trailer park a few blocks away from the office. He handed me a key and said, "We can't have ya staying at the hotel all summer. Here, this is your place."

I unlocked the aluminum door of the trailer and stepped inside, expecting a dingy, dark interior like the trailer my grandfather lived in. It turned out to be brand new and brightly lit. Jeff jutted his chin down the hallway, "Take the bedroom at the end of the hall. You have a roommate but she's never home. S'pretty much all yours. Oh hey, and here!"

He handed me a much larger and thicker bronze-coloured key and said, "This'll get you into the office after hours. Just make sure you lock up at night when you leave."

My own trailer. My own office key. My heart jumped into my throat and I choked out a rushed "thanks!" as Jeff pulled out of the driveway. It took me less than a minute to run back to the office and let myself in. The entire building was dead silent. I croaked out a soft, "hello?" that got no reply. No one was here in the 50,000 square foot building except me.

When I was sure all the blinds were closed, I ran around the building in my bare feet feeling the new velvety commercial carpeting under my toes. I climbed onto the conveyer belt and crawled on my hands and knees, riding it through a tunnel into the basement. I poked my nose into every computer box and scrutinized every computer part I could find in the cavernous storage room. I hooked up a set of brand new Altec Lansing computer speakers to my workstation and blasted out music that echoed through the building. Suddenly being alone wasn't so terrifying – it was amazing!

When I left the building at 2 o'clock in the morning, the midnight sun had barely sunk below the horizon and the sky above was a smoky mauve. I could hear the same group of kids outside chasing one another on their bicycles. I do not remember opening the door of my trailer or collapsing on my bed, but when I awoke the next morning it was past 9 o'clock and I was late for work.

Late for work. Shit. I had never been late for work before. I scrambled for clothes on the floor but I had neglected to wash any of my laundry since I had arrived a week earlier. I threw on a pair of sweatpants and a tee shirt and hoped no one would notice my dishevelled hair.

When I got in to the office, Mac nodded at me without his eyes leaving the computer he was working on.

"Little buddy. Jeff's looking for you."

My heart sunk. Rather than ride out the storm I thought I could take refuge in the service area until it had passed. Apparently not.

Jeff barged into the service area and his voice grew heavy, "You're an hour and a half late, and you look like a fuckin' bum. I can't have ya showing up to work like this, and late too. What if a customer came in and saw ya? They'd wonder what a shitty operation I was runnin' here."

I gulped and cried out, "Customers don't come back here so what's the poin—"

"I don't give a shit! Get cleaned up and come back after lunch. And change your clothes, Christ." He stomped out of the service area. My face was bright red and my chest heaved. I walked out of the building and tears streamed down my face as I made a bee-line for my trailer. I felt like a little kid again, living in a big, scary, adult world. I felt like I had let down Jeff, Mac, my uncle who had got me the job, and my parents. I was a complete failure.

One load of laundry later I slunk back into the service area and moodily took my spot at the repair bench. Mac nudged me with his elbow, "Sometimes he's like that. Don't worry about it little buddy!" Despite myself I broke out in a sheepish grin and choked back a large frog suddenly caught in my throat. Jeff sat down with me at the restaurant that evening and he continued on as if nothing had happened.

"Hey, you busy tomorrow night? How 'bout I teach you some VB? Ever done any programming with VB?" he asked as he chewed a mouthful of fries.

"What's VB?"

"Visual Basic. Super keen. You're gonna dig it."

The next evening and for the next few weeks after work, Jeff and I sat down at a lone computer in the far corner of the building. Although I had some experience with BASIC, *Microsoft Visual Basic 4.0* was a whole new way of thinking about giving the computer instructions. My experience with coding up to that point meant typing instructions line-by-line and much later adding a visual user interface to it – sort of like building the wooden frame for a house first, and only at the end adding things the homeowner interacts with like sinks and toilets and door handles. *Visual Basic* turned that workflow on its head. We began by building the user interface *first* – checkboxes and buttons and drop-down lists – and only afterwards added programming instructions that breathed life into the interface.

Our first program was a dialog box that said, "Click OK to continue", with a small, grey "OK" button below. I learned how to detect the user's click on the OK button I had added, and then learned how to dismiss the window using a few simple instructions. Although I understood the concept of giving a computer instructions using BASIC commands, my experience with the language largely proved to be a hindrance. VB was a whole new way of thinking about computer programming.[57]

---

[57] BASIC is premised on a line-by-line set of instructions not unlike a player piano script. BASIC programs tend to become enormously convoluted when complex, conditional experiences are necessary. The language was meant to teach people the basics of programming and was never meant as a means for making large, involved programs. *Visual Basic* took a much different approach that relied upon a concept called "object-oriented programming" (OOP). OOP imagined the program as a collection of objects with common behaviours that could be easily replicated. For instance, all buttons shared behaviours like accepting single-clicks, whereas icons shared properties like having

Jeff turned out to be an incredibly patient teacher, and sat beside me for a couple of hours every evening and guided me through the process of building a photo gallery program. It was like having a driver's education instructor sitting alongside me, quietly making suggestions as I did all the driving.

Visual Basic 4.0 taught me an entirely new way of thinking about programming computers. My experiences with BASIC on the Tandy TRS-80 and Apple // and TI-85 had taught me that computers were player pianos that read a sequence of ones and zeroes in a logical sequence, from left to right, top to bottom. *Visual Basic* taught me that programming a computer could be more like constructing a fantasy world, full of creatures and buildings of different kinds of shapes – each with different ways of acting and reacting to the user. The programmer's job was to arrange these creatures and buildings on a stage, give them speaking roles, and link them all together in a coherent story. The user's job was to poke and prod at each creature on the stage, and the creatures would react exactly in the way I had told them to. In other words, programming was just a form of scripted theatre.

That's not to say I was thinking very philosophically about programming back then. I was just shocked that our photo gallery program actually worked! It allowed the user to drag'n'drop a bit-mapped image (BMP) onto the window and store the image as a record in a database that could be called up with the click of a button.

I thought little of Jeff's surprising generosity at the time. I thought that he saw me like a little brother, and was feeling guilty about yelling at me and was trying to make up for it by

---

graphics and accepted double-clicks. *Visual Basic* exploited OOP concepts that allowed the programmer to add buttons and icons and menus to a window with a few clicks of a mouse, whereas BASIC would have required the programmer to hammer out hundreds of lines of code to achieve the same result. VB made the software developer think as a user *first*, and as a coder *later*.

teaching me something cool. It was years later, when I began programming my own games, that my full appreciation of Jeff's gift became apparent. When I encountered my first fully object-oriented programming language in my twenties, it felt like a homecoming. It took a long time before I realized that I owed my familiarity to the hours spent with Jeff coding VB scripts. It would be decades before I got to thank him properly for his dedication and generosity.

The Wiz Introduces HotJava

One day as I sat with my adult co-workers talking about Jeff's latest business exploits over lunch, Jeff suddenly stood up and said, "Hey, let's go see The Wiz!"

We walked across the street and I breathed in the heavy, smoky July air. There were fires burning across the boreal forest and everywhere it smelled like a cedar sauna had caught fire. Jeff led me to a corner of the building with a single room that housed a man named Gary, a man whom Jeff affectionately called, "The Wiz."

Gary was a short, bespectacled man with a quick smile and excitable yet warm demeanour. Despite there being less than ten employees in the building, Gary was one of the few that didn't socialize much with the rest of us. He spent all of his time in his dim office with a single desk lamp and two large 17-inch NEC monitors. The monitors cost over a thousand dollars each, and he was the only person in the office with *two* of them plunked side by side on his desk. Even Jeff didn't own one.

Gary swung around on his chair and smiled, "Hey guys! Come check out what I'm working on!"

There were sprawling pages of white text against a black background on each monitor. It appeared to be some kind of programming language but it was far more advanced (read: obscure) than the *Visual Basic* programs I had written earlier. I had no idea what I was looking at.

Jeff sensed my bafflement, "Gary's been working on the sequel server dee-bee. Setting all that up for our billing, finances, you name it. Pretty keen stuff."

Gary shook his head, "Oh no no no. That's all done now. I'm doing something *way* cooler!"

His eyes lit up with a sparkle as he launched a new web browsing program called *HotJava* and we watched as a web page slowly loaded. A large grey box appeared in the middle of the window and I could hear the computer's hard drive grind away.

It took over a minute before, from the right side of the page, a little triangular figure painted in the colours of a penguin appeared. It danced, hopped and flipped across the screen until it disappeared on the left side. It was hilariously well animated and smooth, like a video game.

"They call it Java. It's the coolest thing – works on Mac, Unix and Windows. It's going to change everything. And now it's running just great on our Apache server. I hear they're going to add support for Java applets in the next beta of *Netscape Navigator*."

Gary reloaded the browser window and we watched the little figure dance across the screen again. He commented, "Just think: soon we'll have live audio and video on the Web. Not just text and GIFs."[58]

I did not understand the relevance of the little animated figure beyond being impressed by it. I had no idea what Java was, but Gary's excitement over the software suggested it was going to be the Next Big Thing with computers and the Internet. As it turns out, he was right. Not only did Java sweep across the Internet, but *Netscape* – the World Wide Web browser software – overnight became the software of choice for most web surfers. Gary was living at the bleeding edge of the Internet movement.

When we left I asked Jeff why Gary had been sequestered in his office.

"Oh, I didn't tell ya? We're launching Internet service this winter. Dial-up service to as many towns as I can get access to. We get our upstream and downstream from Northwestel's big pipe in Yellowknife, beam it out here over microwave, then beam it out to end users over microwave again. The latency sucks, but we've got more bandwidth than we need."

---

[58] GIF: Graphics Interchange Format, created by the online service CompuServe in the 1990s. This became the favoured image format on the Web for many years until it was eclipsed by the JPEG and PNG formats. GIFs are still used extensively today because they support simple animations.

My mind spun in circles for the rest of the day. SSI Micro was going to be the North's first Internet Service Provider, and I was in on the ground floor. I thought back to the racks of computers humming away behind the service area and finally understood their purpose: they were being prepared for the ISP launch in a few months. The computer repair job that I had so proudly dedicated myself to suddenly seemed insignificant. I had the chance to help build a little chunk of the vast, global network we were calling The Internet.

Stan and the Meat Slicer

Although I had shyly avoided interacting with most of the sales staff prior to that point, I made an effort to get to know them before I left the north for the fall school semester. Most of the sales staff turned out to be computer nerds themselves, and had flown in from all parts of the country and overseas just to help Jeff launch his company.

One guy I badly wanted to talk with was Rod, who handled residential sales and support calls. Rod was nerdy, thin, and absolutely in love with all things *Star Trek*. I was a closeted *Star Trek: The Next Generation* fan at the time and secretly wanted a buddy to geek out with. But every time I went to Rod's desk he was either gone or immediately excused himself to use the bathroom, complaining of stomach pains. I began to wonder if – like me – Rod was extremely shy, or if he just didn't like me very much. Rod stuck out to me as the kind of guy that could become a great friend once I got into his circle of trust. I relented after trying several times and now only politely nodded a good-morning to him every day. I promised myself that next summer, if there was going to be a next summer at SSI Micro, I would make more of an effort to get to know him.

The sales department also had a friendly man named Stan who handled corporate sales. Stan was a blustery, choleric kind of guy with a vein always throbbing on his temple and his eyes bulged out slightly, like he was always prepared to have a massive coronary episode at any given moment. His loud, jocular voice and linebacker build made him the centre of any conversation, and he was a pro at telling dirty jokes. Stan was hard *not* to like.

One day Stan walked into the service area and saw I was installing RAM in a new machine. He was breathing heavily as usual and said, "I gotta get my eyes on something else for a bit, I'm sick of spreadsheets, Christ. Here, lemme do that for ya!"

I backed away from the workbench and Stan shoved his

knobby fingers into the guts of the 486 and snatched up a four meg SIMM of 72-pin RAM. The retail price of this module was a shade under two hundred dollars at the time, and I was always gentle with them lest I accidentally break one. Stan, on the other hand, had no qualms about using force. I watched as his sausage fingers crammed that little RAM stick into the motherboard like it was a deformed puzzle piece. His face broke out into a sweat and eventually there was a loud *ping-whack!* His arms slipped and he fell forward into the case, slicing his elbows along its metal frame. Blood gushed from the slash across his elbow all over the computer and the bench.

"Fuck! Fuck! *Fuckkkkk*!" he yelled as he stomped toward the washroom.

I looked inside of the computer case, now a gory scene. Droplets of blood were smeared across the motherboard, and although the RAM module had somehow survived the force of his bodyweight, the plastic RAM sockets they were supposed to be seated in were now destroyed. I picked up the RAM stick and examined it. Stan had not noticed the RAM was meant to fit into the motherboard in only one direction, and had been forcing it in backwards. Mac walked in and shook his head at the grisly crime scene.

"*That's* why we don't let Stan in here, little buddy."

Promotion to Assistant Pig-Keeper

It was during my last week at SSI Micro that Mac gave me a field promotion to Chief Engineer of Technical Support, aka. the guy that had to answer the black phone. The black phone at the end of the workbench rarely rang more than once a day, and every time it rang it filled me with dread. What if a customer asked me a technical question that I couldn't answer? What if Mac wasn't around to take over if I became flustered? What if a customer figured out this was just some dumb kid pretending to be a computer technician?

Fortunately that never happened. In fact, I was surprised at how little customers knew about their three thousand dollar computers, and how much more I knew about their machines than they did. Even though computers were becoming commonplace in North America, the north was the very last place to have them. As far as I know this was also the only technical support line for computers north of the 60th parallel too.

I cut my teeth on troubleshooting technical problems with Ma and Pa Kettle with the usual array of questions. Is the computer plugged in? ('Of course it is! Oh wait, no it's not…') Okay, now double-click the left mouse button. ('What's the mouse? Do you mean the mole? We call it a mole here.') Your computer game has no sound? Have you tried turning up the volume on your sound card? ('Sound card? I thought this thing was supposed to come with everything!') The tone and content of these calls are likely familiar to anyone who had worked in IT before, or has tried to help an elderly relative with their computer over the phone.

One support call during my last week in the service area stood out and still makes me smile to this day. On my second last day, Mac handed the phone to me with an exasperated look on his face and said, "Here buddy. *You* talk to her."

I put on my warmest and sweetest voice, "Good afternoon,

SSI Micro. How may I help you?"

The customer had the voice of an older, affluent lady. Rich people were always the worst to deal with.

"Oh, thank God! That last guy didn't know *anything!* You better know what you're doing."

I glanced at Mac who rolled his eyes.

I tried not to giggle, "Ah heh… I will do my best. What can I help you with?"

"Well my computer won't scan a document I have here. I want it to scan my document."

I told her that it was likely some small overlooked snag and we would iron it out together. I walked her through some simple starter questions: is the scanner's power light on? What happens when you press the button to scan? Just a sound, and then nothing? What scanning software are you using?

Twenty-five minutes later fear-sweat began to build on my brow. I could hear irritation growing in her voice and she sounded like she was going to explode on me like she had on Mac.

I had no idea what the problem was and she was becoming irate, threatening to "send this pile of junk back" to the store for a full refund. It was exactly the kind of situation where Jeff would have to intervene and placate the customer, and later Mac and I would be on the receiving end of his wrath. With a day left in my internship I had no intention of blowing my chances of another summer at SSI Micro.

Something tickled the back of my mind. I asked the customer to read out the brand name of the scanner.

"It says… M. A. G. Inno… vision."

MAG was a popular high-end monitor manufacturer and as far as I knew the company had never made scanning products.

"Okay great. Now can you tell me step-by-step how you're scanning the document?"

She sighed, "Yes. I put my paper up against the glass, and I push in the button in the middle for scanning. It says 'Degauss' underneath the button. It makes a weird sound but the document doesn't come up on the screen afterwards."

Degauss. The degauss button allowed the computer monitor to briefly de-magnetize itself to prevent any annoying purple spots to appear due to interfering electromagnetic fields. Wait, was this person actually trying to scan a piece of paper using the goddamned *monitor*?!

Mac heard the entire conversation and was doing a poor job of masking his snickering. His laughter was infectious and I began to snicker myself.

"I'm sorry to say, but your computer *monitor* can't scan documents. You need to buy a whole separate piece of equipment called a *scanner* to do that."

A long pause, and then her huffy reply, "... Well then, that's no good to me!"

She hung up.

Mac and I died laughing and spent the rest of the afternoon derisively mocking the customer. Jeff came in at the end of the day to lambast us – apparently the customer called him to complain that we were "not helpful" on the tech support line. When we explained what had happened, Jeff broke out laughing despite himself.

"Next time this happens, pass the call to me. You *should* have just *sold* her a scanner, man."

Intel Overdrive Chip and Last Day at SSI Micro

My last day at SSI Micro felt like I was attending my own funeral. Everyone I had met, including Rod, came to say their goodbyes. They treated me like I had been a part of their family – like I was one of them, a lonely adult who had gone astray in life and ended up wrangling computers in the dusty one-horse town.

Jeff was the last to see me off and handed me a cheque and a gift-wrapped box as I boarded the Greyhound bus. "Don't open it until you get home. And phone me if you're up here next summer. We'll figure out a job for ya. The ISP should be up by then."

When I got back to the acreage a few days later I opened the mysterious gift. It contained an Intel Overdrive 486 DX4-100 MHz CPU chip. I almost fainted.

I couldn't get the chip installed quickly enough into the empty CPU socket on the PS/1's motherboard. After enduring years of Andrew's scornful remarks about my IBM PS/1, I had a half dozen nasty remarks ready for him and his pathetic Intel DX2-66 MHz PC. Man, revenge was gonna be sweet.

My vicious retribution fantasies were soon sunk by a curiously dark monitor and shrieking *beeeee-eeeee-eeeeeep!* from the PC speaker on boot. I re-seated the CPU in its socket and rebooted to the same dead screen and blaring noise.

I skimmed through the PS/1 technical manual and re-read the instructions on Intel Overdrive CPU installation. The manual patiently explained that there were two versions of the Intel Overdrive CPU: "ODP" and "ODPR". The *ODPR* replaced the old CPU and sat in the existing socket. The *ODP* version used a secondary "upgrade" socket and ran alongside the existing non-removable CPU. My family's IBM PS/1 had an empty overdrive socket required on the motherboard, which meant that I needed the *ODP* version of the chip.

I plucked the Intel Overdrive chip from its socket and

examined the fine white lettering imprinted on the black heatsink's surface.

`DX4`*`ODPR`*`100`

No! No! No! No!

It was impossible to believe. Due to some minor technical difference between products, my dreams of turning the PS/1 into a powerhouse were ruined. I called Jeff who was less than thrilled about the error, as the product was not returnable. He told me to send it back to him and he'd send me a cheque for the value of the chip, and I could go out shopping for my own CPU upgrade instead.

A week later a cheque for two hundred dollars showed up in the mail. The Intel Overdrive CPU had cost over $350 at retail, but thanks to his relationship with Ingram Micro – a wholesale distributor of computer parts – he bought the CPU for half that. As far as he was concerned, it was a $200 gift. But for me, as a retail consumer, there was no way I could afford to buy the CPU at a store, so I deposited the cheque into my bank account. It stung to know that I had come *this close* to owning my dream machine.

1996: Grade Twelve

Ultima IX and Ultima Online

I was now in the twelfth grade and hungry for a new Ultima experience. I began scouring web sites for hours, using my mother's university dial-up account and visits to the campus computing lab for anything "ultima". It was a dozen hours before I came across a few important leads. The first lead was a fuzzy, hazy scan of three screenshots taken from an article in a German computer game magazine. One screenshot showed a high-resolution 3D rendering of a stone staircase in a medieval tower. The level of visual detail impressed me as it reminded me of games like *Myst* where the game was played as an interactive slideshow of pre-rendered 3D images.

However, the screenshots I was looking at were clearly described as being "in-engine" renderings – meaning that the computer was actively rendering each polygon on the screen in real-time. In-engine rendering meant that the player could change the camera angle or zoom in an out on objects, instead of being stuck with a pre-rendered image that the developer chose. A second screenshot showed a cord of firewood neatly stacked; alongside it an axe was buried in a wood-chopping stump, all within steps of a cozy medieval cottage. These textured, arresting 3D graphics went far beyond the visuals I had seen in 3D games like *Wing Commander* and *Mario Kart*. I suspected that whatever this game was, it was going to be a game changer for the 3D gaming market.

It was then that I caught the subtitle below the screenshots: "Early production models from *Ultima IX*". I gasped. This was going to be the next Ultima game in the series? Here, take my money! And here's my computer and box of hockey cards too!

Take all of it!

And then I read the rest of the web page: the screenshots were taken from an early "alpha" version of the game which was nowhere near complete. According to the web page, it would be at least a year before I'd see *Ultima IX* on the shelves.[59] Like my prospects of having a girlfriend any time soon, my chances of playing *Ultima IX* existed only in an adolescent imagination fuelled by a couple of sexy photos printed in a magazine. I slumped down in my seat. I needed to consult with the official source for an *Ultima IX* release date.

Origin Systems' official web site had no information on the game; in fact there was little information beyond the company's logo and information for investors. It was definitively a *corporate* web page, as the idea of game "community relations" did not exist on the web yet. A single line of text at the bottom of the news page caught my eye: it described an upcoming experimental online experience.

Unbeknownst to me a tiny skunkworks team at Origin Systems had been messing around with a networked multi-player version of *Ultima VI* – a game already several years old. This hacked version of *Ultima VI* allowed a few Origin employees to adventure together in Britannia and kill monsters and collect loot. The multiplayer version of the game had never been released to the public, and existed only as a fun hack for employees to tool around with.

---

[59] *Ultima IX: Ascension* had a far more turbulent development process than many other computer games. The game's engine was rebuilt twice to compete with other 3D games that had come on to the market, as well as 3D accelerated video graphics cards that were popularized in the late 1990's. The alpha version shows in magazines never saw the light of day as it was a non-3D-accelerated or "software rendered" game engine. The move to 3D proved disastrous for the newly acquired Origin Systems and its owner Electronic Arts, adding three extra years of development time to the game, which finally shipped four years later with serious bugs and rendering speed issues. The *Ultima* series effectively ended with not a bang, but a whisper.

The idea of a multiplayer *Ultima* languished as a proof-of-concept until Richard Garriott, creator of the *Ultima* series, convinced the CEO of Electronic Arts to fund a minuscule development team to explore the potential of a multiplayer Ultima game. According to the book *Dungeons and Dreamers,* Richard put together a small team with a $250,000 budget tasked with cobbling together a much more elaborate version of the engine that allowed *many* players to play together simultaneously.

The project grew from a couple of hackers to a dedicated team that built servers and new artwork for the game; eventually the project evolved to the point where hundreds (and later: thousands) of players could potentially play together simultaneously. This growing project, first known internally as *Multima,* was renamed to *Ultima Online.*

All I saw that particular day was a single link to a new web site and I followed it. The web page sang out to me like a 19th century paperboy on the corner of a gritty London street: "PRE-ALPHA TESTERS WANTED!" The company was looking for people to play the new *Ultima Online* game and were inviting the general public to submit applications. There was a small submission form that asked a few basic questions about my computer's technical specifications and my e-mail address. I hit the submit button after entering my vitals and got a terse response, "Thank you for your submission! We will contact selected applicants in the coming months."

My mind raced in circles. What was it going to be like? Would the game look like *Ultima VII or VIII or IX?* Or would the game be more like a BBS door game or an Internet-based MUD?[60] How

---

[60] MUD: Multi-User Dungeon. Although I had little experience with MUDding, these text-only games had existed on the Internet for over a decade by 1995. MUDs were text-only role-playing environments similar to the BBS door games I had become enamoured with a few years earlier. Players could explore a territory, kill monsters and find treasures whilst developing the skills and abilities of the character, all in

many other people could I play the game with? Did I play as the "Avatar" – the saviour protagonist of the earlier games in the series? What was the storyline about and did everyone else play through the story at the same time? Was the malevolent arch-nemesis called "The Guardian" a part of this game as he was in *Ultima VII* and *Ultima VIII*?

The next day I raced to school to brag to Andrew about the juicy new info I had uncovered thanks to the World Wide Web. Just imagine! *Ultima IX* was to be rendered in three dimensions! And even crazier – another *Ultima* game where I could roam Britannia with other people at the same time!

I droned on and on about the possibilities of these two games, and his attention flagged and eventually grew into annoyed disinterest. I had not realized that the day I had scooped *Ultima VII* from Willy I had brashly stepped into his personal gaming territory. Uncovering new information about the Ultima series before he did was akin to a colonial invasion and declaration of war. The tension lurking under the surface of our friendship was beginning to float to the top but at the time I had no idea I was overstepping gamer-nerd boundaries. To Andrew this was almost marital infidelity – I was practically hitting on his hot wife in front of him as he stood there cuckolded.

Despite every effort I made to convince Andrew to sign up for the upcoming *Ultima Online* pre-alpha test he was nonplussed. None of my other school friends were interested either; to them, games were something to be played with other people in the same room. Playing with other people remotely over telephone lines was *weird*. My growing obsession with computer games and the Internet was quickly running me out of friends to share any of my passion and excitement for them.

---

a world comprised of ASCII text. MUDs were different from BBS door games in one respect: MUDs could support hundreds (if not thousands) of simultaneous users who could speak with one another in real-time. MUDs were a crucial influence upon the development of future online RPGs like *Ultima Online, EverQuest* and *World of WarCraft*.

In the end I did the one thing I knew how to do: instead of changing my tastes to suit my friends, I began looking for new friends. I wanted to find people who were just as wound up about Ultima games as I was. It would take four lonely months before I came across a group of Ultima fanatics. I found them all the day I played *Ultima Online*.

Ultima Online Pre-Alpha Test

It was February and the snow was melting around our acreage, the poplar trees and pussy willows were on the verge of showing their delicate buds. I sat in front of the computer and gazed out the window absently watching geese landing on our frozen pond as they migrated north, a few days early and visibly confused by the dark ice.

I had all but given up on the prospect of the *Ultima Online* test I had applied to months earlier. Although I checked my e-mail every single day, Origin Systems was completely silent on the development of the game.

Then, one day, I received an e-mail notice from an administrator at owo@origin.ea.com:

```
From: Edmond L. Meinfelder
Subject: Ultima Online Pre-Alpha Testing
Date: Friday, February 16, 1996 9:07 PM

Well done my friend. By applying to test the pre-
Alpha version of Ultima Online, you not only get to
experience and exciting new world, but also help us
make the world more stable and enjoyable for all.

There are a few things you should know, however. Pre-
alpha means the game is not finished -- far from it,
in fact! Almost daily, the look and feel of Ultima
Online changes. For example, the lands seen in the
pre-alpha test will be fairly flat, but the final
game will have rolling hills, mountains and cliffs.
What you see now is not what you will get later, but
instead, merely a taste of what is to come.
Combat, skills and most of the game-system are in
their primal stages. You, as a tester, are not only
welcome to comment on what you see, but encouraged to
do so; please keep this in mind when you visit us
online. Despite the early state of the gaming system,
we plan to include a few quests and some interesting
things to do.
```

The setting for the upcoming test features only a map of the city of Britain, which is limited to 250 players at one time. We regret this limitation, but at this early stage we do not yet have multiple maps up and running. In the future, Ultima Online shall support a huge number of maps and players, all limited solely by the number of computers available to run to the server software. Ultima Online will be the largest Ultima ever.

Right now, the Ultima Online client only runs on Windows '95. Perhaps later we will port the client software to many other operating systems, but for now Windows '95 is a requirement. Another requirement is Internet conductivity. Your machine must be able to send and receive TCP/IP packets to and from sites on the Internet. If you can run either Netscape or Mosaic, chances are very good you can play Ultima Online. Because Windows '95 is a substantial operating system, we recommend a system with the following requirements:

Pentium 60, 486dx4-100 or better
12 megabytes of RAM
Slip/PPP or direct Internet connection connect at 14.4k bps or better
PCI Video
CD-ROM Drive, double-speed (or faster)
16 bit Sound Card (or better)

Please note these optimum requirements are for our currently unoptimized software. In fact, we padded the above requirements with a wide margin for error. As a tester, another of your jobs is to tell us how well the client software works on your system.

As we get closer to test-time, you will receive another electronic mail message with information on obtaining the client, reporting bugs, and commenting on the state of the game. Barring unexpected delays, the test date is sometime in mid-March. For now, we shall use your email address and a password to allow entry onto the game.

There is no charge to test. After all, you are helping us to create a more solid product, and for that, we thank you. so, get ready to step into a new,

```
but familiar world and stay as long as you wish. We
sincerely hope you like our new vision of Britannia.
The Ultima Online Team.
```

I knew immediately what it was and my eyes skimmed through the enthusiastic, stately notice: I had been accepted as a pre-alpha tester and the test would begin in two weeks. Later, an e-mail arrived with a link to the pre-alpha "client" – the piece of software that would give me access to the online game. I gasped at the size of the download: it was a single ZIP file of fifteen megabytes! It would take my 14.4K modem over three hours to download the game client.

For most testers the large file was a minor annoyance. But for me the size problem was crippling, because my mother's campus dial-up Internet account had a maximum two-hour limit. This meant that there was no way I could download the entire client to my hard drive in one shot; back in those days there was no such thing as "resuming" an interrupted file transfer. I fretted over the problem for days.

In the end there was no way to download the whole client to my home PC over the phone lines, so I turned to my old standby method of acquiring software: via the campus computer lab. It took a few hours of fiddling, but I managed to "split" the fifteen megabyte client into ten equal-size 1.44 megabyte chunks using a program called ARJ, which were then copied to ten high-density 3.5" diskettes. The file-splitting trick was courtesy of the clever BBS pirates who had recently run into the same problems trading large games over the phone lines.[61]

That evening I unpacked the hefty client on my PS/1's hard drive and I immediately ran the program to find out what the game was like. Unsurprisingly, the client did absolutely nothing until it was able to connect to an Internet server. As Origin

[61] Although largely forgotten today, one of the first MS-DOS based multi-part archiving programs was not the popular "PKZIP" compression program, but rather its worthy competitor "ARJ". It took several years for PKZIP to add multi-part archive support.

Systems had not made the Internet server publicly available to players, the client just sat dumbly awaiting a connection until it timed out. It was excruciating – like buying a brand new car with an empty gas tank and no gas station for miles around. Yeah, I could climb inside the car and press the pedals and honk the horn, but it felt like I had bought a three thousand pound paperweight.

Although it was strictly forbidden to use the family phone line before my appointed 9PM slot, I painstakingly cleared it with my father and sister and mother that I absolutely, positively, needed the phone as soon as I got home from school for the rest of the night. I promised that I would never make this request again (an abject lie) if they only granted me permission just this once.

My stomach was in knots as I dialled in to the campus modem pool. Was this even going to work? Was there a manual I could refer to somewhere that would teach me how to play the game? What was the interface like?

As my mind raced I was jarred out of my stupor with the sound of a busy signal. I dialled again. Busy. Again. Busy. I spent the next two hours hitting the redial button trying to get a connection to the university. I felt like crying in agony, imagining that the test was going to be over by the time the miserly campus modems let me access the Internet. As it turns out, the pre-alpha test was scheduled precisely during an exam week at the college and students were feverishly raking the modem pool across hot coals desperately trying to complete term projects.

Finally I got a connection and glanced at the clock: I had lost over two hours of my evening just getting online. I rushed to launch the client and was prompted with a very rudimentary character creation window – a simple kind that only asked for the name of my character and allowed me to modify a few character statistics like strength, dexterity and intelligence. I clicked a button to login to the server and waited anxiously. The screen went black for a minute and I held my breath. 14.4K was considered the slowest acceptable modem speed for the game which recommended a blazing 28.8K modem.

Meeting Britannians in the Pre-Alpha

The first thing I remember seeing was a large stone temple with brown roof tiles and dead naked bodies everywhere. Well, they were *sort of* naked. The bodies were all identical and sexless and all were wearing white Huggies. A grin spread across my face. I looked at my character centred on the screen from the familiar isometric perspective used in the prior Ultima games: I was dressed as some kind of vagrant, I held a hatchet in one hand, and there was a brick-shaped leather backpack on my back. I wore ratty breeches and a puffy shirt that looked none too clean either. There was no way I was "The Avatar" of the previous games who had always been portrayed as a knight in shining armour. Nope, in this version of Britannia I was a dishevelled, filthy bum.

I watched other characters casually walk around outside of the temple and followed them around. I clicked to walk my character south of the temple, and three full seconds later my character took a jittery step south. The lag in the connection, either due to my modem or line noise or Origin's server, was so bad that I could not walk at a normal pace. Meanwhile, people zoomed past me as if they were on speed. It was intolerable taking a single step every few seconds, but I had little choice; I persisted in slogging my way outside of the temple southwards.

As I passed inns and shops I began to recognize my surroundings: I was in the fantasy medieval city of Britain, the capitol of Britannia and the seat of Lord British's palace. My slow-motion walking tour of the city was exciting at first, but it took a full hour before I got to the suburbs – a trip that should have taken a couple of minutes at most. I fidgeted with the mouse and wondered what the heck I was supposed to *do* in this game anyway? Prior Ultima games centred on a saviour protagonist called "The Avatar" whose role was nothing less than saving the world. The *Ultima Online* pre-alpha test came with no instructions nor introductory cutscene. There was no overarching plot that sent me off on a grand quest to kill an evil sorcerer or protect the world against a malevolent entity or unearth a sacred artifact. It was simply a world of characters running around talking to one another.

I walked towards a bridge and a vibrantly coloured knight walked up to me. Their emerald green plate armour made me look like a down-and-out drifter.

"Hail sir!"

I smiled and replied in the same polite pseudo-medieval Britannian patois I had learned from *Ultima VII*, "Good morrow to thee."

The knight would have bowed if he could have and said, "Dost thou wish to join me for an adventure, sir?"

Before I could think up a clever response phrased in courteous, playful jargon, my fingers hammered out, "YES!"

The knight momentarily dropped his chivalrous mannerisms too and replied, "Okay cool. Follow."

He obviously was on a much faster connection than I, and sped off behind a building north of the temple. I lost him immediately and he kept having to return to let me follow his turnings. It was like I was driving Archie's backfiring jalopy trying to follow a Lamborghini through New York City. It took almost ten minutes to walk just a few screen-lengths north, where the knight had dropped several items on the ground.

"Here, take all this," the knight gestured to the pile of equipment.

A minute later I was dressed in identical green armour to the knight: a green helmet, green plate armour, a curved green heater shield, and a jolly bright green skirt.

Returning to my Britannian formality I thanked them for the equipment, "If I may ask, generous knight, what is thy name?"

"LaWizard Dragon. T'is my pleasure."

I introduced myself with equal parts formality and goofy excitement. LaWizard must have sensed my enthusiasm for either his companionship or the game because he immediately suggested we form a guild of companions: we would call ourselves the "Green Skirt Guild" or GsG. I smiled; I had made my first online friend. Despite knowing this was a completely imaginary fantasy world enabled by modems and computer servers and programmers, the connection I made with this person *felt* real and I was bursting with pleasure.

When I watch people play online games today the fundamental excitement of anonymous social exchanges seems all but lost. No one thinks anything of saying hello to another player, or being invited out to a "raid" to kill a clutch of monsters, or joining a party for an expedition into a deep dungeon. These social exchanges are about as exciting to most players as seeing strangers in a crowded subway station. But in 1996, the idea of *talking* with another people in a Ye Olde English vernacular that existed only in a fantasy medieval world in a series of computer role-playing games, which existed only on an Internet server located thousands of kilometres away, in real time, was absolutely orgasmic for a lonely dorky teenager. The instantaneous interactive graphical chat alone made the *Ultima Online* pre-alpha test an unforgettable moment in my life.

Minutes later, LaWizard and I ventured forth for our first battle with a clutch of orcs who held a bridge in the southwestern portion of Britain. Before I even swung my mighty axe the screen went black, and I awoke on the floor of the temple, wearing only a pair of white Huggies like everyone else. Apparently when a character died in the game they were automatically resurrected in the temple. An orc had hewn me down during a moment of extreme Internet lag.

I opened my backpack to retrieve my spare axe and some gold to buy myself new equipment, and found my pack was emptied of its contents. My face flushed and I felt a wave of nausea. I had lost all of the gorgeous green equipment LaWizard had given me only minutes earlier! As it turned out, when a character died in the game their corpse was left with all of his or her equipment intact in it, ripe for pilfering from marauding bands of orcs or thieves. It was my job to run back to my place of death and retrieve my things before someone else had the pleasure of doing it.

I walked back to the bridge where I had died.[62] The orcs were gone now but the bridge was scattered with the bodies of other unfortunate souls. I searched the nameless corpses for my equipment to no avail and eventually walked away with someone else's axe and clothing. I ventured over the bridge into the farmlands surrounding the city and noticed a rabbit minding its own business in the grass. A couple of dozen axe hacks later, the rabbit uttered a death shriek and I searched its corpse for loot. I found a ham. Yes, the dead rabbit was apparently made of ham. I next attacked a deer, which almost killed me in the process, and when it died it also yielded a shoulder of ham. I then began scourging the farms around Greater Pre-Alpha Britain murdering innocent creatures and taking their hams.

I heard a soft click at the back of the computer that jarred me out of my daze. It was the modem disconnecting. Damn! It seemed like only minutes had passed but a glance at the clock revealed that my two hours of university-rationed Internet time was up. I had been so engrossed in the world that I had not only missed supper with my folks, but my sister was already drawing a bath and getting ready for bed. I hit the redial button and scooted to the kitchen while the modem dialled, and returned with a bowl of *Froot Loops* just in time to see the campus dial-in SLIP login prompt appear.

The rest of the night was consumed with exploring Britain and killing animals and chatting with Britannians and rebuilding my collection of green armour. Due to my slow connection there was no way I could hope to survive combat with high-level monsters like orcs but I could at least enjoy medieval fantasy Britain as a tourist. I fell asleep at the keyboard and awoke at 2am before stumbling off to bed.

---

[62] Fellow pre-alpha testers (and later, *Ultima Online* beta players) will remember this infamous bridge as "The Bridge of Death" (BoD) named after the hundreds of players slaughtered at the site by orcs.

I only got a few hours of sleep that night and awoke early enough to get online before my parents could put an end to my phone line hogging. It was a Saturday and now hundreds of players were in the world, murdering every creature – and player – in sight. It was a bloodbath. One mage by the name of Malicious Dragon had found a way to wreak havoc outside of the temple. He had discovered that the "Darkness" spell created a circular black splotch on the screens of every player in his vicinity. The spell was meant to obscure the view of enemies so that the spellcaster could beat a hasty retreat. The nasty black smudge blocked out everything in the centre of the screen like a smoke bomb and took minutes to disappear. As a powerful sorcerer Malicious discovered that he could cast the spell several times in quick succession, thus blacking-out an entire area of the game for every player standing there. He covered the entire temple area of Britain with Darkness – the area where dead players were resurrected. Players who awoke in the temple rose to completely black screens, crying out helplessly that they couldn't see. Malicious cackled away insanely at his hijinks at the edge of the temple and typed out a smiley emoticon to me as I watched. Although the word did not exist yet, it was the first time I had witnessed "griefing"[63] in an interactive online game.

The *Ultima Online* pre-alpha test, demoed at the 1996 Los Angeles Electronic Entertainment Expo (E3) trade show, lasted three days. The test ended with a royal address from Lord British himself, as played by Richard Garriott – the creator of the Ultima series. Lord British stood upon the ramparts of Castle Britannia and addressed the dozens if not hundreds of players crammed in front of the walls. A screenshot taken at that moment shows me,

---

[63] Griefing: a player who exploits a bug or feature of a game in order to annoy other players.

once again dressed in glorious Green Skirt Guild raiment, standing at the edge of the screen trying to force my way closer to the wall. Seconds later the server disconnected me. It was overloaded with people and suffering from horrific lag, which everyone complained about and littered the screen with messages about it. I gave up trying to reconnect to the server after a dozen failures and never got to see Lord British's stately address to his loyal (and disloyal) subjects. A few minutes later the server was shut down and the E3 pre-alpha test was over.

Lord British (center-top) addresses his lagging subjects during the pre-alpha test. Screenshot courtesy of Moongates.com and David "Auric" Hernly.

I had hoped the pre-alpha test would sate my hunger for more Ultima, but it only increased my appetite. In the coming weeks I scoured the World Wide Web for more information about *Ultima Online* and *Ultima IX*. I was not alone. *Ultima Online* themed message boards sprang up overnight and Usenet discussion groups were ablaze with buzz about the pre-alpha test. This game was going to change everything we knew about computer games and every Ultima fan wanted to be in on the ground floor. It was in those growing days of excitement about the game that I discovered Internet Relay Chat and found a community of like-minded Ultima fanatics. These fellow nerds became my friends, enemies, lovers, guildmates and confidants, and they defined my social life for the next few years.

Within weeks of the pre-alpha test two web message boards, "Andrew's Place" and "LaWizard's Chat Zone" became communal town squares for the pre-alpha fan diaspora. It turned out that my fellow Green Skirt Guildmate, LaWizard, was also a technowizard and knew how to set up a message board using the primordial UNIX tools that defined the World Wide Web of the 1990s.

Web boards in the 1990s were much different than the complex message board software used today. Today, if a person wants to post a message on a community message board, they must first sign up, select an alias, password, enter their e-mail address, pass some annoying anti-robot security question, and get approved by an administrator. Afterwards a new user is given the lowest level of security clearance to post on the board until they have proven that they are not going to generate spam or annoy other people with childish remarks. Users can edit typos in their messages and delete erroneous posts with ease, and can even write private messages to other board members. Members often receive automated e-mail that notify them when someone posts a reply to their message.

In contrast, a WWW board of 1996 was little more than a web page with a submission form at the bottom. The HTML form, backed by a "CGI script" often written in the C or Perl languages, allowed anyone to enter their name, type up a message, and hit the submit button. Their message would immediately be added as a link to the Web board's main index page for anyone and everyone in the world to read. Deleting an erroneous message required the system administrator to manually edit the HTML tags of the index page and remove the offending link. There was nothing preventing an annoying person from spamming the board with nuisance posts, or writing messages using someone else's name. The only person who could edit posts was the server administrator which meant that members had to be incredibly careful when posting an opinion; anything posted was immediately public and potentially incendiary. There were no automated notification e-mails that let you know when there were new messages; the only way to see if there was a reply to your message was to hit the "refresh" button in Netscape Navigator and wait for the web page to reload.

All of these features of early Web boards must sound – to today's Internet users – unbearable. But Andrew's Place and LaWizard's Chat Zone exploded with activity because the opportunity to write messages to other Ultima fanatics far outweighed the technical irritations. Every minute there were at least a dozen posts added to each board during peak hours. These two boards became my prime attraction every evening, and I contributed my two cents to the writhing gelatinous mass of speculation about *Ultima IX, Ultima Online,* and Origin Systems.

And boy did these boards generate opinion. Not only did the boards attract fans of the Ultima franchise, but they also created a fan base for the boards themselves. Fans immediately declared their allegiance to one board or the other, and both Andrew and LaWizard only encouraged posters in their devotion by playing equal parts beneficent fathers and cruel overlords. Users became so absorbed in their religious zeal that some planned secret "takeovers" of the enemy board and grouped together to it with messages. It was good, dirty, childish fun.

After a few days I saw a reply to one of my messages from LaWizard Dragon himself. He had recognized my alias and welcomed me as a fellow guildmate to his board! I wish I could say that I played it cool and pretended like we were old war buddies by nodding a polite hello and heading over to the nearest pub for a pint. But I was a lonely teenager and being acknowledged publicly as a friend of the server administrator was like being ceremonially knighted in front of a gaggle of shit-raking peasants. I replied to LaWizard's greeting with the most sycophantic tone I could muster and bowed formally (yes, I really wrote "*bows to thee*" in the reply) to the man I considered my guildmaster. Thankfully he was not too embarrassed by my public display of fealty and invited me to a more intimate venue for conversation. In his usual concise conversational style he wrote,

```
Posted by LaWizard Dragon at 10:16:44 on April 28,
1996
Hey,
I remember you. Come by #ultima on EFnet IRC.
-LaWizard
```

It took a few minutes to figure out what the message even meant. As I have mentioned before there was no search oracle like Google to query with a random technical question. Discovering the meaning of an acronym might involve hours of research just to determine which searchable database to consult in the first place. Fortunately, the word "IRC" meant only one thing to the denizens of the Internet at the time and I tracked down its meaning fairly quickly from an online hacker dictionary: it meant "Internet Relay Chat".

IRC turned out to be a protocol, or a set of protocols, that lived on a different layer of the Internet – sort of like how the FTP, e-mail and Usenet protocols occupy their own separate layers of services.. all served over the same network of wires. IRC enabled users to gather in a single virtual space – chat rooms – and talk with one another in a text-only environment. Live chat rooms served over the World Wide Web were still in their infancy thanks to the slow growth of Java, and IRC was already years old by this point. IRC was a far more complex approach to chat than Web chat, requiring the user to first download an IRC client, then choose an IRC server to connect to, then join a chat room or "channel", before any chatting happened. This convoluted process dissuaded the majority of Web users of the late 1990s from ever trying IRC… this meant that most IRC users were technofetishists like myself. The high technical barrier to entry meant that only the nerdiest of the nerdy hung out on IRC… and like any dedicated bar fly, they always landed at the same place every night.

I downloaded the only IRC client that seemed straightforward enough to use: a Windows 3.11 client called *mIRC* (pronounced "murk"). Thanks to its user-friendly nature *mIRC* showed me that "EFnet" was short for an extremely popular server called "Eris FreeNet" at efnet.org. I connected *mIRC* to EFnet and joined the #ultima channel just as LaWizard had instructed me.

IRC turned out to be a blend of the intensely intimate Bulletin Board System cultures and wildly eclectic anonymous Internet chat room cultures. Upon entering the #ultima channel my chat window flooded with text, scrolling line-by-line like a player piano script. It was unbelievably similar to the multi-node BBS chat I had seen years earlier.

People were chatting excitedly about all kinds of things simultaneously and it was difficult to tune into any particular conversation thread. There were at least five different discussions happening concurrently between thirty participants, turning the chat window into a haphazard flood of text that took a while to decrypt into separate conversations. One group of people was discussing the latest news about the upcoming id Software title *Quake* while another was debating the effectiveness of spells in the *Ultima Online* pre-alpha test; a third group was cracking puerile dick jokes and a fourth group spoke in-character as eloquent, chivalrous Britannians. Figuring out who was addressing whom was a skill in itself.

I was overwhelmed by the beehive of activity and did the only thing I thought would be appropriate for a channel full of Ultima fans. I bowed formally and introduced myself with a silly "Good morrow to thee all!" The first to reply were the renaissance faire types who responded with their most courtly expressions of welcome. Their warmth was equally offset by the cool "supz" and "yo" I got from the majority of the channel's inhabitants. Obviously there was some kind of a division between those who wanted to simply play Ultima games for entertainment, and those who wanted to live in the fantasy world of Britannia. This cultural difference within the channel respectively mapped to the difference between how my school friend Andrew perceived Ultima, and how I did. He was into the games for the combat, dark narratives and black comedy. But I wanted to *live there*.

LaWizard eventually noticed my presence in the channel and sent a private chat message and welcomed me to #ultima. He explained that the channel was a mix of pre-alpha expats, "posers" who claimed to be in the pre-alpha but had clearly never set foot in cyber-Britannia, and there were a handful or Origin Systems employees who dropped by the channel occasionally. I asked him who these Origin employees were and he replied coolly, "Sorry dude. Can't say. Private."

It did not take long to discover who these secretive employees were, for they did not work hard to conceal themselves with their choices of "nicknames" or online aliases. The ostentatious nicknames they chose went by an implicit naming convention: Lord_Gimli, Lord_Pall, Lord_Hades… the honorific denoting their lordly status as *Ultima Online* administrators. It was also clear that they had absolutely no interest in discussing official company business in the channel either, and any prodding for news about *Ultima IX* or *Ultima Online* made the inquirer the subject of an immediate and brutal public booting.

Unlike the sovereign nation of Australia which (as far as my years of cultural research from *The Simpsons* has taught me) punishes civil delinquency with a kick to the rear with a wingtip shoe, getting booted from an IRC channel was a very public and embarrassing, symbolic act of punishment.

Internet Relay Chat servers have a built-in permission system that enables the owners or "operators" of a channel to manipulate the chat room in certain ways. The intent of these permissions is to allow operators to moderate discussions by kicking out and even banning troublemakers, while awarding "ops" status to trusted friends. Getting the boot from an IRC channel was no worse than having someone hang up the phone on you, and just meant that you would have to rejoin the channel a few seconds later. A minor technical inconvenience.

But the symbolic aspect of a public booting had sociopolitical consequences. As we see in William Golding's *Lord of the Flies*, adolescence and rampant abuses of power are synonymous with one another, and inevitably lead to a class system based on popularity and fear. Ops were considered no less than Olympian gods thanks to their powers, for they had the ability to discipline, punish or reward anyone they saw fit to. Were you pestering an Origin employee about the upcoming *Ultima Online* beta test? Kicked. Begging for ops from an operator? Kicked, then if you returned to the channel too soon, banned. Even speaking in full Britannian lingo with thee's and thou's was only tolerated to a point in #ultima, and some of the more fickle operators awarded a guest's courtliness with a boot to the bum. All of this added up to a channel where teenage and middle-aged Ultima fans alike vied for popularity and climbed social ladders toward sacred op-dom.

It didn't take long to adjust to the intimate yet transient culture of #ultima after my experience with BBSs. There were the original founders of the channel who held their ops designation with polite dignity, yet who suffered no fools; there were the role-playing Britannians who dropped into the channel randomly to swap chivalrous banter with one another; there were the tech-gamer barflies that had no interests beyond playing computer games and building new computers to play games on. I fell somewhere in between the last two subcultures and found myself speaking Britannian while swapping tech tips on RAM and hard drive installation.

The majority of inhabitants appeared to be in their twenties, all holding jobs or living in college dormitories. There was even a group of friends and drunkards who lived together in a shabby apartment in Toronto, Canada, under the name "The House of Rassilon". It felt to me like an eclectic group of adults, and I lived in abject fear that one of these twentysomethings would out me as 'just some dumb kid' who lived in his parents' basement.

I was never outed. It turned out that my quick typing and

accurate spelling concealed my relative immaturity. It helped that my IP address and domain name identified me as originating from a college campus and for the first year in #ultima everyone else thought I was a college student just like they were.

Finally I had discovered a place where I could talk with people who cared about computer games as much as, or even more than, I did. We had a place where we could share stories about the pre-alpha test, and show off our war scars like old online veterans. There was no risk of being overheard by classmates or parents who criticized our hobbies for being childish wastes of time. Finally I had a home to call my own.

As much as I loved talking about computer games with other nerds, playing them was even better. Within days of finding #ultima I began to search the EFnet server's list of active channels and found out that a large number of IRC channels had little to do with chat. In fact, it appeared that for many users IRC was simply a means to swap files with other people. It was like the Internet itself had grown as a means for distributing warez; whenever a new tool or service opened up a pirate was on its heels discovering a new way to amass and distribute booty!

The developers of the IRC protocols had created a tool called "Direct Client Connection" chat or DCC. DCC allowed two users to directly connect to one another, instead of having their messages routed through the IRC server first. DCC chats were important for private conversations where people needed an uninterrupted flow of chat, as EFnet servers infamously crashed or "split" from one another and interrupted conversations.[64]

---

[64] An IRC server "split" occurred when one of EFnet's servers became detached from the other servers on the network. IRC networks like EFnet were not single servers; they were a huge wide area net of geographically distant servers that all connected to one another through a common protocol. This WAN topology was important because it allowed individual users to connect to the server geographically closest of them, thus reducing network latency. In turn, the local server linked up with other nearby EFnet servers and formed a massive global network. A message that originated in Thessaloniki, Greece might bounce through eleven servers across Europe before it landed on a server in Toronto, Canada. Although today the Internet is an incredibly dense network full of interconnections between backbones and many alternate routes between destinations, in the 1990s the Internet was a much more fragile and sparse network. A collapse in a backbone route between Arlington, Virginia and Toronto, Canada might mean that you couldn't access *Yahoo!* for a few hours (or days!) until the disruption in the network was repaired. Server splits sometimes occurred when a major route between two IRC servers was disrupted, rending apart the

DCC chats were perhaps better known for one additional feature the programmers created: two users could swap files with one another.

It didn't take long for pirates to come up with ingenious ways of exploiting DCC file transfers. It was one thing to find a friend to swap a couple of games with over a DCC chat, but it was quite another to devise a method for widespread piracy to hundreds and thousands of greedy leeches like me. The invention of IRC "bots" proved a critical step toward making IRC a main hub for the distribution of warez that eventually overtook BBS piracy.

If you haven't interacted with an IRC bot before, imagine it as a computer program that is meant to ape another human being sitting at a computer in a chat channel. A bot responds to textual commands similar to a text parser in a 1990s adventure game like *King's Quest* or *Zork*. The technologies are one and the same: a command like "pick up gold ball" in *King's Quest IV* does the same thing as an IRC bot command like "!downloadwarez". When the computer interpreter in *King's Quest* reads your command, the player's character Rosella picks up the gold ball. And similarly, on IRC when the bot reads your command, it does your bidding.

In this case, the bot programmer has made the bot respond to a specific magical command word: !downloadwarez. The bot sits along with all the warm-blooded creatures in an IRC channel like #warez4all and waits for someone to trigger its magical command word. When the codeword !downloadwarez is written by a user in the #warez4all chat window, the bot launches a

---

servers and making each server into a private island. During a split the users on the Thessaloniki server could only speak to other Thessalonikians, while the users on the Toronto server could now only speak to other Torontonians. A split left each group of people beached on their own IRC server until the route between the two servers was fixed, and the chat channel could be "rejoined". Griefers often took advantage of server splits in order to "take over" or seize channels.

private DCC chat connection with the user.

Here's what the chat window looked like when a warez bot initiated a DCC with me:

```
Hottest Juarez in #warez4all since 1993!
No ratios!
No limits!
No shareware!
No freeware!
100% 0day
You are user 8/16.
Menu:
L)ist philez
D)ownload
U)pload
Q)uit
```

If the text interface of a DCC bot chat reminds you of a Bulletin Board System, it's because they were almost identical in design. The only difference was that IRC bots were stripped down to the bare essentials necessary to pirate software. Each bot functioned as a tiny server, hosting a few dozen or hundred files, carefully curated by its owner. Some bots featured 0day games, others were devoted to "oldwarez" (aka. abandonware), and a handful were devoted to pirating commercial applications or "appz" like *Lightwave 3D* and *3D Studio*.

The most popular IRC bots were illicitly hosted on powerful servers with huge hard drives and fat internet pipes without the knowledge of the server administrator; these bots could support dozens of simultaneous users. In comparison, my spindly 14.4K modem could at best support a single file transfer at 1.3 kilobytes per second. IRC bots were labours of love, like a child building a robot out of spare parts in their parents' garage; no one was making money from IRC piracy. Bots were often built just to impress compadres in the channel and gain the grudging approval of operators.

I was *not* one of those codehappy geniuses who designed a brilliant IRC bot and unleashed it upon the world to serve up pirated software just for the fun of it. I was more a slovenly leecher who obsessively joined any channel with "warez" in its title seeking free files. I began to multitask and chatted in #ultima while waiting for DCC file transfers to complete, and my phone line use skyrocketed from just a couple of hours a night to the *entire* night and some of the morning. My only limit became the PS/1's 384 megabyte hard drive which filled up within weeks, and I was forced to save new downloads to floppy disks. This was becoming a problem.

A "New" Fax Machine at the Junk Yard

The amount of time I was spending online grew geometrically every week and things became tense in the household. My sister was now dating Willy, the guy who had given me his copy of *Ultima VII*, and complained that she was missing phone calls from her boyfriend. The issue of the phone line finally came to a head when a neighbour drove over to the house to tell my father that his phone line had been busy the entire night. Everyone knew I was the perpetrator, and a major change was in order.

Like every other time I was in technological trouble with my parents, I was called to the kitchen table for an uncomfortable conversation. My father was furious that he was missing calls from neighbours and surmised that he'd likely been missing calls from his business clients as well. My mother was less concerned about the phone line itself and more about the amount of time I had been spending on the computer. I sat silently and stared at the kitchen table blankly; it felt more like an intervention than a conversation. I felt attacked. Who were *they* to tell me how I should spend my time outside of school? What was wrong with playing computer games and spending time on the Internet? I certainly could be doing worse things like drinking booze and going to parties with my underage friends like so many other farm kids did.

My mother sighed and spoke in a caring but exasperated tone, "Sometimes I wish you *would* go to a party. You need to be around your friends."

I gulped and felt acrid guilt rise into my gorge. It was true, I hadn't spent much time with my friends lately and even elected to skip out on our weekend trips to the City to watch movies at the theatre. Deep down I knew that something was wrong but as far as I was concerned computer games and Internet Relay Chat were as good, if not better than, spending time with corporeal human beings. The majority of my friends appeared to have outgrown games, my friend Andrew no longer wanted to swap shop talk about Ultima and Wing Commander, and the only people who cared about games as much as I did were the inhabitants of #ultima.

As the conversation steered towards my psychological well-being my father appeared uncomfortable and returned to his fatherly wheelhouse. He stared at me with his penetrating bulbous eyes and stabbed his finger at me, "Look here. You're only gonna be on there for two hours a night from now on."

I felt like vomiting on my shirt. I spent at least six hours a day on the Internet in past weeks, sandwiching school in between marathon online chat sessions. An interesting conversation in #ultima might take two hours just to get rolling; often it took over an hour to wait for an available download slot on a warez DCC bot. I might as well not bother dialling the Internet at all for a piddly-ass two hour session! This was the kind of cruel human rights abuse that the United Nations existed to prevent, and I was sure the Canadian Charter of Rights and Freedoms had something to say about this kind of intolerable childhood hardship. Only Russians or Italians could appreciate the harsh dictatorial regime I was living under!

My plans for a coup against the Monarchy of Mom and Dad were thwarted a couple of weeks later for the most unexpected reason.

If my father's business had struggled to get on its feet since we had moved south, now it was mortally wounded and hemorrhaging money. Clients refused to pay their bills and subsequently my father wasn't paying his either. Government tax collectors and businesses alike sent notices of arrears to our house which my father left unopened in the oak office desk. Despite the financial chaos my father continued to make extravagant purchases on credit, hoping for the day that his business would recover. A wiser businessman would have found the source of the bleeding and staunched the wound, but my father's recent mental and physical health problems only led to more anxiety-driven spending.

One day after school I received a call from my father asking me if I knew anything about Brother brand fax machines. I told him the only thing I knew: Brother made pretty good computer printers.

"Okay. Well, I'm on my way home with a fax I just bought. Don't tell your mom."

He sounded excited; a bad sign as far as I was concerned. He had a poor record with fax machines and this was no doubt another one of his business cost-saving schemes pregnant with technological disaster. I immediately thought back to an incident years earlier when he had purchased a fax machine for his business…

I was eleven and we had arrived at a large nondescript metal warehouse with a sign planted in the ground in front of it that read, "Government Surplus Auction". We stepped inside and looked into a dimly lit cavernous space with a hundred feet of metal shelving. Piled on the shelves were objects of varying sizes, each with identification number tags hanging from them. It looked like a morgue for industrial machines.

A skinny balding man dressed in a tie and short-sleeved shirt stood behind a filthy counter with a cash register and a telephone. He looked as if he had not seen a customer in years, and a decent meal in longer. He introduced himself and waved us over to the orderly yet dungeon-like warehouse.

Need a pneumatic jackhammer to break up concrete? Check aisle A4. Want a ten year old tilting hospital bed for grandma? That's in C2. Used fire extinguishers are in aisle B, but you have to get them recharged yourself at the fire station. Need an electroencephalograph? Well, boy I have a deal for you – there's a row of them in C4. Actually, aisle C is all medical stuff.

My father hated salespeople and regarded this man with disdain and expressed it in his terse reply, "I'm lookin' fer a fax machine."

"Oh, those are over in D behind the computer stuff. Somewhere near the back we've got a couple."

Computers, you say?!

I am not sure what I had imagined but when I thought of

computers and a government auction, but I surely thought I would find massive DEC PDP-11 mainframe computers sold by the pound, or *least* the decaying hulks of CRAY XMP supercomputers left out to pasture after mandatory retirement from the secret service.

Instead I found a row of ancient computer monitors, all the same make and model: thirteen-inch amber monochrome CRTs with serious phosphor burn-in. In fact, the burn-in (due to leaving a static image on the screen for hours) was so bad that it revealed the monitors' original purposes. They all had the hazy remnants of numbers and tables – some kind of government accounting system running MS-DOS or UNIX. Aside from a huge printer called a "plotter" that was almost four feet long, the computer aisle of the government surplus auction was devastatingly boring.

My father looked all over for the fax machines and found nothing until the salesman walked over and pointed at two large blue Samsonite suitcases, "Those two there. They're both the same. Both work fine too."

My dad hefted the cleaner looking suitcase off the shelf with a grunt and clicked it open. Inside was a massive metal contraption more at home in a steampunk novel than on an office desk. It looked like an oversized typewriter without a keyboard; it had a large metal drum that spun freely on a spindle. The machine occupied the entire bottom half of a suitcase large enough for a two week-long vacation. Neither my father nor I had ever *seen* a real fax machine in person before, so we naturally assumed this was what they looked like.

My father tried to look nonchalant, but was clearly as confused as I was about the machine. "You're sayin' it works right? I don't want to drive home and find out the fuckin' thing's broken."

The salesman cooed, sensing the fish taking the bait, "Oh, *sure!* We test all of our items before they go up for auction."

Before my father could try to argue over the price, he saw the price tag hanging off the suitcase: "FINAL SALE: Buy-It-Now

$20". All the way home my father chattered excitedly about his new purchase. He picked up the handset of his massive Nokia car phone and called my mom to tell her the good news. He was as excited about his twenty dollar fax machine as I was about a new computer game. For once in my life I knew exactly how my dad felt. His enthusiasm was infectious, and even *I* was becoming excited about this bizarre contraption.

When we got home I carried the suitcase to the den. It weighed over fifty pounds and required that I squeezed both of my hands into the plastic handle of the suitcase just to carry it. I had to push aside the Amstrad just to fit the suitcase on the oak desk, and I propped open the lid with a heavy metallic snap.

In the light of the den I could now see more clearly what he had bought. Glued to the inside of the suitcase lid was a two page foldout of instructions printed with tiny red letters describing how to send and receive a facsimile. There had to be at least fifteen steps to receive a fax, and sending a fax was even more complicated. Of course fax machines had to be complicated – you were sending paper over a phone line for God sakes! My father told me to read the instructions and get everything set up for his first transmission.

Aside from the metal drum (a printing apparatus? A scanner?) the machine had a large power supply integrated into one corner and two suction-cup looking objects in the opposite corner. The instructions described the suction cups as "acoustic couplers" that accepted a telephone handset. Acoustic couplers were vacuum-forming cups of rubber that sealed around the mouthpiece and earpiece of an old handset. Presumably the fax machine sent and received paper over the telephone line through the acoustic coupler. Presumably.

It took me almost an hour to read through the instructions and flip the levers and press the buttons involved in getting the contraption ready for use. My father had already invited over my friend Chad and his father to witness the fabulous machine at work, which was my father's rather unsubtle attempt at neighbourly bragging.

Everyone stood around me as I wrapped a sheet of paper around the metal drum and fixed it into place. I plugged in the machine and the drum spun rapidly, smacking the paper against the metal parts of the machine with a *thwap! thwap! thwap!* every second. My father called a friend who owned a fax machine and pre-arranged to have a fax sent to our home.

When the phone rang I quickly picked it up and pushed the telephone handset into the coupler with a rubbery *smuck!* and heard the faint screech of audio signals. Nobody breathed. How long was this supposed to take? A minute? Five minutes? An hour?

After five minutes of watching the paper flapping around uselessly on the drum I unplugged the machine. We tried again several times to make some kind of sense of this electromechanical nightmare; absolutely nothing was printing on the piece of paper. Eventually Chad's father spied the manufacturing date in the corner of the instructions and howled, "Jim, this thing was built in world war fuckin' two!"

My father and Chad's father disappeared into the kitchen for a beer. My father was clearly dejected at his twenty dollar boondoggle.

Chad's father teased my father mercilessly about it. "Hey Jim, I betcha the museum downtown would buy 'er from ya! Ha ha!"

The next morning I found the fax machine guts dumped into a garbage can outside. My father had kept the blue Samsonite suitcase for his travel needs. I never mentioned the fax again and neither did he.

So, years later, when my father called me from his car phone with excitement in his voice, and told me that he had bought a "new" fax machine, you can imagine my tired groan. Given our family's desperate finances no doubt he had found some kind of "deal" that he imagined would save him hundreds of dollars in the long run. I was afraid to ask how old the machine was, thinking of the fifty-pound beast in the blue Samsonite suitcase.

It was a pleasant surprise when he arrived home with a slim *new* box containing what I recognized as a real, post-World War, fax machine. It was indeed a Brother and it did not feature an acoustic coupler nor large suitcase, although it was not the "plain paper" kind of fax machine we take for granted today. It was a fax that used a roll of special thermal paper, like the kind you'd see in a receipt printer. I hooked it up and a minute later I was sending a fax over the phone lines to a friend of my father's. My father's face brightened when he heard the phone ring a few minutes later and received his first fax – a hastily scrawled "IT WORKED" from his friend. He watched as I played with the configuration menus on the tiny LCD screen, pleased that *I* approved of his purchase. He had finally made a technology purchase on his own that had lived up to my exacting standards. And one that none of his neighbours would razz him over.

That night the gears must have been grinding in my father's head because he announced that he needed a second phone line for his beloved fax. Like the fax machine itself, he was justifying the additional cost as a necessary business expense, thus bypassing my mother's recent push for financial austerity. When my mother objected anyway, he shrugged and said, "I'll write it off on my taxes". He neglected to mention that he had not paid his taxes in years.

He could see that I had a million questions about the second phone line, and before I could open my mouth he said, "You can use it for your computer, and your sister can use the main line. But when I need it you're gonna get off."

My. Own. Phone. Line.

Let's contextualize this new development for a moment with a bit of cultural analysis. Jane Jacobs, the eminent writer of two commentaries on modernity – *The Death and Life of Great American Cities* and *Dark Age Ahead* – has a lot to say about urban planning and technology. One of her arguments is about traffic management and highway development. She notes that major cities like Los Angeles often try to solve their traffic congestion problems by building highways with more lanes, less sidewalks and complex crisscrossing overpass systems. Jacobs argues quite persuasively that these planning measures do not actually reduce congested traffic but in fact *increase* congestion over the long run. As highways become wider and faster this temporarily increases the total carrying capacity of vehicles, which only attracts more drivers and more vehicles in the long run. A congested two-lane highway is a frustration. A congested ten-lane highway is a nightmare. Humanity abhors a vacuum.

I bring up Jacob's analysis of urban traffic problems here because my father made the same mistake about telephone lines as the city of Los Angeles did about roads. He thought that adding an extra phone line would free up valuable phone time in an era where call waiting and voicemail were nonexistent. He thought there was *no way* one human being could completely saturate a phone line 24 hours a day.

How wrong he was.

For the rest of that month the only thing preventing me from being online 24 hours a day was the two hour limit imposed by the campus dial-up service. As soon as I got home from school I began dialling and redialling the modem pool until I got a connection; even my eating and urinating schedules began operating on a two-hour cycle. Windows 95's built-in Dial-Up Networking (DUN) system had an automated redial function that ensured I would never need to sit at the computer manually clicking the "redial" button ever again. I could dial, walk away and watch cartoons, and return when I heard the sexy screech of a modem handshake, like a mythical siren luring a sailor to his doom on the shoals.

IRC and #ultima became a home within a home and I became one of its barflies. Conversations speculating about an upcoming *Ultima Online* beta test announcement exploded into a cacophony of opinions, and the channel grew to over a hundred users at its peak. Several regulars left to form their own channels on other IRC networks like BeyondIRC and UnderNet. EFNet's #ultima remained to be the original, official home of all things Ultima.

The social relationships I had developed on IRC became more real to me than the real home and school relationships I had at the time. Several people in the channel became the only close friends I had for the remainder of my high school years, as I spent more and more time talking with cyberfriends and less and less time talking with my real life friends. Marriages and divorces both real and virtual, romantic escapades, infidelities, guild defections, face-to-face meetups at geeky conventions like GenCon, and other social dynamics developed within the IRC channels I frequented.

Channels. I was now a member of several Ultima-related IRC channels that had forked from #ultima over the past year. I do not recall the end of the eleventh grade nor do I recall much time spent with Rob, Donny, Trevor or even Andrew. When the second phone line went live in our house the real world existed only to feed, clothe and educate me, and the real fruits of social experience were modulated bits over a noisy phone line.

Ultima games still mattered to me, but like the other people who spent too much time on IRC our cyber-socializing became an end in itself rather than a means to share our love of computer games. By now I was hopelessly dependent upon the relationships I had made online and my family and friends were helpless to intervene. The term "Internet addiction" had not even been coined as a pop psychology term and here I was in the throes of it.

A Death in the Family

It was the first time in my life that I was guaranteed summer employment and I could smell the commercial carpet at SSI Micro over a thousand kilometres away; all it took was a single phone call to my old boss Jeff confirming my arrival date.

"Sure, c'mon up North, we're working on some new keen stuff!"

I was to arrive on the first Monday of July. I had a week to get together my things before I could immerse myself in computers 24/7 for two glorious months. It was like summer camp except *they* paid *me* to stay!

This time I came prepared with a suitcase instead of a garbage bag, jeans instead of jogging pants, a bunch of sci-fi novels, a copy of *MechWarrior 2*, and a pile of pirated games I planned to swap with my old co-worker Mac. It was going to be a damned good summer.

My mother had been working on a research project for her Master's thesis which involved interviewing northerners, and she timed her trip so that both of us could make the drive up north together. When we arrived in my old home town thirteen hours later I stayed the weekend with my uncle Fred, enjoying a few languid summer days before my job started. Early Monday morning we packed up my uncle's Aerostar van with sandwiches and his faithful Dalmatian and made the drive to Fort Providence.

As we drove together we caught up on each other's lives as we always did: girls, technology, science, girls, computers, school, girls, family gossip and girls. Of those six categories I had much to report on five of them. I was ashamed to admit that I had not dated anyone in high school and *definitely* had not had sex yet. No doubt my uncle found this puzzling. He had grown up in a generation where sex, cars, drugs and rock'n'roll defined adolescent life; computers and technology back then were for old white guys in business suits.

As we got closer to Fort Providence he steered the conversation toward SSI Micro. "Oh hey, you heard about Rod right?"

Rod? It took a second to jog my memory. Right: Rod. The *Star Trek* nerd from SSI whom I thought had avoided me – excusing himself to the bathroom every time I tried to make small talk with him. I tried to play it cool like I had been best friends with all of the staff there, "Oh right, Rod. Nice guy. What's he been up to lately?"

"Rod died." The words left his lips without expression, like he was reporting on the morning weather.

I gasped. "What? How?"

"He stopped showing up for work in the middle of last winter, so Jeff went to check on him. He found him curled up in his bed. Jeff said he had shrunken down to nothing but skin and bone and he had been dead there a while. Jeff called his parents and they flew down from Ontario to bury him. He was close to his mom and dad and he had told them he had been the happiest of his whole life working in Prov. I guess he had intestinal cancer and didn't tell anyone about it. He was twenty-nine. Can you believe that?"

I looked out the passenger window at the spruce trees whirring by for a long time. Why hadn't Rod told anyone he had cancer? Was he shy like me and too embarrassed to bring it up with his friends? What if I had made more of an effort to get to know him? Would he have told me about it and perhaps sought treatment? My stomach was tied in knots and I felt like crying my eyes out for him. He was a lonely guy and deserved to live a long life, and had died alone in a frozen, crummy aluminum trailer in the middle of nowhere at the age of 29. All of it felt wrong to me.

Then it hit me: he died of intestinal cancer. All the times Rod had excused himself to the washroom, all of the times he complained that his stomach was bothering him, all the times he disappeared for an hour and returned to his desk looking pale. It had nothing to do with him not liking me or not wanting to talk

Star Trek with me. When we last spoke he must have been going through the late stages of his cancer and had nothing to ease the pain he was going through. Rod had slowly died in front of my eyes and I had blamed *him* for not wanted to get to know *me*.

I do not remember the rest of the drive to Fort Providence and when I stepped into SSI Micro later that day the carpet felt different to my feet. Rod's desk, six months after his death, was left vacant and the whole building felt emptier and less exciting. Most of the same staff had remained with a few exceptions – Gary ("The Wiz") and his wife Grace had completed their contracts with the company and migrated south to Australia. The blustery salesman Stan had disappeared into the nether and in his place was a friendly young German guy named Reiner, who took up odd jobs around the company trying to cover his room and board. Mac and his wife Kasia stayed and warmly welcomed me, both choking back tears when I asked about Rod's passing. Even Jeff's infectious excitement for new technology had given way to a careworn crease on his brow. It was not quite the fireworks I had hoped for upon my arrival; it was more like coming home to family after a year spent in college.

A few days later the initial shock wore off and I settled into the comforts of living in a giant computing facility again. The rack of Internet servers hummed gently behind me as I answered tech support calls and repaired the occasional computer. When Jeff found out that I had experimented all year with Internet services over the campus dial-up, he began training me to manage the company's BSD UNIX server.

Over the past year, SSI Micro had flourished into a 24/7 subscription-based Internet Service Provider, riding the massive wave of enthusiasm people of the North had for Internet access.

* * *

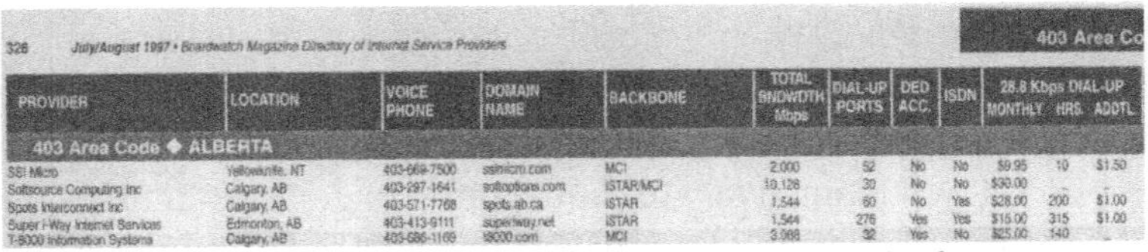

326 July/August 1997 • Boardwatch Magazine Directory of Internet Service Providers

403 Area Co

PROVIDER	LOCATION	VOICE PHONE	DOMAIN NAME	BACKBONE	TOTAL BNDWDTH Mbps	DIAL-UP PORTS	DED ACC.	ISDN	28.8 Kbps DIAL-UP MONTHLY	HRS.	ADDTL
403 Area Code ◆ ALBERTA											
SSI Micro	Yellowknife, NT	403-669-7500	ssimicro.com	MCI	2.000	52	No	No	$9.95	10	$1.50
Softsource Computing Inc	Calgary, AB	403-297-1641	softoptions.com	ISTAR/MCI	10.128	30	No	No	$30.00	–	–
Spots Interconnect Inc	Calgary, AB	403-571-7768	spots.ab.ca	ISTAR	1.544	60	No	Yes	$28.00	200	$1.00
Super I-Way Internet Services	Edmonton, AB	403-413-9111	superiway.net	ISTAR	1.544	276	Yes	Yes	$15.00	315	$1.00
T-8000 Information Systems	Calgary, AB	403-686-1169	t8000.com	MCI	3.088	32	Yes	No	$25.00	140	–

A clipping from Boardwatch magazine (July 1997), showing SSI Micro's dial-up Internet offerings.

When Jeff showed me the big fat Internet pipe (in reality: a thin telephone wire) that SSI Micro fed its customers from, I gasped.[65] It was not nearly as fast as the campus network, but at 768 Kbaud - just shy of a megabit per second - it was at least fifty times faster than my home connection.

The speed of our connection proved a godsend when, a week later, Jeff announced that one of the employees had set up a publicly accessible *Quake* "deathmatch" server on our network. This meant that anyone on the Internet could connect to our server and play this insanely popular first person shooter with other people. Within a day word spread through SSI Micro's clientele and several of our customers were playing deathmatches until the wee hours of the morning.

---

[65] The BSD Unix server in 1996-1997 was a Gateway 2000 Pentium 90, which handled all traffic for World Wide Web, FTP and shell accounts. The server connected to a Livingston Portmaster 2e terminal server, which in turn was connected to dozens of US Robotics Sportster 33.6K modems. The Yellowknife point-of-presence server 44 dial-in lines, Hay River point-of-presence served 12 lines, and our Fort Providence location server a meagre 4 lines. This was all fed to southern Canada via 768,000 baud leased line from CA NET Edmonton, equivalent to the speed of half of a T1 line. Source: https://web.archive.org/web/19970524131924/http://www.ssimicro.com/ourgear.htm

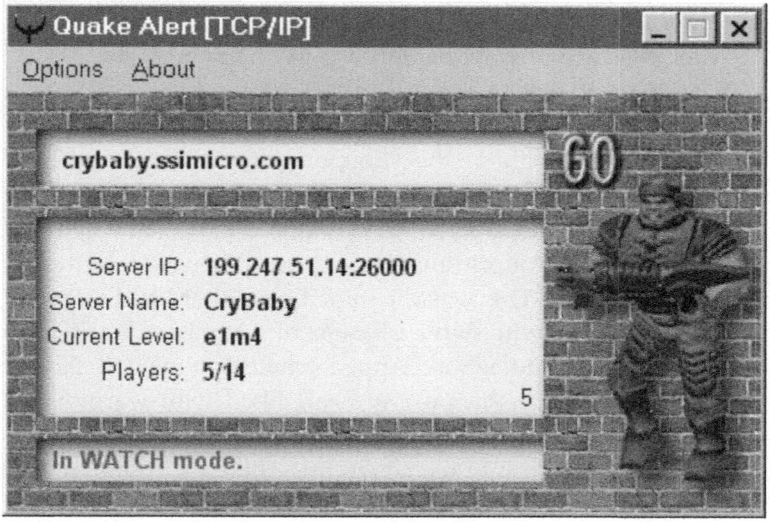

"Crybaby" was SSI Micro's Quake Deathmatch server; a luxury I abused frequently.

I pulverized the competition. In the average two hour match I racked up over a hundred kills whilst my competitors could only frag me a couple of times. The other players became suspicious, thinking that I was either a bot or was exploiting some kind of cheat with the server. The truth was far simpler: owing to the fact that the server was a few feet behind me, I had the best connection in the house. While my competitors had "ping times" or latencies of 250 milliseconds or more, I consistently pinged-in under 20 milliseconds. This meant that an event in the game took approximately ¼ of a second to reach a customer's computer and make it back to the server, while my computer had an almost instantaneous response time. I could annihilate the enemy before they even realized they had walked into the same room as me. It was a bloodbath and everyone, except me, hated it.

It was past 2 o'clock in the morning when only one other player was left in the game and we began to chat instead of shooting at one another. I asked him if he was an SSI Micro customer.

"Yup. Well, actually my parents are. My name's David."

"Cool. Nice to meet you."

I explained that I was an employee and that I was working for the company throughout the summer. After a few minutes of swapping pleasantries, the conversation became more intimate. It turned out that not only were David and I the same age, but we had even grown up in the same town. When he told me his last name I gasped. This was the same David that I had attended elementary school with, whose basement I had been terrified in over Halloween, and whose Amiga I had first played *Indiana Jones and the Last Crusade* on. My heart filled with warmth as I not only reconnected with an old friend, but realized that both he and I had grown into teenagers that shared a common love for computer games. It brought a sense of continuity and humanity into a passion that was too quickly becoming a solitary pursuit.

We promised to stay in touch, but after the predictably lop-sided *Quake* deathmatches wore thin and I returned to my acreage before autumn, we parted ways once again. That year I left SSI Micro quietly, the summer a blur of Quake deathmatching and FTP server maintenance.

"Free" Dial-up Internet Access

When my final year of high school began in September I had barely noticed it. I was far more concerned about my social standing among the #ultima cronies who were now forming a secret invite-only guild that had Origin Systems employees as clandestine members. If only I could worm my way into the guild! It would enshrine my name in the history of *Ultima Online*!

The two hour time limit was – in my mind – a barrier to entry into this secret *Ultima Online* guild. Regulars in the channel teased me daily about my frequent disconnections from the channel; many of these people chatted from the convenience of a hardwired Ethernet network located in their college dorm rooms. I so badly wanted to fit in with them that I was willing to do *anything* to appear as elite as they were.

My need for acceptance and approval from these dorky twenty-somethings led to a financially catastrophic decision in the twelfth grade.

In the 1980s and 1990s the Internet was basically only accessible from specific North American university, college and military labs that were linked together via a huge network which snaked and coursed its way through many states and provinces. Dial-up accounts at sufficiently large universities were the only way to get online from home, provided as a service to staff and students so they could complete their work remotely. I was one of the lucky few kids who had a mother who attended a large university, and this gave us Internet access from home during a time when less than 1% of the Canadian population had any kind of Internet access.

This situation is unimaginable today – Internet Service Providers (ISPs) are ubiquitous no matter where you are in the world; most ISPs deliver their services over cable, ADSL, cellular, fibre optic and satellite. In the mid-1990s there were only a couple of privately run ISPs in the City and the monthly rates were outrageously high as the service was targeted at businesses. It took a couple of years for residential dial-up Internet service to become affordable to the average family.

My financially insolvent family could not afford these monthly fees, on top of the two private phone lines they were now paying for. So when an opportunity came up to get Internet access *for free* I jumped on it without a second thought about the meaning of the word "free".

My mother had been volunteering for an international aid organization funded by a larger Federal government initiative. The organization's purpose was to research policies for funding aid programs in developing countries all over the world. When my mother told me her organization was connected to the United Nations I became intensely proud of her. Imagine! My *mom* was on a council that made decisions about what countries would get millions of dollars in funding to help build schools, drill water wells, and house people.

One day my mother called me into the office because she needed help with the computer. She told me that the organization's council kept one another abreast of meeting schedules via e-mail and needed help setting up her new e-mail address. A few minutes of wrangling with *Eudora* – a wildly popular and well-built Windows e-mail client – proved successful and I proudly showed her the new e-mail address she could send and receive mail from.

"Oh, and I need you to set up this new number they gave me."

She handed me a slip of paper with a phone number, user ID and password. I stared at it and could hardly believe my eyes. It was the login credentials and phone number for a private ISP in the City. In under a minute I had the PS/1 squealing and squawking at a strange new modem fifty kilometres away. No busy signal! Just an instantaneous Internet connection that used a new protocol called PPP.

I barely heard my mom when she touched me on the shoulder lightly and said, "Don't use it too much okay? It's for my work."

At first I tried to alternate between calling the campus dial-up modem pool and using the new ISP number only occasionally. She had mentioned nothing about monthly fees and I assumed, self-deceptively, that the organization she volunteered for had a budget of millions of dollars and no doubt handed out unlimited Internet access to all of its valued staff like it was toilet paper.

It was past midnight when I finally hit the Disconnect button on the Windows 95 Dial-Up Networking window and noticed the elapsed connection time: 6 hours 19 minutes. Unbelievable! I had suffered no random disconnections nor two hour time limits! This was the panacea I had been searching for since I had received the 14.4K Sportster modem, and it cost my family *absolutely nothing!*

The warm pink glow of the magical Internet connection lasted a couple of months into my first semester of the twelfth grade. My mom came home in a curiously somber mood one Sunday after a weekend-long meeting with the aid organization she volunteered for, walked straight into the den and looked at me.

"Come outside with me for a few minutes. We are going to talk." Already I could sense a difficult and embarrassing conversation; I suspected she was going to tell me she was divorcing my father.

We walked up the driveway slowly and she said nothing for a few minutes. Finally I asked her what was going on.

"You've been using my Internet account?"

An accusation, not a question.

"Yeah, you told me I could..."

"How much are you using it?"

I could already feel her trap ensnaring me, prepared two months earlier when I was handed her login credentials. I tried to scurry away before it was too late, "Well, not much really, just when I can't connect to the campus Internet..."

An abject lie. I was connecting to her aid organization's Internet account every single day for five to ten hours a day. Sometimes I even left it on all night to download particularly large files.

She paused as I spoke and her eyes penetrated mine and sensed the lie. "More than that. Did you know that someone has to pay for all that?"

I swallowed and croaked out what sounded like a 'no' and shifted around on my feet unsteadily. I could see where this was going.

"It was very embarrassing for me this weekend you know. At the meeting the chairman asked why our Internet bill was so high and no one knew why as they rarely used it. And *I* only used it once or twice. Then I thought of you and all that time you spend at the computer. Do you know how much their bill was last month?"

I sighed and tallied up the costs in my head. I guessed that my Internet connection costs would be over a hundred dollars for the month. A hundred bucks was going to take a huge chunk out of my dwindling summer job earnings. The trap crafted with such care had finally sprung and I had to chew my leg off to escape.

"No. How much was it? I can pay it back mom."

"It was eight hundred dollars."

My head swam and I felt like retching. The driveway became impossibly long and the poplar trees around me closed in and squeezed the breath out of my chest. Eight. Hundred. Dollars. It was more than I had made the entire summer working at SSI Micro.

"And yes, you are going to pay them back for all of it." Her tone was abrupt but not unkind. She could see how shocked I was at my mistake.

I stuttered and stammered that I would, somehow, and almost barfed as we walked back to the house.

"My son, you've got to learn how to control yourself. You're on that Internet too much." She was now calm and the hint of compassion in her voice washed over me like a tidal wave.

I began to sob, completely ashamed of myself, not only for having cost an international aid organization hundreds of dollars, but for my lack of discipline. I felt like an addict outed during an intervention by a loving family member who felt helpless dealing with my addiction. I had finally reached a point where my addiction was now hurting other people and it was time for my mom to intervene.

In the end she worked out a deal with the organization. In lieu of the Internet fees that had blown their entire year's budget for e-mail access, I would do volunteer work for them. I would build the organization a web site and take care of any of their computer technical problems for the rest of the year. It was the best plea bargain I could have hoped for.

Months passed and I waited for my chance to repay my debt. Like any other non-governmental organization the crisis was replaced by another more urgent one and everyone there forgot about the pesky kid who ran up a phone bill. No one called me for troubleshooting help and I never built them a web site. I was off the hook, but to this day never stopped feeling guilty about it. Sorry mom.

Toshiba 4800CT 486 Notebook

After years of financial stress and strain, my family finally got some good news. Over the summer my mother secured a relatively lucrative research contract in my old home town. The influx of cash meant that the tensions over money visibly diminished, at least for a while; it also meant that my mother needed to bring a computer up north with her to get the work done. Before she finished telling me that she'd need to take a computer with her I already had her research contract money spent in my imagination.

She gave me a budget and a goal. "I have to keep it under fifteen hundred dollars. And it needs to have a printer. And a modem so I can get e-mail up north."

I thought it through. The Internet boom of the mid-1990's had done more to put IBM-compatibles in peoples' homes than computer games and productivity software combined over the past decade. The IBM PS/1 we had purchased two years earlier for thousands of dollars was now being sold at half its price, with twice the RAM, CD-ROM drive, hard drive space and processing power. Fifteen hundred dollars was a very respectable budget for a 486-based desktop PC in 1996, and might even squeak my mother into Pentium territory. I flipped through my most recent issue of *CD-ROM Today!* – a monthly magazine that came with a CD-ROM disc packed inside – for ideas on what she might buy. I stumbled across a two-page spread comparing the latest laptops from Hewlett Packard, Apple and Toshiba. What about a laptop instead?

The prices for new laptops were astronomical, fetching over $4000 for some of the latest models with colour LCD screens. If bleeding edge technology was out of our league, then the next best thing was to buy a heavily discounted past-generation model. My mother and I arrived at the Future Shop electronics chain that afternoon and I ushered her over to the laptop section of the store. The laptop section was new, opened only a few months earlier, showcasing portable computers like they were diamond rings.

And to people like me, they were. Laptops were computers only seen in the movies, carried by cartoonishly rich supervillain-hackers in shiny aluminum briefcases hand-cuffed to their wrists. Employees polished the glass display cases hourly, removing the greasy handprints of urchins like myself.

The prices were all over the place. An entry-level laptop with a passive-matrix monochrome LCD screen topped out my mother's budget at $1500. It turned out to have a sprightly 386-DX processor but had no opportunities for upgrading; its measly 2 megabytes of RAM were soldered on to the motherboard and its tiny hard drive was buried somewhere inside of the case.

Laptops in those days weighed in at about 10 pounds and were about four inches thick. Compared to the average ultrabook-style laptop sold now, this was about five times heavier and five times thicker. It felt like carrying around the Oxford English Dictionary, and strained the buckles of any leather laptop case.

I could see hesitation building in my mother's face as her eyes scanned across the price tags. She said, "I don't know. I don't think I need one of these."

Over the years I had learned a bit about negotiation. Luring her with vague promises of efficiency and time-saving technology was not going to work here. I had to appeal to her common sense, the kinds of everyday problems a laptop might solve for a working mom living away from home.

"But mom, you're going to be going up north and you don't know if you'll have an office there. And you don't want to be packing a big computer around with you everywhere you go," I wheedled.

"Mm." Her lips formed a razor thin line. She was getting wise to my negotiation tactics and could smell my rationalizations a mile away. I led her over to an outrageously overpriced new IBM tower with a Pentium processor. It had a gigantic *one gigabyte* hard drive, 32 megabytes of RAM, and a seventeen-inch monitor.

It weighed in at $4995.

"I guess you could go with a new desktop instead... But they are a little expensive..."

"WHAT!" she roared. She flipped over the IBM tower's price tag and looked like she was ready to stomp out of the store.

It was the oldest trick in the book used by only the slimiest salespeople: the "door in the face" sales method. The method made a pricey purchase appear reasonable in the face of an outrageously overpriced option. Want to convince your spouse to buy you a new Toyota for $16,000? Show them a BMW for $60,000 first; then allow *them* to 'persuade' you to look for a cheaper car.

We wandered around the store for another fifteen minutes and I could tell she was becoming frustrated – she hated shopping. I had to make my move before she pulled the plug on the whole operation.

"Mom, your work is paying for your laptop right?"

(Your. Laptop.)

"Well, it's not my work – my contract is paying for..."

I cut her off sharply, "So you won't have to put it on your VISA at least." Ah, it all sounded so logical.

I could see her heels dragging in the mud, hauled closer to the inevitable purchase in her future. I walked over to a middle-of-the-road Toshiba laptop. It had eight megabytes of RAM, a colour active-matrix TFT screen, a 200 megabyte hard drive, and a 486 DX2-50 processor. It was a little powerhouse packed into a white plastic brick, and it cost $1995, five hundred dollars *over* her budget.

"If you get this one mom, you'll never need to upgrade it ever. And I bet you can talk the salesman into a free printer." Ah, future-proofing. The second-oldest trick in the book.

Either I had worn her down or the hour perusing Future Shop had, because all of a sudden I could see her carefully constructed levee collapse under the pressure. She waved over a salesman, and yes, he *could* throw in an ultraportable Canon inkjet printer with the purchase of a new laptop.

"Mom? Didn't you say you need a modem too? This one looks okay..."

She gritted her teeth as I passed her a small box containing a 24 Kbaud modem made for laptops using an architecture called PCMCIA. The credit-card sized modem cost her another hundred bucks, and I beamed: it was almost two times faster than the 14.4K modem in my PS/1. Heh heh.

The complete package – laptop, printer, and modem rang in at over $2200 after taxes at the counter. Even with the healthy budget she had for a new computer this was well beyond what she had planned to spend. On the drive home I nervously picked at the tape of the laptop box. I did not want to open the box myself, feeling a pang of guilt that I had once again bamboozled my mom into another extravagant tech purchase.

"You can't wait to get your fingers in there can you? Go ahead, open it! At least we'll know if it works before we go home." She sounded resigned and almost happy, like she had bought it just for me. Decades later, I suspect a part of her did.

Today in the average North American home you will likely find a laptop on the kitchen table, a tablet device idling in a child's backpack, and a laptop or tablet charging in the living room. Few people purchase desktop computers today unless they have an urgent need for high horsepower gaming or graphics work. *Mobility* has become the primary value of computing among a host of older values like personal comfort, performance and upgradeability. For the average person today the more compact, energy efficient (underpowered) and lightweight the better.

But in 1996 the value of mobility was unfamiliar to the average person who had no experience with the *concept* of using a laptop. The computer was understood as a monolith that occupied an entire corner of the kitchen, family room, office, child's bedroom or basement and created its own space around it. Families would often call the place the "computer room."

In my family's case the computer always sat in the centre of a huge oak teacher's desk, with a hulking printer to its right, and its peripherals splayed around it with wires hanging like tentacles. A row of neatly organized computer games filled one shelf of the bookcase behind a large tilting 1970s leatherette chair that acted as the "computer chair". The computer gathered a whole way of life around it in the way that a kitchen table does in a dining room.

Learning how to use a laptop in the 1990s did not mean learning how to use its weird trackball or dealing with its finicky LCD screen with 5-degree viewing angle. Learning how to use a laptop meant discovering how a mobile computer could fit into one's life. It meant, for instance, that I could now sit in the living room playing games as my parents watched a movie. A laptop meant that my mother could write her Master's thesis on the kitchen table while I chatted on IRC on the PS/1 in the den. It brought an end to the arguments between my sister and I over who was using the computer because she could always play *Hoyle's Book of Games* on the laptop.

A laptop effectively reconfigured the personal spaces of our home without knocking down a single wall. But today, for the most part, people already take for granted the value of mobility and fluidity in the house. "Laptop thinking" – mobility and individual possession – is an assumed part of the affluent modern life. Everyone is *expected* to have a tiny computer of their own.

A healthy family might have managed the new social divisions that individual ownership of a computer brought into the home. But anyone can see how even a healthy family is impacted by taking a look at people standing at a bus shelter today. Instead of complaining about the weather or how late the bus is with strangers, the vast majority of bus-riders today gaze into the glass of their mobile devices like they were crystal balls. Mobile technology – laptop-thinking – makes people alone together.

But an unhealthy family living through financial and domestic strife compounds the problem of isolation exponentially. Arguments and fights between my mother, father, sister and I were the only social currency we had left. Arguing over who was using the computer or phone line was at the very least a social exchange that drew us together into a common space, even if that exchange was ultimately negative in tone. In the short space of six months multiple phone lines and multiple computers allowed everyone to vacate our collective hell into an array of lonely personal hells. The home was no longer a place of overlapping tensions that could be expressed between suffering people, but a place where everyone suffered alone together.

So it is not difficult to imagine how a seemingly benign technology purchase tore apart the strained seams of an already failing marriage. My mother departed for the north a month later with her laptop and printer in tow, and began work on her research contract. My father recruited my grandmother to make the trip south to look after my sister and I, as well as help with chores around the acreage. If my mother's presence created tension between my father and her, her absence exploded into outright fights between my father and everyone else.

After six months my mother returned to the house, several thousand dollars richer and visibly happier than I had seen her in years. My sister and I regaled her with stories about my father's enraged meltdowns and made her promise to never leave again. We felt like we had been abandoned and blamed her for it.

Much of the blame was quickly forgotten because the Toshiba laptop was finally home again. I carried it around the house like a teddy bear, playing games like *Destruction Derby* on it. The laptop had an Intel DX-class processor that was capable of playing all of the amazing games I had drooled over for the last two years. The only rule my mother decreed was that, under no circumstances, could I take the laptop with me to school. I broke that rule exactly once, sneaking it into my backpack on a day where my mother was away for meetings. I showed *Destruction Derby* to my friends at school hoping to impress them, and became so paranoid that someone would break it or steal it that I drove home early from school just to put the laptop back.

In the end the Toshiba laptop lived up to my promise: my mother never once had to upgrade it through its entire lifecycle, and still runs perfectly using its original hardware and software nearly 30 years later. I booted it up once a couple of years ago, eager to see if the thing worked after years of bit rot in a dingy basement. The machine grinded and clicked through its boot sequence as if it were built yesterday. It was like opening a time capsule: every file was in its place. *Destruction Derby* and *Hoyle's Book of Games* still had their icons on the desktop, mIRC still had my old login credentials for EFnet, and Dial-Up Networking still had the phone number to the aid organization's Internet Service Provider. I closed the laptop's screen with loud *snick*, reburying its treasures for another time.

1997: Graduation

The Untimely Death of the IBM PS/1

Christmas had come and gone and my high school graduation was fast approaching. With the laptop back in the house I somehow cajoled my parents into letting me move the PS/1 desktop computer into my bedroom, and the Toshiba laptop took its place on the oak office desk as the family computer.

There were other changes too. mIRC went from one among many of my Internet applications to the *only* application I used daily. It may be hard to believe now, in a time where people surf for hours endlessly perusing aggregator sites, but by 1997 the World Wide Web had become less compelling to me than it had been a couple of years earlier. IRC had completely overtaken Web message boards, FTP sites and warez and Usenet groups. All of my online time was spent in a single place: #ultima.

I was vying for operator or "ops" status in #ultima by showing up each day and sucking up to the ops whom I considered to be no less than demigods. Even though I was back on the two-hour dialup limit after the "unlimited" dialup fiasco, once again I still managed to squeeze in a solid eight hours of IRC every day after school. The phone line my father had rented as his business fax line was completely saturated with bits of textual chat data instead of the facsimiles he intended.

That all came to a halt one day when the clickity-clacking beast of an IBM keyboard died on me. All three tiny LED lights on the keyboard lit up and stayed on, frozen, instead of briefly flickering to indicate the keyboard's health; the keys were completely non-responsive when the computer booted into MS-DOS. After a half dozen reboots and plugging and unplugging and cleaning out the PS/2 keyboard port, I pronounced it dead. I called my father who was in the city buying lumber for his business, and told him that we needed a replacement keyboard *now!*

He became irritated, "How much is that gonna cost me?"

"Probably twenty bucks. They're not that expensive dad." (A white lie. They were at least thirty.)

"………. Well, alright. We'll see if I have time."

It seems silly to think of it now but those few hours sans-PC felt like being stranded on a desert island or locked in a dark closet. For the first time in years I was totally offline not by my own choice and anxiety crept into me. I had no way of contacting my friends online, and worse, I couldn't even pass the time waiting by playing *Wing Commander III* or *MechWarrior II*.

When my father came home a few hours later with a new keyboard I was visibly relieved. It was a light plasticky keyboard that looked and felt nothing like the big iron PS/1 keyboard that must have doubled as a flail in feudal times, and the keys had none of the spring-loaded *thwack!* that my fingers had come to expect. But, like any heroin addict worth their dope, any junk is good junk… and any keyboard with alphanumeric keys and a PS/2 connector would do the job.

I looked at the connector dangling from the end of the new keyboard cable. It was a large round DIN-style connector that would never fit in the comparatively tiny PS/2 port of my computer. *Shit*.

It was a Monday. Neither my mother nor my father planned to make a return trip to the city until the weekend, and they sure as heck weren't going to make a special trip just to spend money on another computer part. I had pushed my luck by asking for the keyboard in the first place.

I needed a cable that converted the DIN connector to a PS/2 connector. But where?

My mind reeled iterating through a hierarchy of decision trees as I tried to find some kind of solution. Call one of my friends? None of their computers had PS/2 ports. Steal one from the computer lab at school? All of them were Macintoshes and used

Apple's proprietary connector. Build a PS/2 connector myself? I didn't have the parts to...

... wait a sec, I *did* have the old keyboard which had the proper PS/2 connector on it already. Maybe I could cut off the old connector and splice it to the new keyboard. After all, a PS/2 connector was just a miniaturized version of the DIN connector, right? It probably worked like fixing a broken a headphone jack – just connect red wire to red wire, white to white, black to black, and voila, a new connector! Boy genius saves the world from impending technological disaster once again.

A *real* genius, or at least a six-month-old chimpanzee of average intelligence, would have searched the Internet with the laptop upstairs to find some kind of schematic that described how to *properly* interface a DIN keyboard with a PS/2 connector. But the anxiety of having computer downtime had overwhelmed my ability to use monkey cognition and I pushed ahead with exploratory surgery instead.

It only took a few snips with a pair of wire cutters and some deft wire twisting. I stared at the exposed ends of the new DIN keyboard's cable wires: it had a couple of extra wires that the PS/2 connector did not have. Some of the wire colours matched up – red to red, white to white, purple to um.. magenta, black to uh – stripy grey? How about I just tape these dangling blue and green wires off? Who needs those pesky extra wires anyway? I bet the nerd who designed this thing over-engineered it anyway.

Now I had a brand new keyboard with a tangled mess of wires hanging off of it, but at least the keyboard now had a PS/2 connector on the end. Time to light this candle.

I plugged it in and hit the power switch on the PS/1. There was sharp metallic *pop!* and the computer's green power light instantly dimmed to nothing. Fuck. Fuck. Fuck!

Oh well. I guessed that at worst I had just fried a brand new keyboard and was out thirty bucks.

I unplugged the keyboard and hit the power switch again. Nothing. Not a peep from the computer. Oh, God. Painful memories of the Amstrad's last gasping beep instantly flooded back into me. I hit the power switch several times to no effect. The PS/1 was now completely dead and there was nothing I could do about it. The Amstrad debacle had left me with lingering guilt about lying about its final moments. I had no choice but to explain to my parents that I had just fried our two-year-old computer all by myself. My father had not even finished paying off the credit account he had purchased it with years ago.

As I had learned to do over the years, breaking bad news to my mother was far easier than to my father who always erupted into fits of rage. I explained my botched surgery to her and watched her eyes grow narrow and the breath hiss out of her lips.

"This is the last time. We *told* you not to mess with that thing."

"I know. I'm sorry mom. I just-"

She cut me off, "You wait here."

She stomped off to her bedroom and I heard her rifling through stacks of paper. A few minutes later she came downstairs with a carefully folded pamphlet from Future Shop containing a faded receipt and warranty card. She handed me half of the papers and we began digging through the fine print together.

A warranty! I had forgotten that after the Amstrad's end my father insisted that we buy a computer with a three year full replacement guarantee, which had cost him another three hundred bucks. I had argued this was a waste of money (why not spend that extra cash on a bigger hard drive or RAM?) but he insisted it was worth it on a computer that cost him three grand.

Was he ever right about that. Later that week my mother took the PS/1 to The Future Shop with the receipt in tow. With a full year left on the warranty there was no question that they were going to have to fix it. When the repair technician asked what was wrong with the computer I put on my best inscrutable face and said, "It doesn't turn on for some reason."

Ahem.

A week later a technician from the store left a message on our answering machine explaining what would happen next.

He said, "Damndest thing. We tried everything and the motherboard is completely dead. We saw some damage around the keyboard port but otherwise there's nothing physically wrong with it – all of the other parts are working. So we're going to order a new motherboard at a cost of six hundred dollars. Don't worry – this is all covered by the warranty. It should be ready in four weeks. We'll call back."

The only thing *I* heard in the message was the phrase "four weeks." My mother was busy completing her research contract on her laptop all day, and I was in no position to ask her to hop off so I could chat with my Internet buddies. Four weeks of no *Wing Commander*, no IRC, no warez, no FTP sites. And worse, the *Ultima Online* beta test was quickly approaching; there was a chance that I would miss the beta test application day.

My impatience had turned a minor inconvenience into a month of guaranteed misery and it was all my fault. Monkey logic would have told me to just wait the month out and things would be okay, but I had a far better idea: when in doubt fix life problems with money.

For obvious reasons a loan for a new technology purchase from the Bank of Mom and Dad was out of the question. I was going to have to fund a new computer purchase completely on my own. Thankfully I had two things working in my favour: I had hung on to a good chunk of my summer earnings from SSI Micro, and I had not yet spent my Christmas dough.

This computer purchase would have to be different than when my family bought the Amstrad and the IBM. Thanks to my training at SSI Micro I planned to buy the computer hardware piecemeal and put it together myself. I flipped open the Yellow Pages phonebook and began making calls to every computer store in the city. The handful of computer hardware stores that existed three years earlier had swelled to over a dozen and this created intense price competition. If A-COM Computers dropped its price by a few bucks on a 16 meg stick of RAM, B-

TECH Computers would follow suit a few days later. B-TECH would drop its prices on power supplies and Baby AT form-factor cases, and A-COM would drop its prices accordingly. There was no price list posted on the Internet so the only option was to call the store and ask the salesperson to read back their prices part by part over the phone. I could even haggle if I knew one store was cheaper than another for certain parts. I estimated that by scrimping a few dollars here and there I could save a hundred bucks on an entire computer.

I must have annoyed more than a few salespeople because I did not know exactly what I could afford in the first place. RAM and hard drive prices fluctuated daily and the $200 four megabyte RAM SIMM I had purchased a year earlier was now half its price. I had just under $500 in my wallet and this was going to be a tight squeeze. Every place I called (some more than once with the hope that a salesperson would take pity on me and offer a deal) rang in a new base-model Pentium PC at over $750.

I persuaded my mother to drive me to the computer store that had the best prices on individual components. When I got there I explained that I *had* to build an entire computer with a budget of $500. The salesperson, who was no more than twenty years old, chuckled and said he was broke too.

"Alright, man, here's what you do. There's no way you can build an entire machine for that. Just buy the bare bones. Get a cheap Pentium CPU, the most RAM you can afford, a new motherboard, video card, and re-use your old hard drive, modem, CD-ROM, sound card and monitor. That'll bring you in at just under five hundred."

That would have been fine, but my old computer parts were still in the possession of the service department at Future Shop. I would *still* have to wait weeks to get the PS/1 back from the repair technicians before stripping it down for parts. My mother was waiting in the car for almost an hour and I sensed she was going to barge in to the store any minute, demanding that I leave.

I paced around the store anxiously for a minute wracking my

brain. Five hundred dollars was easily the most I had ever spent on any single thing in my life, and as far as I was concerned I would never see that kind of money again. In the end a rationalization won me over: I either was going to go home today with a new computer, or I would watch that five hundred bucks drain slowly from my wallet over the rest of the year with magazine, CD and game purchases. Time for a huge capital investment! It would, um, stimulate the economy.

"Okay. I want a Pentium 133 with 16 megs of ram and a video card. Oh and I'll need a Baby AT tower case with a power supply too. The cheapest ones you've got. Do you have all of that in stock?"

The salesman broke out into a grin and said, "*Allll riiiight!*" He was about as excited as I was. In the 1990s only computer nerds worked at computer stores, and watching someone buy a new piece of hardware was akin to one junkie watching another shooting up a colossal dose of heroin. The only thing better was having it for yourself.

He came back with a box of computer parts wrapped in plastic anti-static bags, neatly stacked together. My heart pounded as he rang each one into the cash register: two hundred, three hundred, four hundred and seventy-five dollars! I blew a year's worth of earning in one shot and I *still* had no solution to the problem of a missing hard drive. My hands shook as I pulled the box of parts onto my lap in the passenger seat of the car.

My mother glanced over at the nondescript box on my lap, "My son. You have to be more careful with your money. How much was all that?"

I sighed and replied with a vague answer, "I know. It came out to more than I thought."

When I got home I enjoyed every second of assembling the new computer: the new metallic smell of the boring beige AT case, the shiny new sticks of RAM, the gleaming green motherboard with a beautiful Intel Pentium chip riding high in its socket, and the folded black power cable that would take years to smooth into softer, flatter curves. But it just sat there on my desk in my bedroom like an empty house. I had none of the other necessary hardware to boot it up. For the next week I woke up in the morning and stared longingly at it like an old photograph.

In a stroke of sheer luck, a technician from Future Shop called three weeks *earlier* than expected. They had a motherboard for the PS/1 shipped in from a local store and the repaired machine was ready for pickup! The next evening my father brought it home and after a single boot-up to make sure it worked, I stripped it bare of almost all of its components. The Sound Blaster 16, MKE double-speed CD-ROM, modem and hard drive all found new homes in the unremarkable beige Baby AT tower case. The nameless Pentium 133 was born from the organ donor that preceded it. The IBM PS/1 was no longer a part of my life.

The PS/1 was shoved into the closet alongside its departed Amstrad cousin, and a new white metallic mini-tower sat on the desk. The jump from a 33 MHz Intel 486 processor to a Pentium 133 was a four time increase in raw computations per second, just as the PS/1's 486 CPU was a four times increase from the Amstrad's 8 MHz processor. But to me, in some ways more important than the increase in clock frequency, was the change in processing architecture. The Pentium processor had a fully functional FPU or "floating point unit" that could do complex numerical calculations very quickly, versus the 486 SX processor that had this capability nerfed by the manufacturer. The Pentium processor opened up a whole new landscape of games and programs that ran sluggishly or did not run at all on my old 486.

It is difficult to characterize the sense of thrill and power that comes from building one's own computer from off-the-shelf parts, even more so for a teenager with limited funds. I had plenty of prior experience rebuilding and modifying Gateway 2000 computers at SSI Micro, but the situation was fundamentally different. The Gateway 2000 machines arrived at my workbench pre-assembled from the factory, and only needed minor modifications like a new video card, RAM or modem.

Building a computer from scratch was more like going to a junk yard and constructing a roadworthy vehicle out of scrap parts scavenged from the piles of metal. The AT mini-tower case functioned as the frame for my little car. The 200-watt AT power supply and its bundle of yellow, red and black wires was its fuel tank and wiring harness. The CPU was its engine, lowered carefully into its socket. The motherboard screwed comfortably into place on the frame just as snugly as a transmission and exhaust system would.

There is an economy of design when it comes to building a functional and aesthetically pleasing computer that looks good from both inside and outside. The hard drive, CD-ROM and floppy drives could be installed in any one of the four 5-1/4 inch bays; this required the builder to carefully think through a configuration that would minimize the amount of loose wiring snaking through the case and impeding air flow. Does the computer look better with the drives stacked together in the bays, or should I leave a single bay of space between them for better air circulation? Should the CD-ROM be on its own IDE bus, or should I share the same IDE cable as the hard drive and run it in "slave" mode? Should I connect the PC speaker cable to the motherboard, or remove the aggravating beepy-boopy nightmare from the case completely? What order should I put the ISA expansion cards in? Neatly stacked together from the first slot onward, or separated from one another with an empty space? What can I use to bundle together the loose power supply wires with so they look a little cleaner inside of the case?

After years of being told by my parents in no uncertain terms that I was *not* to probe around inside of the computer's case, I finally had a machine that begged to be twiddled with on a daily basis. It was *my* computer and like a 19th century mad scientist I was free to rebuild my machine in any way I saw fit. Over the next few weeks I agonized over designs that maximized the form and function of my new Pentium. Every day after school I re-arranged the components inside of the computer and then stood back to appreciate the difference it made, like I was standing in an art gallery admiring a painting.

In today's age where the computer has become a toaster or Cuisinart, pre-assembled in a factory thousands of kilometres away, the sense of ownership that came from building one's own computer has all but vanished. For the majority of computer owners today, the computer is a disposable appliance that holds no personal value beyond its function. In 1997, despite its plain appearance, the Pentium had become an extension of my person. If other teenaged boys my age were customizing their muscle cars and trucks, this was the closest thing I could have to a pure expression of myself as a dorky kid.

I gazed at my creation. It was the first time I had built a machine out of off-the-shelf parts that I had bought and scavenged myself. The Gateway 2000 machines I had built for SSI Micro had proprietary Gateway-branded motherboards, and the Amstrad and the IBM were both full of proprietary parts you could never find in a computer shop. The machine in front of me had no brand name, no particular country of origin, and it bore no sign of its ancestry aside from the organs I had surgically removed from its predecessor. The computer was *me*.

And the differences weren't all under the hood. This new mini-tower case had no art-moderne countenance like the angular rationality of the IBM PS/1, nor the gentler form-fitting curves of the Amstrad's desktop case. It *did* have one thing more important than good looks however: it was purely my creation, born from Frankensteined parts and the contents of my entire chequing account. I dug through the contents of the motherboard's empty box and christened my boring beige box with a blue sticker that suggested pride and precision in its craftsmanship: *Intel Inside*.

The first boot was a delight. The Amstrad and the PS/1 had no formal BIOS settings that could be tinkered with, but this motherboard came with a generic Award-brand BIOS that lit up the screen with a yellow and green Energy Star logo on boot. There were dozens of settings that let me re-assign drive letters, change the drive boot order, or mess with IRQ assignments.

Computers were slowly making the transition away from using physical "jumpers" on the motherboard and its ISA cards. A jumper acts like a light switch – it connects or disconnects two electrical contacts. When a jumper is on, some setting on the motherboard is enabled, for example like turning on the PC speaker. When a jumper is disconnected, it is off, and consequently the PC speaker is disabled.

In this new motherboard, the manufacturer was moving towards a "jumperless" design that shunted the work of messing with physical jumpers on the circuit board to toggling settings in the BIOS. Instead of prying at tiny pieces of plastic the size of grains of rice on the motherboard, changing a setting (like turning on or off the PC speaker) was simply a matter of toggling a setting in the computer's BIOS at boot. On this particular motherboard there still were a dozen jumpers, but at least a few of the critical settings were now configurable in BIOS.

Getting the old IBM PS/1 hard drive to work with the new motherboard was a different story. Today we live in an age where the majority of hardware is designed as PnP or "plug and play": you buy the accessory, plug it in and a few seconds later the computer recognizes the hardware and you're off to the races.

But in 1997 PnP was more commonly referred to as "plug and pray", because most often it did not work at all as advertised. If you bought a new modem, there was a 50% chance that Windows 95 would recognize it. There was a 25% chance that a new Sound Blaster would work on first boot without configuration, usually because it conflicted with some other piece of hardware in your computer. And with hard drives there was a 0.1% chance that the hard drive would work without tons of fiddling with the hard drive's jumpers and settings in the computer's BIOS.

The move to plug-and-play, jumperless, motherboards caused headaches in particular because the transition was half-hearted. New motherboards like mine still had a mix of both jumpers and BIOS settings, and these often created conflicts with one another. The combination of conflicts between jumper settings and BIOS settings was particularly infuriating because one was never sure what the cause of the problem was.

The result was always the same: the computer would fail to recognize the hard drive and it would yield a "NO OPERATING SYSTEM" error on boot. That's because in 1997 there was no "auto-detect" setting in BIOS, and the BIOS required the user to manually enter settings that exactly matched the hard drive's specifications. You may or may not recall some of the arcane terms used back then to describe a hard drive's design: Heads, Sectors, Tracks, Cylinders, Size. These terms described the layout or "geometry" of a hard drive. Providing the exact numbers for each of these settings to the BIOS was like giving a map of the city to the motherboard. If you gave the motherboard the map for a different city, the computer would get lost and no longer recognize addresses properly, and fail to read or write data to the drive. The correct map told the motherboard where to go and how to get there, and even the tiniest mistake was fatal.

It took an entire day to track down the source of the problem. I checked and re-checked my geometry information and it was correct, so at least that was eliminated as a possible cause of death. The problem turned out to be the "Master/Slave" jumpers on the hard drive and CD-ROM. Now long forgotten, the Master and Slave jumper settings allowed two drives to co-exist on the same IDE bus. That is, you could daisy-chain together two drives so they could share a cable together, thus allowing the computer to have twice as many drives as it would normally have. I had left the drive on "Master" mode as I intended to let the CD-ROM become its "slave" on the same IDE bus.

However, I had forgotten something strange about the Sound Blaster 16 and MKE CD-ROM I had pillaged from the PS/1: the CD-ROM used the Sound Blaster as its own personal IDE bus. Yes, the Sound Blaster *sound* card functioned as a data bus for the CD-ROM. It was a rather ingenious piece of design back in 1993 when the computer was built, because it meant freeing up the PC's single IDE bus for the hard drive. But in 1997 this was no longer necessary, as every motherboard came with at least two IDE buses that allowed for up to four attached devices.

With the machine built and bugs ironed out it was finally able to detect the hard drive and boot to MS-DOS. My first stop was to try out all of the games I owned that had punishing system requirements, such as *Wing Commander III* and *BioForge*.

Nearly a year had passed since I had emptied my wallet prematurely to buy *BioForge* and it had been collecting dust on my shelf the whole time. The time had finally come to see it played at the full frame rate, and with 16 megabytes of RAM the load times were unbelievably quick. The pre-rendered introduction video no longer stuttered, and the bionic protagonist no longer limped around in slow motion. In fact, *BioForge* appeared to be more of a fast-paced action game than the "Interactive Movie" advertisement on the box led on. The first minute of the game required the player to break the protagonist out of his prison cell by bashing the living crap out of a hovering nurse-bot. Twenty years later I can still hear the echoes of the nurse-bot's mechanical voice endlessly repeating "SUBJECT MUST STAY IN BUNK. RECUPERATION IS MANDATORY. SUBJECT MUST COMPLY WITH ALL INSTRUCTIONS." After a few punches and kicks the nurse-bot exploded into a thousand flying fragments repeating "THIS UNIT IS SHOCK RESISTANT…" as its death shriek. This dark bit of humour tickled the part of me that *Space Quest III* had awoken years earlier.

This first puzzle set the tone perfectly for the rest of the game. A minute later I had broken out of my prison cell and was heading for a cell across the hall containing a blue-skinned figure stomping around muttering nonsensical phrases. As I approached his cell, the figure turned around and gestured at me with a large blue arm and barked, "If you've come for the fork you'll be sorely disappointed!" As he turned I noticed that his other blue arm had been torn from the socket and lay in a pool of blood near the force field bars of his cell.

If this was like every other adventure game I had played, the severed arm would have only been window dressing, meant to add to the mood but not to the interactivity of the game. I walked up to the blue severed arm and tried to pick it up, expecting nothing. Unbelievably, my character picked up the arm and wielded it like a bloodied club! I smirked and walked up to the blue hunchbacked bionic figure expecting to have a long conversation in the traditional dialogue tree style seen in the majority of adventure games and RPGs. Instead, the goateed blue bastard started attacking me! With little else to do, I took a swing at him – and to my shock and absolute delight, my character started *beating the man to death with his own severed arm.* I beat him to a pulp with it feeling little remorse and looked around the room. Sitting on the floor behind the body was a large metal fork. I took it and cackled darkly. Whatever this game was about, *BioForge* and I were going to get along just fine.

Although I had played *Wing Commander III* many times over the year, playing it at its full Super VGA 640x480 resolution gave it a level of visual realism I had never seen before on a computer. I was finally able to watch the cutscene videos without the skips and pauses that had plagued my relatively weaker 486. Beyond the visual quality, the transition from cartoony animated characters in *Wing Commander II* to live actors in the cinematic sequences had both lost something and gained something. The smooth and life-like animation and bright colour palettes of *Wing Commander II* had given way to natural human movement and a darker cinematic colour palette, and some imagination had been lost in the translation. But a few top-notch performances from actors Mark Hamill, John Rhys-Davies and Malcolm McDowell breathed new life into the rather tacky comic-bookish dialogue. On the 486 the game drove like a broken down Corvette set on blocks in my driveway: I could see the potential in it but did not have the cash to take advantage of its horsepower. On my new Pentium 133 the game shone and felt like a completely immersive interactive experience, truly like being cast in a sci-fi film. After trying to chew through the indigestible rinds of so-called "multimedia" games for the past two years, it seemed that Origin Systems had hit the nail on the head as far as interactive movies went.

I spent the rest of the day re-installing every game I owned, seeing how they fared on the new hardware. As happy as I was with the shocking speeds there were some surprising disappointments. Almost all of the Sierra adventure games no longer worked properly – they ran too fast on the Pentium and no longer triggered critical plot changes at the right points, making the games unfinishable.[66] The *King's Quest, Space Quest and Quest for Glory* series were among the worst offenders and it meant waiting years before I could play these games to completion again. The LucasArts adventure games were thankfully spared from these bugs and thus remained on my hard drive indefinitely: *Sam and Max Hit the Road* and *Day of the Tentacle* were just as playable on a Pentium as they were on a 486. This compatibility issue spoke volumes about the differences in programming chops between Sierra On-Line developers and the LucasArts developers. At the end of the day my 384 megabyte IBM hard drive was full to the brim and for the first time in weeks I was excited about the prospect of gaming again.

---

[66] Years later these plot trigger problems in Sierra On-Line games became known as "timer bugs". Timer bugs are caused by the way many Sierra programmers chose to trigger events in the game's programming script. Devoted hacker-fans learned how to patch out these bugs with esoteric assembly language fixes to the game executable. But it would be years before a few adventure game fans would create these fixes. In the meantime a crucial utility called "Mo'Slo" emerged as a stop-gap measure for playing very old games on new Intel CPUs. Running MOSLO.COM would force the CPU to slow down and allow many games to run at the correct speed, thus preventing the timer bugs from occurring.

Ultima Online Beta Application Day

One morning as the snow was melting in the late winter sun, I received a private message from a friend in #ultima. He had received word from an Origin employee that the *Ultima Online* beta test was going to be announced in a couple of days. The URL to the beta test application would be posted publicly, and prospective beta testers were expected to flock to the web page and claw their way to the "submit" button like riff-raff at a Black Friday sale. The upcoming beta test was arguably the biggest news in gaming on the Web at the time, and we all knew that Origin's web server would buckle under the load of applicants when beta application day arrived. There was a good chance that many of us would miss out on submitting beta applications due to either heavy web traffic, or the fact that many of us would be at school or work when the website went live.

The op I was chatting with about this problem, Citizen_X, was a congenial and outgoing guy from Houston, Texas. He told me he was not hugely interested in the UO beta himself, preferring playing games with just a handful of people or chatting on IRC for the sake of talking with others. The idea of a massively multiplayer online role-playing game played with thousands of anonymous CHUDs from around the world seemed like a step backwards to him. He was far more interested in the text-based MUD games that had been around for a decade already. I staunchly expressed that I was still excited about the *UO* beta and champed at the bit for my first taste of Origin's new masterpiece. Without warning, Citizen_X pasted a link into the chat window.

```
<Citizen_X> http://www.owo.com/beta/signup.cgi
<Citizen_X> have fun ;)
```

I gasped and pasted the URL into my Netscape Navigator window. The page loaded. It was the beta application signup page, ready and waiting a full day in advance of the official announcement.

Thanks to some friendly cajoling from one of the #ultima operators, one of the OSI employees had leaked the URL during a private DCC chat. In exchange for the beta application URL, the op had promised that the URL would only be circulated among fellow #ultima ops and not into the general public. Being a long-time channel op, Citizen_X was among the few in the know, and he had given me the link out of pure generosity despite the fact that I was not an op myself.

YES!

What type of processor do you have?	
What type of sound card do you have?	
What is your favorite type of game?	
What is your second favorite type of game?	
What online services do you use regularly? (Check all that apply.)	AOL CompuServe Dwango INN Microsoft Network GEnie MPG Net MPLAYER Prodigy Playnet Ten WOW Direct Internet provider
What percentage of your total gaming time is spent playing multi-player games?	
What percentage of your total gaming time is spent playing games online?	
Which information source are you most likely to turn to for games? (Check all that apply)	Web sites Newsgroups Advertisements Magazines Store Clerks Friends Demos Other

A screenshot of the Ultima Online beta test application form.

I re-read the beta application page several times, poring over the questions it asked about my computer's specifications and my qualifications. I agonized over how to answer each question. Would I be penalized for specific hardware? What if they wanted someone with more software testing experience? What if the test was only open to Americans and not Canadians? Would former pre-alpha testers get preference over those new to the game? Was my 14.4 Kbaud modem too slow?

In the end I had no choice but to answer each question honestly and pray for deliverance. I clicked the submit button and anxiously waited for the server to accept (or deny) my page-long submission. Just like the pre-alpha test application, the server's response was terse:

```
Thank you! We will be contacting successful beta
applicants in the coming months.
```

It would be another painful waiting game to find out if I was among the chosen ones for the upcoming test. The next morning the beta signup page was officially posted on OSI's web site and prospective testers flocked in droves, crashing the server several times. A few days later the company announced that they had many times the number of applicants they had expected to receive and would have to modify their plans for an "open" or public beta test accordingly. This likely meant making cuts from the massive pool of applicants. The next few weeks were excruciating as I set my Eudora e-mail client to check my e-mail every two minutes just in case Origin Systems came knocking on my virtual door. For a long time there was no knock.

Chris Roberts Visits IRC

The wait was killing me. My obsessive speculations with other fans about the upcoming beta test were even beginning to bore *me,* and I turned to other pursuits to pass the time. Illicit pursuits.

On my weekly scan of the EFnet channel list for warez I came across a new channel that immediately sparked curiosity: #ultimawarez. I joined and was greeted by a handful of buccaneers who were in the midst of a conversation about UNIX accounts and FTP servers. I listened silently until I asked if any of these folks were familiar with the *Ultima* franchise of computer games. One pirate, by the name of SDarkness, replied tersely, "duh. that's what we named the chan after."

I confessed that I was a huge fan of the series and that I spent most of my time in #ultima with other fans. The group of friends in #ultimawarez turned out to be refugees from #oldwarez which – as the name implies – was focused on pirating old computer games (what would later be called "abandonware"). This new channel was to become our home-away-from-home.

My new channel was everything that #ultima was not. Some of the regulars openly talked about stealing UNIX account login credentials, using them to swap warez, and a few even privately traded credit card numbers. Credit card number theft or "carding" was a territory I had no experience with nor wanted any. In those days many credit card numbers were used to purchase time on long-distance carriers like Sprint which would allow the pirate to trade files on distant BBSs. I made it clear that I was only here for the *Ultima* games and talking about anything Origin Systems.

One day SDarkness announced that he had a new UNIX server account "root" or administrator password and was eager to do something fun with it.

```
<SDarkness> spoofing time. anyone got a channel they
```

```
wanna fuck with?
```

My mind raced through the different channels I was frequenting on the EFnet and BeyondIRC networks. There was only one that came to mind: #wingnut. The channel was full *Wing Commander* fans that drove me nuts with their obsessive conversations about their favourite Origin Systems game. They argued over what I considered to be meaningless minutiae, like whether a Confederate class heavy cruiser could destroy a Kilrathi Kamekh-class capital ship or whether certain characters were Kilrathi spies in the *Wing Commander* universe. As far as I was considered these were the kinds of computer game nerds you'd never want to sit around on a subway train as they collectively spazzed out about their obsession. Talk about the pot calling the kettle black, but I didn't see it that way at the time.

In a moment of pure viciousness I suggested #wingnut to SDarkness and gave him a thumbnail sketch of the channel's regulars and operators.

```
<SDarkness> wing commander eh? watch
```

I idled silently in #wingnut and waited for SDarkness to join, thinking that he was going to "take over" the channel or harass the regulars by spamming the channel with nonsense. Instead, someone new joined the channel:

```
* Chris_Roberts <croberts@origin.ea.com> joined
#wingnut
```

All chatter in the channel suddenly ceased. Someone typed "*gasp*" and a few others uttered "seriously?" and "wow". The channel's leader, an older man by the name of Eagle, greeted Chris_Roberts reverently and welcomed him to #wingnut. Even I was spellbound until I received a private message from Chris_Roberts:

* * *

```
<Chris_Roberts> ;)
```

SDarkness had "spoofed" or plagiarized a legitimate origin.ea.com domain name! On IRC, when joining or leaving a channel a person's domain name was always listed alongside their name – announcing to the channel just who this person was and where their connection originated from. For the vast majority of users their domain names were set by their Internet Service Providers and there was no (easy) way to change this. SDarkness had somehow gained root (administrator) access to a UNIX server somewhere on the Internet and had hacked it to modify his originating domain name. To most UNIX hackers today a spoof like this one is barely worth mentioning, but to myself and to the regulars of #wingnut it was a master stroke.

And SDarkness had picked just the right person to spoof. Who was Chris Roberts? The *real* Chris Roberts was the creator of the *Wing Commander* series of games. The games featured an elaborately crafted space opera story grafted on to an impressive space combat simulator, and had enthralled computer gaming enthusiasts for years. For fans of the series, Chris Roberts was as famous as *Ultima* series creator Richard Garriott. In a culture of obsessive fan-nerds, *Wing Commander* aficionados were rabidly fanatical in a way that even *Ultima* fans could never live up to.[67] Having Chris Roberts visit your IRC channel was like having George Lucas politely knock on the trunk of your treehouse in 1985 and announce tea time with R2D2 and C3PO.

For that reason alone, these friendly folks went apeshit. They jumped at the chance to ask Chris Roberts every dorky question they had about the game series, bombarding him with tiresome factoids, speculations and suggestions for future games. SDarkness indulged it all and basked in the glory:

---

[67] Recently, Chris Roberts ran a crowd funding campaign for a new *Wing Commander*-style game called *Star Citizen*. Roberts raised over 900 million dollars from individual donations – many of which made by lifelong fans of the original games.

* * *

<Chris_Roberts> Slow down folks. I'm writing all this down.

He even announced that a character in one of the upcoming *Wing Commander* games would be named after a lucky #wingnut fan. As he kept jerking their chains I rolled around in my office chair clutching my sides and typed out new private messages to him that he could use to taunt the channel.

The jig was finally up when SDarkness went too far, announcing that the company had filmed "Hobbes" – a Kilrathi tiger-like character featured in the second and third games of the series - in uncensored sex scenes with actor Mark Hamill, which were hidden as easter eggs in *Wing Commander III*. The chatter promptly died in the channel, and Chris_Roberts departed a few seconds later, promising to return at a later date. When the channel's leader Eagle finally saw through the ruse he summarily banned "Chris_Roberts" from ever visiting #wingnut again.

It was the kind of mean-spirited prank that only a confluence of technological development and adolescence could have imagined in 1997, and would inevitably become a commonplace occurrence 15 years later when social networking and celebrity became a common currency for North Americans.

A day later, the channel operator Eagle found out that I was responsible for orchestrating the hoax, and I was banned for life from #wingnut with good cause.

Ultima Online Goes into Closed Beta

On the #ultima IRC channel, word went 'round that Origin was planning two beta tests. The first test would be a "closed" or invite-only beta test consisting of testers hand-picked by Origin. The second test would be an "open" beta or public stress-test in which Origin would open the floodgates to everyone who applied. I thought I was a shoe-in: as a pre-alpha test veteran I felt I had the absolute *right* to be in the closed beta test, as I was clearly far more devoted than the average fan.

The test was to happen over a couple of days, apparently timed as a media event at the 1997 Electronic Entertainment Expo (now called the "E3") in California. The E3, alongside the Consumer Electronics Show in Las Vegas, was the largest computer game exposition in the world where publishers showed off their latest and greatest games. Developers and publishers from around the world convened upon this Mecca to show off their wares and garner media attention – usually from magazines like *PC Gamer* and *Computer Gaming World* and *PC World* to promote their titles. Origin planned to show off a live demonstration of *Ultima Online* at the E3 where the media could watch players explore Britannia in real-time. I was sure I would be among the three thousand guinea pigs selected for the mad experiment in game marketing. Only 250 of us could play simultaneously, so I had to be Johnny On The Spot when the server opened.

One day in June, days before the E3, a few of the #ultima ops let word slip that they had received official closed beta test CDs from Origin and were installing the game as they spoke. Only a handful of people in the channel were chosen for the closed beta test, and I was not among them. I was crushed. It felt like the thousands of hours of fan-devotion I had invested in Origin were all for naught. I felt like they thought I was just some kid that wanted to play the hot new Ultima game, and they didn't understand just how deeply rooted I was in the world. I raged at the missed opportunity and made my fiery opinions public, posting angry messages on an Ultima fan Usenet discussion group to other disillusioned Ultima fans. It got to the point where my childish whinging earned me a few kicks from the #ultima operators.

The public bootings only enraged me further, and I took a break from Internet chat for a few days. I wanted nothing to do with #ultima or Origin Systems or *Ultima Online*. I went out with my high school friends to watch movies in the City and brooded morosely about my ill luck. I re-installed *Wing Commander: Privateer* and flew my Tarsus space ship around, working as an illicit drug courier buying and selling "Brilliance" and "Ultimate" at space stations in every quadrant. I cruelly hunted down Retros, snuck past Confederate cruisers, and made friends with space pirates. At least in *this* universe I could earn some respect and admiration.

My tantrum ended a week later when real life kicked me in the face. I had finished my final examinations for college placement and was impatiently waiting for the last semester of my high school life to end, when my sister got into a serious car accident.

I was sitting in Mr. G's Physics class, waiting out the afternoon clock, when I was called down to the office. I received a call from the hospital and shook as I listened to a doctor slowly explain that my sister had rolled our car on a dirt road with my prom date sitting in the passenger seat. I hung up and began running down the street to the hospital, located a few blocks away. Tears streamed down my face as my feet pounded the pavement, expecting to be brought into a morgue where I'd be shown a body on a steel gurney.

When I arrived at the hospital a few panicked minutes later both my sister and my prom date were scraped and bruised but miraculously spared of serious injury. At home that night I found the car towed into the yard – a 1988 Pontiac Grand Am – torn in half. The police told my parents that it was a miracle that anyone survived the crash. My parents vacillated between being thankful my sister was alive and admonishing her for causing the accident. I attended my graduation ceremony that night and numbly celebrated the end of my high school experience. For once, I stopped thinking about computer games for a few days, and thought instead about how my sister had almost died.

The Ultima Online Public Beta Announcement

A week later Origin announced that the closed beta test had been a success, and the upcoming public beta test was just around the corner. The open beta test would happen in July, but there was a catch: Origin had not expected such an overwhelming response to the application, and the number of potential testers far outnumbered the amount of CDs available. Rather than turning away beta testers, the staff at Origin came up with a solution that proved to be far more controversial than anyone might have expected. The company asked testers to foot the bill for CD duplication, by mailing-in two U.S. dollars to for a public beta test CD.

Today the idea of paying to beta test a hot new game is not even remotely controversial. Steam's "Early Access" stream where people pay to play games while they are still in alpha stages of production is evidence that many gamers have no moral qualms about paying to test a company's product.

Rarely do pay-to-test schemes trigger the kind of public conflagration I witnessed on the Internet in 1997. People were outraged that Origin Systems was requiring people to pay for CD duplication and shipping fees to participate in a beta test. Enraged Netizens compared it to walking into an office and telling the hiring manager that you were willing to pay *them* for the pleasure of doing a menial desk job. To many the move was irresponsible and unethical and only enflamed anger at Electronic Arts, the evil entity that had ingested Origin Systems in an acquisition years earlier, now flexing its corporate muscles. To some, including myself, Origin Systems (and in particular its founder Richard Garriott) was no longer the knightly defender of the moral virtues we had grown up with; the company had become just another bureaucratic organization trying to make it big in a cutthroat corporate ecosystem.

Two American dollars.[68] While I hurled flaming invectives at Origin via Usenet discussion groups and on IRC channels, promising a boycott of their products and trying to convince others to do the same, I quietly asked my mom to write a cheque paid to the order of Origin Systems, Inc. I was beginning to believe that I had an online public image to maintain: that I was a moral crusader out to defend what was right and point fingers at corporate wrongdoers. Secretly though, I sure as hell wasn't going to miss the beta test over two measly bucks! (And judging by the number of fellow fans that raged at Origin over the pay-to-test structure, I was not the only one who was pulling this ugly, two-faced move.)

I biked over to the rusty green community mailboxes a mile away and deposited the proverbial cheque in the outgoing mail slot. It hit the bottom of the box with a hollow thunk. How long was it going to take to get to Austin, Texas? How would I know that they received the cheque? On the mile-long ride home my mind raced through hundreds of unlikely scenarios that could befall my precious cheque before it reached Origin's offices. What if our mailman – a sluggish, friendly, phlegmatic man with a large gut – let it fall between the cracks of his truck seat while he was taking it to the post office? What if my mother's cheque bounced? Would a miserly bank manager stamp it "NSF", getting me booted out of the beta and my mother sent to a poorhouse?

For two weeks there was no word from anyone at Origin Systems and fans like me awaited any news about the beta with bated breath. Little did we know that *Ultima Online* was a skunkworks project undertaken by a tiny team of dedicated MUD and RPG fans that were breaking new ground in game genres. We had no idea that Electronic Arts had little, if no, interest in the game and had chronically underfunded the project from the beginning. The two dollar duplication and shipping

---

[68] Those outside of the United States, Canada or Mexico, paid $10 USD.

cost paid by fans made the public beta test possible at all, as Electronic Arts would not front the money for it.

Origin Systems staff were working around the clock trying to ready the game in time for the massive stress test, and the idea of a "community manager" to address fans' concerns was only in its nascence. We were starved of information and many worried we had flushed two bucks and our hopes and dreams down the shitter.

All of a sudden a few people in Texas began receiving CDs. A few friends in #ultima put the CD into their flatbed scanners to prove to everyone they had received them, and this whipped up the game-playing Internet into a frenzied storm of argument. Why had these folks received their CD's first? (Proximity to Austin, Texas). What happens if I live in Denmark or Australia – will I miss the test due to slow postal delivery? (Yes.) Should I have put extra money into the envelope for express shipping? (No such thing.) Who can I call to find out if my disc has shipped yet? (Please, don't call.)

I recall some of these questions in a far more civil manner than the way they were originally posted, which looked more like this:

```
> WHERE THE F*&*$! IS MY CD I PAID FOR?
> CALLING OSI CUSTOMER SERVICE RIGHT NOW FOR MY MONEY
BACK.
> BOYCOTTING OSI GAMES 4EVER. WHO'S WITH ME?
```

Finally, after the storm of angry e-mails became unbearable, Origin proactively sent an e-mail to testers:

```
Hello again, Prospective Ultima Online Beta Tester:
First, we would like to apologize for any confusion
that may have ensued after the previous, somewhat
imperfect mail-out. Some of the people who were on
our mailing list either received several empty
messages or nothing at all. We can only apologize for
the problems inherent with sending one mail message
```

to 30,000 persons, and then send out another message. Now, that we have gotten that taken care of, we can get down to business.
We would like to thank you for showing the interest and taking the time to apply for the upcoming Ultima Online beta test. We hope to conduct the Beta Test sometime in December or January. We can only ask that you be patient and grant us the time to make the Ultima Online world as perfect as possible.
This is just a reminder to those of you who may have forgotten to send in your payment. If you have sent in your payment and are confirmed on the web page, then thanks and well see you in the test. If you have sent in your payment but are not confirmed on the web page, then there is no reason to panic. There can be several explanations as to why you are not confirmed:
First, it takes our Accounting Department a couple of weeks to properly credit each account once that payment has been received. It is possible that we have your payment, but have not been able to properly process your payment.
Second, there have been some problems with multiple payments being made in one envelope or with one check. We have had some trouble properly processing these payments. If this is the case, then you will want to fully explain your situation, include a list of all applicants names, mailing and e-mail addresses, and send this information to multima@origin.ea.com. We will look into it.
Third, we cannot control the speed of conventional snail mail. Several factors can control when we receive your payment, one being your mailing location. You need to keep that in mind before considering that the payment may have been lost.
Lastly, if you sent your payment in over 4 weeks ago and still are not confirmed, then send us a message to multima@origin.ea.com because the payment may have been misplaced on its way to Origin. Of course, we hope that this is not the case, but there is little that we can do. You may need to check with your bank to see if the check was cashed, and then consider sending an additional check.

```
If you have not sent in the payment, then there is no
reason to send us an e-mail. It isn't because we
don't want to hear from you, but we do want you to
hurry and send in your payment. As you well know (or
maybe not), you will need the software CD in order to
participate in the beta test. You will need to send
in your payment as soon as possible. If we receive
your payment before our deadline, then you will
receive a CD for the beta test.
```

The sense of amused exhaustion from the UO team dealing with the new glut of fans was palpable.

The waiting game was killing me, and I knew the timing would be tight. Each day I biked to the green mailboxes so I could check the mail just as the mail delivery truck departed for other farms. For a week and a half I opened the mailbox to utter despair. If the CD did not arrive in the next four days I would miss the test. Then, three days prior to the test, I opened the mailbox and inside was a square, white, cardboard sleeve. It had the look of something official. I flipped it over in my hands and read the return address: Origin Systems, Inc., Austin, TX, USA. My hands began quaking and I cycled the whole way home screaming goofy nonsense. I felt like the hero of *Charlie and the Chocolate Factory,* who had finally won his golden ticket.

Binge-Playing Ultima Online in Public Beta

I do not remember the five minutes it took to get home from the mailboxes, but I do remember the words I yelled when I threw open the front door to the house:

"Mom! It came! It came!"

My mother laughed and shook her head at the seventeen year old shrieking with joy at the flimsy piece of cardboard in his hands. I looked like a five year old who was given a discarded refrigerator box for his birthday and treasured it more than any other gift.

I gingerly peeled open the sleeve and slipped out the beta disc. It was glorious: a stylish black and white affair pressed on a proper silver layer of blessed magic. Although the cardboard sleeve was adorned with naught else but a "beta key" serial number that provided me with access to the test, the entire package felt official and proper. After months of doubt it felt like it was the best two bucks I had ever spent in my life.

While I ran the game's installer I dialled up and joined #ultima which was abuzz with chatter. It seemed that others, both in Canada and the United States, had received their beta discs too. Everyone was glowing with excitement, aside from many international friends who were shit outta luck due to slow snail mail.

Some #ultima regulars began renewing their allegiances to fellow guildmates whom they planned to go on adventures with in a few days. Others were excitedly arguing over the implications of the game's pre-rendered 3D cinematic introduction which suggested an underlying story for the universe the game was set in; those who had not seen it chastised them for revealing spoilers. One of the more technically oriented operators began hex-editing the game's executable program, hunting for Easter eggs and possible ways to exploit the game.[69] And there were a few who clandestinely made back-room deals with Origin Systems staffers in exchange for in-game benefits like gold, armour and prestige. Everyone had a stake in the beta, and those left out due to geographical disabilities sat at the sidelines begrudging the sour grapes they had been handed.

The second the game finished installing I launched it and was greeted by the familiar Origin Systems logo cinematic. It was the same pre-rendered 3D logo video used in *Wing Commander III* and gave me the fuzzy electrical feeling that I was about to witness magic. A few seconds later the introduction cinematic proper began and I was riveted to my seat for a couple of minutes.

The introduction cinematic was gorgeous – the 3D characters and environments were rendered in a precise, realistic fashion that I had never seen before on a computer.[70] The music, narration and visual storytelling all conspired to create an experience that utterly decimated my months of bitter kvetching at Origin Systems. For all their missteps with fans and corporate wrangling with Electronic Arts, Origin had not lost a single ounce of the magical talent infused into their games. True to their corporate motto, Origin had once again succeeded in

---

[69] Hex Editor: a program that translates a file's sequences of binary bits into human-readable numbers and letters. The word "hex" is short for "hexadecimal" which is a Base-16 numeric system computers use, comparable to the Base-10 numeric system most people in the world use. (Think of a computer as a machine that can count on its sixteen fingers). Hex Editors not only allowed a hacker to look at a file's structure, but also allowed them to modify the data in the program. Hex Editors were most often used to modify game executables to create cheats or hacks that gave characters extra lives or super strength. In some cases, Hex editors allowed hackers to discover Easter eggs that the original programmers left behind to impress or delight others.

[70] The fantastic 3D introduction was created by visual artist Denis Loubet, who had designed much of the manual artwork and box cover art for Richard Garriott since the beginning of the series.

'creating worlds'. If the intro was *this* good, the game must have been a hundred times better, I thought.

And it was. Sort of. The beta test went about as well as most beta tests could go: servers were jammed with players, players were randomly disconnected in the midst of fighting a creature (or another player), cheaters discovered ways of destroying the in-game economy by hoarding metal ore and gold and fancy shirts, player-killers (PKs) roamed the lands rampantly slaughtering innocent newbies, and hundreds of players unacquainted with the finer points of Britannian etiquette treated the game like a massive teen chat room.

Imagine the beta test period as a week-long television marathon of your favourite show. The only evidence it ever happened were the bags of potato chips and empty cans of pop and chocolate bar wrappers strewn around your coffee table. Specific memories of each event and episode grow foggy and by the end of the marathon it all feels like a bit of a blur.

That was the beta test for me. Gorging on anything leaves one with a sense of emptiness – that one never really took the time to savour each morsel of the experience. I barely recall specific events or details in the 18 to 22 hour marathon sessions I'd play the game in between snatches of restless sleep.

The parts I do remember are fragmentary: running full-tilt from a PK as she chased me through a dense forest in Yew, firing a dozen arrows at me with a majestic *thwop!* each time she released her bow string; stepping into the entrance of Dungeon Deceit and witnessing piles of bodies accruing on the cave floor as a mad mage fired bolts of lightning (the spell: *corp por*) in every direction; buying my first horse only having it die a minute later at the hand of a huckster who fed it a poisoned apple; joining a standoff at an Orc Fort between my motley crew of guildmates and an opposing guild who tried to claim the fort for themselves; watching a wild timber wolf chase down and kill a deer completely on its own volition; quietly chopping down trees and hunting birds north of Trinsic so I could fletch my own arrows; and once I even kissed a guildmate's character in the seclusion of the forest and felt a pang of excitement at my first kiss, even if it was just virtual. The entire experience is an amalgam of discrete images that follow no discernible plot.

There *was* one event that I remember well however, because it became a part of the mythos of *Ultima Online*. Twenty years later the event is still recalled as a momentous occasion in any MMORPG.[71] It was the day that a player murdered Lord British.

In the Ultima series the kingdom of Britannia has always featured a character by the moniker of Lord British. The role-playing alias of Richard Garriott, Lord British is usually depicted as a kindly Arthurian father who dotes upon his loyal subjects as if they were his children. As the protagonist of the series, the player known as the "Avatar" shares a close bond with Lord British, and is often sent out on quests by this benevolent dictator.

But as is wont for any rebellious child presented with a father-figure in a magical universe without real consequences, there is the oedipal urge to murder him; as such "killing Lord British" became an ongoing gag in the Ultima series. Even though Lord British is immortal by design, the developers of the series always created a secret method for murdering the patriarch and consequently breaking the game. Each game featured some devilish and intricate and often hilarious technique for regicide, and knowledge of these dark magicks marked the division between the true Ultima mage and mere weekend warrior.

When *Ultima Online* entered beta, there was a quiet conversation amongst members of a highly clandestine guild called "The Ravens of Fate". The RoF was comprised of a select few #ultima operators who were friends with programmers and

---

[71] MMORPG: Massively Multiplayer Online Role-Playing Games were an offshoot of the textual Multi-User Dungeons (MUDs) that had been online for years. MMORPGs were "persistent" worlds that remained active after users logged off, creating continuity and 24/7 access in a time where most multiplayer games were the equivalent of one night stands.

designers at Origin. It was rumoured at the time that some Origin staffers were even members of the guild themselves; fan favouritism and allegiances to any particular guild was a strict no-no at the company. During beta week, the RoF quietly discussed a method for reviving the age-old tradition of killing the great father of Britannia. But for the first time in the history of the series, the murder would happen in a grand spectacle by hundreds of real people in real time.

As the story went among my #ultima friends, RoF contracted one of the most notorious bug-exploiters or cheaters in the *Ultima Online* realm for the illustrious execution which required skill, guild and absolute amorality. The player went by the name "RainZ" and was personally responsible for the deaths of hundreds of players during the beta test. In a sword-toting Wild West of a beta test, RainZ was indisputably the Billy the Kid of our fantasy world. Not only were his exploits intelligent and executed with surgical precision, but his ironic sense of humour and imagination for miscreance was impeccable. RainZ was the perfect hit-man for Lord British, and what better place to do him in than in a large public ceremony? At the end of the beta test, Lord British announced he would address the world's commoners from the parapets of his castle. Unbeknownst to the beloved and haughty king, the date and time of his demise were set.

It was the last day of beta and the servers were jammed with players trying to squeeze a few more hours out of the game. I arrived late for the royal proclamation and tried to edge my way in to the perimeter of a laggy crowd. It was a repeat of the pre-alpha's good-bye address: absolute chaos. I barely could make out the edge of the ramparts, and the lords who stood upon them: Lord British (played by Richard Garriott himself), Lord Blackthorn (played by designer Starr Long) and other Origin luminaries. With the clamouring crowd of knights and ladies and paupers and jongleurs around me dressed in all colours of garb, the event resembled a medieval renaissance faire. Or a public hanging.

The crowd was unusually unruly and loud. In *Ultima Online* chat messages appeared above the heads of players and my screen was cluttered with dozens of variations upon "MOVE!" and "I'M STUCK!" and "LAG!". The crowd was packed in so tightly that no one could move, and the only option was to teleport oneself out of the madness if one was skilled in the magical arts. As a swordsman and a bowyer, I had no such training and had to ride out the waves of lag, frozen in place.

Lord British began addressing his loyal – and disloyal – subjects. The crowd fell silent for long enough to just make out his words among angry shushes. Suddenly I was disconnected from the server and my face flushed with anger. The worst possible time! It took over a minute to reconnect to the server and I was greeted by the same crowd I had seen a minute earlier; now everyone was making a racket about the server crash.

With an 'ahem' and a stammered apology Lord British continued his huffy speech from the balustrade, urging calm amidst the chaos. A few feet ahead of me was a robed character. He began chanting an incantation that I recognized as "Fire Field" (*in flam grav*) – a deadly spell that player-killing mages used relentlessly during the beta due to its unbalancing effects on other players. When any offensive spell was cast upon another player within the boundaries of Britain, automated guards suddenly teleported to the offending mage's position with their halberds set to 'kill'. But this robed mage was cleverer than your run-of-the-mill swordspell killing newbies for kicks: RainZ had chosen Lord British as his target.

Lord British unknowingly played his own part in the assassination. As RainZ casted Fire Field, the King chortled at the puny spell, confident that his immortality would protect him from the incantations of a mere hedgewizard. But RainZ knew something that Lord British, apparently, did not: our dear old King had lost his invulnerability status during the server crash a minute earlier.

Here's what I remember from the pandemonium that ensued after the spell was cast: a long stripe of fire appeared on the parapet where Lord British stood, and seconds later LB's body lay as a corpse on the stone floor and a ghost stood in his place. The scene proceeded in a series of still photographs seconds apart as the server lag intensified.

People began screaming "HE DIED" and others cackled mercilessly at the assassination of their medieval dictator. I rushed to load a screen capture program to photograph the chaos but by the time my program was ready the server had crashed once again. I had missed the magic moment by mere seconds.

When the server came back up, Lord British once again stood as a living body, appearing flustered and frustrated. Behind the scenes at Origin Systems, as ex-Origin staffers recalled over a decade later, a tiny mistake had led to the successful regicide. The server software behind the game required the server administrators or "Game Masters" to manually turn on invulnerability statuses for special characters like Lord British. When the server crashed the first time due to the massive overpopulation the administrators had rushed to get Lord British back on his parapet; forgetting to remind him to reset his invulnerability status. One can imagine the look on Richard Garriott's face as his beloved namesake gave up the ghost in front of his eyes; ex-Origin staffers who were in the room at the time recall he was not a happy king.

To this day some believe that the murder was an inside job: that an Origin employee and RainZ conspired to remove the invulnerability flag at the perfect time and place for the most explosive public spectacle. RainZ denies having help from anyone on the inside and swears that the prank was a 50/50 mix of pure luck and Richard Garriott's unfamiliarity with the game. But whatever truly happened that day behind the scenes, the result is incontestable: RainZ made MMORPG history forever by being the first player to successfully murder a (supposedly immortal) in-game king. He had found Lord British's Achilles heel; truly a tribute to the Ultima series.

After *Ultima Online*'s smashing success in the months that

followed, massively multiplayer online role-playing games became far tamer affairs. No one wanted to let inmates (players) run the asylum. Paintings were nailed to the walls, and every sharp corner was sanded down and covered in Nerf. Designers learned to restrict the game worlds to manageable, predictable experiences where players were forced to paint within the lines set before them. No game company wanted to deal with the impossible task of managing the evolving wild frontier that *Ultima Online* had become in only a week of beta testing. A year later, Origin's designers tired of managing the chaos of their own game and withdrew many of the features (and bugs) that made the game a complex ecosystem and designer's nightmare.

For the people like me who cut their online teeth in *Ultima Online*, it became the gold standard by which all future MMORPGs were judged. To this day no other online game has matched the depth and richness and madness that *Ultima Online* offered over that short period, and many players yearn for the sense of absolute freedom that Origin handed out to thousands of people for two U.S. Dollars. Over 25 years later, the game still exists in an official capacity – but it is a sad shell of its former self.

The End of the Ultima Online Public Beta Test

When the beta test ended the party was over for many Ultima fanatics. Those who had flocked to #ultima months earlier departed and planned to return in a few months when the game was commercially released. Others had only just found out about the wildly successful test through online news services and were hungry to hear veterans recall their adventures in Britannia.

I had other things on my mind. While the beta test descended into social anarchy, life had fared for the worst within my household. My father and mother had stopped sleeping in the same room, and my sister was caught drinking at a party with a dozen of her under-aged friends. The household fights and arguments that erupted every month or two had become daily affairs, and I began locking myself in my room the second I got home. I no longer ate with my family at the dinner table and instead brought my food to the computer where I chatted with friends on IRC as I ate.

Sensing my withdrawn demeanour my mother asked me about my plans for the autumn. In her voice I could hear the implicit expectation that I was to attend a university in the City. I nodded apprehensively and later that day was enrolled at her behest in a Computing Science program at the same university all of my high school friends were attending.

The truth was that I didn't care where I ended up, as long as it was anywhere but home. When I received an acceptance letter from the university a month later, I began apartment hunting and found a place that I could afford. On the first of September I packed up my meagre belongings: a garbage bag of clothes, two large boxes of computer games and a Pentium 133. This would be all I needed to start a new life in the big city. The beta of adolescence was over, and life was getting real.

A New Apartment and the End of DOS

It took less than an hour to move my paltry pile of possessions into my new apartment on the squalid outskirts of the City's downtown core. For the first week of university I had no phone, no Internet, no television and only the computer on my flimsy student desk.

When the telephone company hooked up my phone I began hunting for an Internet Service Provider. Now that I had my own line, I did not want to rely upon the university's two-hour dial-up limit. It didn't take long – a half dozen companies had sprung up seemingly overnight in recent months, hoping to cash in on the Internet craze. *Internet Connect* offered top-tier service at a bargain basement price: unlimited hours of dial-up Internet for $19.99 per month.

I do not recall that first month of school because I was on the Internet 24 hours a day. Or, more correctly, the *computer* was online 24 hours a day. When I was at class, my computer was downloading the latest warez so it was ready by the time I arrived home that evening. A combination of IRC and the newly released *Ultima Online* occupied the majority of my day. You can imagine the wonders this punishing online schedule did for my grades.

One day my mother visited with a panic-stricken look on her face.

"Are you okay? Why haven't you called?"

I shrugged, "Oh. Just busy with school. Sorry I forgot to call you this week."

"You haven't called me in a *month*. And every time I try to call your phone is busy."

A month? I thought back: well, maybe it was possible that a month had passed since my last phone call. Later that night I looked at my Internet bill: I had racked up over seven hundred hours of dial-up time over the last month. My phone line had been completely saturated with bits of data. Whoops.

As that first semester of university wore on, the number of Windows 95 games on my desktop surged. The newest games were best enjoyed with one of the new 3D-accelerated video cards that cost hundreds of dollars. Of course, one of my student scholarships was immediately exhausted on a new video card: an S3 ViRGE 3D card which promised modest 3D acceleration on a budget. Another scholarship was blown on a Sound Blaster AWE64 Gold which finally replaced the trusty Sound Blaster 16 that had lasted since the IBM PS/1 days. A new U.S. Robotics Sportster 33.6 Kbaud Plug'n'Play modem replaced my aging 14.4 Kbaud Sportster, which now found itself in a box of miscellaneous computer hardware I was loath to throw out. One piece at a time the MS-DOS only parts that had come from the PS/1 were being replaced by modern hardware that offered better Windows compatibility.

There was no sudden death blow to MS-DOS that marked the end of its days – it simply faded away like my old life at the family farm. By my second semester of university, the Pentium 133 bore no resemblance to the Frankensteined creature it began its life as. It was now a mature machine that had grown new appendages and a new look. It was a Windows 95 box, through and through.

It was in a cold February of 1998 that I looked over a cardboard box that sat beside my computer desk and realized that I had not even opened it since I had moved in months earlier. I opened it up and inside was my collection of MS-DOS treasures that defined my childhood. To my ten year old self they would have been a king's ransom: *King's Quest IV, Space Quest III, Monkey Island II, Quest for Glory, Railroad Tycoon, Sam and Max Hit the Road, Wing Commander: Privateer, Wing Commander III...* but to me they had become a sign of times long past. My computer had not been booted into MS-DOS mode in months.

I picked out a handful of my favourites and stacked them around my monitor like sentries guarding a fortress, with the intention of re-installing some of them soon.

Instead, the boxes faded into the background of my computer

desk and I no longer noticed them. Newer, visually impressive Windows 95 games like *X-Wing vs. Tie Fighter* that put strenuous demands on my 3D video card now graced my desktop. New 3D standards like Glide, OpenGL and Direct3D were now madly dogfighting for supremacy in the gaming market. Origin Systems was re-designing its upcoming *Ultima IX: Ascension* – the game that had drawn me to the Internet years earlier - as a 3D accelerated experience from the ground up. 3D video acceleration in Windows 95 had become the top selling feature of any game, and MS-DOS had become an anachronism.

One day, at the end of my first year of university I looked up at the boxes crowded around my monitor. It looked like a Buddhist shrine left to decay in the elements. My trusty old Tarsus had not flown to New Detroit in a year, the intrepid Roger Wilco had remained stuck on a rotting garbage scow for two, and Princess Rosella had stood for years in the sands of a distant beach with the sounds of squawking gulls and lapping waves in her ears. MS-DOS had come to the end of its days.

Afterword

The Pandemic

My wife and I are an hour away from home, circling through a maze of 1970s-built suburban neighbourhoods, trying to find an address. She squints at her iPhone, shielding her eyes from glare with one hand as she pokes and pinches with the other at the device trying to get a fix on our location.

"Go left here. I think?" she mutters.

"Here? Or up ahead?" The excitement is building in me and the question comes off unnecessarily harsh.

"Here. I dunno. Look for yourself."

My wife sighs irritably and I pull over to the curb, trying to find a single beige house in a cul-de-sac of identical beige bungalows built during an oil boom a generation ago. We were supposed to be enjoying our Sunday together over a cup of coffee at our favourite café, and instead we're fighting with Google Maps. Not exactly an ideal date.

We eventually find the house – a sprawling, single-story bungalow with an older Honda Accord parked on the sloping driveway alongside a U-Haul van. My wife stands behind me as I ring the doorbell, the other hand fishing my wallet out of my back pocket. We've done this ritual together too many times to count, and I'd feel guilty if I wasn't so excited.

A man in his seventies opens the door and welcomes us in.

"Keep on your shoes! We have to steam clean the carpets anyway."

I looked around the empty living room. "Oh, you're moving."

"Yep. My sons are off on their own now. The oldest's in Engineering, the youngest's gonna be a teacher." He sounds proud and I smile approvingly.

I cut to the chase. "So, you've got some computer stuff you're getting rid of?"

"Sure do." He motions around the corner of a low wall, and there are half a dozen huge boxes of equipment and games. My eyes bulge and I shoot a thrilled look at my wife, who giggles despite herself.

"Whoa. That's a lot of stuff!"

"Bought it all when my sons were small, y'know? But when they got older, teenagers, they got into sports and didn't play with it anymore. So it's just been in the basement. My wife and I are moving to a condo, we don't use it. I figured someone could use it. Why send it to the dump?"

I nod appreciatively, "Well, I certainly could use it!"

I hand the man five twenties and haul the treasure out of his entrance, stacking two boxes in my wife's arms. By the time the car is loaded, the boxes have filled the entire trunk and the back seat is loaded to the ceiling. It is a family's hoard of Radio Shack TRS-80 equipment and games, collected and enjoyed for years, now destined for my collection.

We wave to the friendly gentleman who has been spared a trip to the dump, and I chatter nonsensically on the return trip home. I keep saying, "Can you believe I got all this for a hundred bucks?" and barely hear my wife's reply each time.

At home I unpack each box and make a mental inventory of the contents, examining each piece of hardware and software, placing it carefully into separate piles. At the bottom of the box I spy two cartridges that have fallen under a box flap and retrieve them. *Dungeons of Daggorath* and *Downland* – the very first computer games my sister and I ever played – are back in my hands thirty years after I first saw them. My chest feels like it's going to burst open with glee.

After a few days the excitement of my latest find wears off, and I spend hours fitting each piece of equipment into the few remaining nooks and crannies in my collection space. The walls are crammed with every imaginable piece of hardware and software – some from my childhood, and most from the childhoods of others. Each computer game, joystick, keyboard and modem has its origin story. A black variant of *King's Quest VI* came from my friend Wayne when he cleaned out his mother's attic; a pristine copy of *Gold Rush* came from a married couple in Calgary who played Sierra On-Line games together as college sweethearts; I spot Trevor's copy of *Quest for Glory III* which he hated so much that he gave it to me out of spite for it. And now, there are *Downland* and *Dungeons of Daggorath* cartridges which once were enjoyed by two suburban boys who grew up to become an engineer and a teacher. It is not computer gaming memorabilia I collect, but the memories themselves.

My wife and I unpack the last box together and she slumps against the wall, "Okay. That's the last one, honey."

I cram the contents into the hoarding room and close the door behind us as we leave. I'll catalogue and alphabetize them another time. Tonight we have a date at an art gallery, and I'd rather make new memories than live amongst old ones.

Thirty-odd years after my obsession with computer and video games began I am still left wondering why and how they continue to play such a powerful role in my life and the lives of my friends. Many of us now decompress after work with a few minutes (or hours) of PlayStation, Nintendo and PC games; others play new games with their kids. Occasionally some of my old crew – the very same who goofed around with *Dr. Sbaitso* and *Wing Commander* as children – occasionally get together for an evening of *Mario Kart 64*. Games are now at the periphery of most of our lives, a distant second to adult responsibilities like our spouses and children and homes and careers.

And yet, the games we grew up are all still there in one form or another. Games like *Super Mario Bros.* and *Zelda* and *Final Fantasy* are into the umpteenth iteration of the series, while other games like *Mass Effect* covertly imitate the same game play formulas developed twenty years earlier in games like *Ultima* and *Wing Commander*. Online games have come to dominate the gamer consciousness, with *World of Warcraft* and *Ultima Online*, once behemoths in the MMO space, are just two among the thousands.

The people who made the games that defined our childhoods have come and gone too. Richard Garriott, creator of the *Ultima* series, weaved his way in and out of the computer game industry for the past thirty years. After hitching a (brief) stay in space with the Russian cosmonaut program, he returned to helm the *Shroud of the Avatar* spiritual followup to the series, and beat a hasty exit from the industry once again after its failure. The Two Guys from Andromeda, creators of the *Space Quest* series, broke up and reunited twenty years later; and are currently failing to complete a crowd-funded unofficial sequel to their legacy called *SpaceVenture*. Ken and Roberta Williams, owners of adventure game empire Sierra On-Line, exited the industry in the 1990s and circumnavigated the world on a multimillion-dollar yacht. They too returned to game development 30 years later, for a brief time to create the virtual reality adventure game *Colossal Cave VR*, only to disappear once again after it was met with a mixed reception. Other elder developers quietly float around the industry, creating games for whatever console or tablet is currently in vogue.

After disappearing for most of the 1990s and 2000s, independent or "indie" developers have returned in full force – it is no longer critical to work for a giant game publisher in order to become a game designer. Everyday people have the tools at their fingertips to build a decent game in a few weeks, and publish it through dozens of independent publishers. In 2012, I decided to live out my dream and began working as an independent software developer and have enjoyed a 13-year (and counting) career in the industry so far.

The acquisition of software has changed completely. Online services like Good Old Games (GOG) have turned those MS-DOS games put to pasture thirty years ago into a veritable gold mine, letting everyday people play them again on modern computer systems. Digital distribution has made buying a physical computer game in a box an anachronism, and many new consoles are "online only" and have no physical mechanism for reading data anymore.

Chatting about games with friends no longer requires a classroom or playground. There are now hundreds, if not thousands, of podcasts devoted purely to retro computer and video gaming – each with a focus on a particular gaming system or game genre, catering to every possible audience who grew up with a game. Where I once had one IRC channel to talk about games with other kids, live chat software like Discord has created an innumerable selection of gaming communities to choose from. In other words, in the space of two decades the world of gaming changed more than the world of public transportation has in a hundred years.

Throughout these stories I've resisted the desire to use the word "nostalgic" to describe my attachment to these old treasures. And yet the word itches at the back of my mind each time I recall the first time I played a game or used a particular computer system.

To most people nostalgia has a rosy, comforting feeling and evokes reminiscence of the good old days when life was simpler and happier. Perhaps we forget that the word nostalgia, understood etymologically, means "home sickness". For a person whose childhood is a patchwork quilt of joy and guilt and fear and social isolation and excitement, one glance at a sacred treasure dredges up a jumble of feelings. Perhaps nostalgia itself has many levels of expression, and only the most superficial kind is the rosy one people usually speak of. Perhaps there are other deeper expressions, because being home sick is a complex feeling: sometimes sick *for* home, and other times sick *of* home.

Writing this book was an exercise in exploring those complex feelings in the absence of my computer game collection, which sat for years in a massive storage container. In the process of writing not once did I wander among the stacks of my collection and poke around in the contents of each box. Every memoir came from sitting in my chair, staring at the ceiling, and remembering every detail I could about a particular game manual or box cover.

I take this as evidence that the sacred objects themselves – the keyboards, cloth maps, floppy diskettes, covers, posters, monitors, motherboards and feelies – possess no magical ability to trigger memories alone. Object history is, in the end, heavily loaded in the favour of the imagination of the rememberer. My memory, imagination, and conversations with friends and family were enough to reconstruct a fairly accurate remembrance of things long past.

Perhaps the thousands of pounds of treasures I've hauled around and curated and worried over for the past thirty years are, after all, just things. Perhaps my memories are the source of my attachment, and the floppy disks and silicon chips and logoed plastic housings have been reduced to foci for remembrance, like photos in a high school yearbook. Flipping through an old yearbook is truly an exercise in nostalgia; without a person to recall stories of its photos the album is just a meaningless collection of glossy paper and faces.

What happened to that massive pile of cardboard and floppy disks that sat in storage for years? A year prior to the COVID-19 pandemic, I decided to liquidate more than half of the collection to fellow collectors. I went through storage bin after storage bin, paring away games that evoked little attachment or interest, catalogued their contents and then unceremoniously sold them. It took over a year, and by the end the collection shed more than half of its weight, and plastic bins were no longer stacked to the ceiling of our tiny apartment. It was a relief for me, and an absolute coup for my wife, who was tired of plastic bins towering over us in our bedroom.

And then, a funny thing happened two years later. My wife and I bought a house mid-pandemic and moved in. As part of an old ritual, one of the first things I unpacked were the games I had deemed too precious to sell. I bought a half dozen Ikea cube shelves to fill one room dedicated to my office, and began to fill the shelves with games. Occasionally, like an itch on a phantom limb, I couldn't find a game I was looking for – a game I had sentimental attachments to, and swore that I had owned at some point. *The Incredible Machine 2*, *Codename: ICEMAN*, and *Ultima Online Charter Edition* were all conspicuously absent. I opened up my collection spreadsheet and skimmed through the list: I had sold them all during the great purge two years earlier. Damn!

I made a list of the missing games, which quickly grew to over a dozen. I figured: I'll just replace the handful I have the deepest regrets about selling. I found myself once again creating new eBay Saved Searches, talking to fellow collectors, and skimming through local Facebook Marketplace ads.

It has been three years since I made that list, and I've now acquired dozens of games that I regretted selling, and dozens more new ones! I'm now more excited than ever about collecting and software preservation, and curate my finds in collections at archive.org; I play more of these now-old games today than I ever had the opportunity to as a kid.

Didn't I learn anything from writing this book? Wasn't the whole point to relieve myself of the emotional attachments to the physical items, so I could get rid of them, and enjoy the memories I had of the past?

Perhaps this is where computer and video games are inherently different from collecting old bottle caps or coins or photographs. Think of an old family photo or snapshot from a vacation that you treasure. To you, it might evoke happy or sad memories. But to a stranger, devoid of its context, the photo has no meaning. In contrast, an old computer game creates its own context: a player loads up the game, learns how to play it, and makes new meaning as she or he plays.

If that is true, then nostalgia is fundamentally secondary to the more primary experience of memory-making. We can only be nostalgic for something meaningful to us. Freed of the weight of the past, any old game recaptures its ability to entertain and shock and sadden in new ways. It takes only a player with an open mind and heart, not one preoccupied with a personal history (sour, bitter or sweet), to enter into the world a game offers and perceive it newly with fresh eyes. The ways I played games as a child – to escape, to control, to feel secure – can give way to new ways of playing games as an adult.

But what are these new ways of playing and enjoying games outside of addiction and avoidance? What do games look like to a person who isn't trapped in the past? What kinds of games give mature adults meaningful experiences? These I leave as open questions to be answered in the lives of those who play games and create them.

Tonight, laying in bed feeling worn out from a day spent programming, I find myself loading up *Betrayal at Krondor*, searching for some lost treasure in an abandoned dwarven mine.

For once I am not thinking about the time Andrew and I snuck off of school grounds to make pirated copies of *Krondor's* diskettes at his house. Or the time in high school I found out the game had been released for free, and downloaded the entire game from Sierra.com over a 28.8Kbaud modem. Or the time I played through the whole game on an ill-conceived trip to meet my first and only Internet Girlfriend in Columbus, Ohio.

No. Tonight I'm thinking about a treasure chest that I found in a corner of the mine that I had never figured out how to unlock over the past thirty years, and what secrets it might contain.

And I'm having fun.

About the Author

vga256 is an indigenous Canadian social researcher who retired from an academic career in his thirties to pursue his creative dreams. After working in the game industry for ten years as a contracted game developer for indie studios and publishers, he founded his own independent software and game studio: **tomotama**. He lives in Edmonton, Canada, and is a devoted husband to his far more creatively talented wife, and is an obsessive catdad to two furballs named Henry and Kiki.

Find out more at:
www.tomotama.com

Made in the USA
Monee, IL
08 November 2026

67384912R00225